# gatherings

Ceres

Nature's perfect juice.

EMERY
INVESTMENTS

BELLINI

Bellini Custom Cabinetry Ltd.

RUNNYMEDE

RUNNYMEDE DEVELOPMENT CORPORATION LIMITED

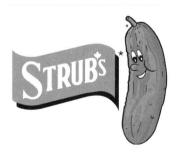

# gatherings

creative kosher cooking from our families to yours

A project by the parents of
Netivot HaTorah Day School

Copyright © Netivot HaTorah 2003

We recommend some ingredients by brand name. Please note that the brand name is a trademark owned by the company which produces that product.

The laws of Kashruth are many and complex. While this is a kosher cookbook, this is not a guide to Kashruth. There may be products that change ingredients or Kashruth supervision over time. Any questions that arise over the products used in our recipes or specific questions about keeping kosher should be directed to your local Rabbi.

National Library of Canada Cataloguing in Publication

Magence, Shawna, 1970-
    Gatherings: creative kosher cooking from our families to yours / Shawna Magence and Carol Lesser.

Includes Index.
ISBN 0-9733607-0-4

Cookery, Jewish. I. Lesser, Carol 1964 – II. Netivot HaTorah Day School  III. Title.

TX724.M338 2003                641.5'676                C2003-904145-X

First Printing, October 2003, 5,000 copies
Second Printing, October 2004, 5,000 copies

Cover and interior design: Counterpunch/Peter Ross
Photography: Chris Freeland
Food Styling: Terry Schact
Printed and bound in Canada: Transcontinental Printing

For additional copies, use the order form in the back of the book.

This book can be purchased in bulk for corporate gift giving.
For details contact:
Netivot HaTorah Day School
18 Atkinson Avenue
Thornhill, Ontario
L4J 8C8
905-771-1234 EXT 303
www.gatheringscookbook.com

# Introduction

It is a pleasure to introduce *Gatherings: Creative Kosher Cooking from Our Families to Yours.*

As editors of this incredible project, we have had the honour of sharing this venture with over 130 dedicated volunteers, all of whom have put their hearts and souls into creating this finished product.

While this project began as a fundraising project for Netivot HaTorah Day School, it has become a tribute to it. Our vision has become a reality.

Gatherings is made up of over 300 mouthwatering recipes that broaden the perception of kosher cooking. All the recipes you find here have been triple tested to ensure quality and reliability. While we have included some traditional recipes, the majority of *Gatherings'* recipes are creative and innovative ones that will impress even the toughest audience.

The title of the book, *Gatherings*, is appropriate because gathering is exactly what we did. The Netivot HaTorah family gathered all the recipes and ideas that are shared in this cookbook. When we have an intimate dinner or celebrate a simcha (occasion), we gather together to celebrate, and food is an integral component of the occasion.

In the Jewish religion having festive meals is actually required for certain occasions. We are, therefore, always looking for creative and original recipes. To some the idea of a perfect recipe may be simple, quick cooking that tastes delicious, to others it is cuisine that looks and tastes gourmet. This book includes something for everyone.

We must thank our families whose support, guidance and taste buds over the past two years has been invaluable. We could have never done this without you all! The Magences – Jeremy, Aitan, Yona, Ahava and Yakir; the Lessers – Stewart, Eli, Aaron, Ayala and Tamar.

To the heads of each committee – Alina, Aryella, Dina, Laurie, Marcia, Roberta and Sharona – words cannot express how we feel about you both as co-workers and friends. Thank you for sharing yourselves with us and for always being available to help or to listen.

We hope that this cookbook will assist cooks both novice and more experienced in adding to their repertoire of recipes to make their gatherings tastier, creative and more enjoyable.

From our families to yours – enjoy!

Shawna Magence and Carol Lesser

# Contents

# A special thank you to the following people

TRACEY COX: photographer's assistant extraordinaire

RABBI ELLIOTT DIAMOND: for sharing the history of Netivot HaTorah Day School with the *Gatherings* readers, from the perspective of a vice-principal and founding parent of the school.

ETAN DIAMOND: author and Netivot parent, for writing the informative and interesting forward for *Gatherings*

BAYLA FORTINSKY: for your enthusiasm, reliability and for your bookkeeping skills

DANA FRANCOZ: for creating an incredible P.R. package

CHRIS FREELAND: photographer not only with a great eye but an extra-special heart

CONTINENT WIDE: for your generous gift of disposable cameras

MELINDA GAITAN: for holding down the fort and creating a new definition for "multitasking"

NORENE GILLETZ: for getting us off the ground and sharing your invaluable advice

GMB CATERING: for sharing the "Strawberry, Blueberry and Rhubarb Crumble" recipe

FAYE KLEINMINTZ: for your excellent office support

EVELYN RAAB: for your long-distance advice

LORI RENNIE: of Transcontinental Printing for making the printing process seamless

PETER ROSS: for leading us every step of the way and of course the beautiful design and layout of *Gatherings*

ROSE LAZAR CATERING: for sharing "Florentine Mushroom Caps and Wheat Berry Salad" recipes with us and for helping make our launch delicious

"SIMPLY ENTERTAINING": the first Netivot cookbook

TERRY SCHACT: for your flair with food styling and recipe editing and for steering us in the right direction

JILL SNIDER: for the final edit and for permission to use "Harvest Apple Spice Cake" (Robin Hood Foods) one of our personal favorites.

OKSANA SLAVUTYCH AND MARC-PHILIPPE GAGNE – OKPROPS: prop stylist who knew how to highlight the food

DR. REUVEN STERN, PRINCIPAL NETIVOT HATORAH DAY SCHOOL: for upholding Netivot's vision and for educating our children

WENDY THOMAS: for stepping in at the last minute to complete the editing and indexing

MIRIAM WEBB: for your passion for the project and incredible persistence in fundraising

TO GRETA REISS, ALAN STEINFELD AND ROBIN SHINER: for dedicating yourselves to Netivot so that all our children can benefit

AND FINALLY TO LORI WOLYNETZ AND THE NETIVOT PARENTS' ASSOCIATION: without your generous gift, this book would not have materialized

# Sponsorship

C.R.A.F.T. Development Corporation, Emery Investments, Finn Contracting Inc., Netivot HaTorah Parents Association, Ceres Fruit Juices

Anonymous, Bellini Custom Cabinetry Limited, Helen & Hy Bergel, Joseph Dubrofsky, Eltor Cable Systems Inc., Excel Heating Services, Roz & Ralph Halbert, Tom Hofstedter & Family, Yehudit & Jonathan Hames, JMH Litigation and Financial Solutions, Marsha & Michael Lax, Carol & Stewart Lesser, Shawna & Jeremy Magence, Nathalie & Charlie Piwko, Publipage Inc., Runnymede Development Corporation Ltd., Elizabeth & Jonah Turk, Lori & Larry Wolynetz

Sandy & David Cohen, Counselling & Healing Services, Vivian & Lewis Dubrofsky, Iris & Michael Halbert, Diane & Barry Kirschenbaum, Sarena & David Koschitzky, Sarah & Larry Krauss, Dina & Shlomie Lebowitz, Linda & Larry Levenstein, Alina & Steve Mayer, Karen & Dov Meyer, Mirco Sales Limited, Elisa & Eli Rindenow, TK & Yossi Rosenblum, Orna & Michael Serruya, Marcia & Jeff Shumacher, Strub Brothers Limited, Aryella & Eddy Weisz, Dr. Michael West, Zoglo's Vegetarian Choice™

Esti & Randy Cohen, Bayla & Gary Fortinsky, Ahuva & Mark Karoly, Rachel & Sharon Kerbel, Shoshanah & Allan Kopyto, Enid Lesser, Dr. Maurice Levitan, Eva & Frank Mayer, Sarah & Morris Perlis, Karen & Mel Rom, Donna & Randy Shiff, Sharon & David Shore, Lea Shumacher, Lori & John Ulmer, Naphtali & Ann Winter, Sue & Larry Zeifman

Zehava & Michael Abramovitch, Tanya Annarili, Elana & Jonathan Aziza, Deborah Begun, Daniella & Ari Bergel, Ilan Bergel, Miriam & Daniel Bloch, Avigail & Aaron Blumenfeld, Sandy & Reuven Brudner, Renee & Lorne Climans, Harry & Helen Cohen, Elite & Avigdor Collins, Tobey & Arthur Crandell, Rose & Leslie Cross, Patty & Charles Dolman, Cheryl & Alvin Einhorn, Amanda & David Eisenstat, Susan & Harley Eklove, Lynn & Steve Ellwood, Honey & Lou Elmaleh, Michelle & Marc Factor, Evelyn & Bernie Farber, Debbie & Amalya Feldman, Elana & Jimmy Fendelman, Marisa & Christopher Finlay, Susan & Aaron Finlayson, Sonia & Abe Fogel, Adele & Joseph Fortinsky, Cyma & Perry Katz, Robin & Tim Gofine, Karyn & Robert Goldberger, Michal & Moshe Goldstein, Marjorie & Gershon Green, Pam & Rob Gross, Tova & Alan Gutenberg, Nicky & Alan Halpert, Michele & Nathan Herrmann, Esther & Marvin Huberman, Yvette & Jordan Ison, Lisa & Joel Jakobovits, Lisa & Edward Jesin, Susan & Gene Jurkowitz, Pershang & Kamal Kamali, Margie & Mark Katz, Simmi & Brian Kleinberg, Rachel & Jack Lefkowitz, Daniel Levenstein, Daniel Magence, Ruthie & Michael Mammon, Sheryl & George Markus, Joyce & David Muller, Becky & Ari Neugroschl, Roberta & Marvin Newman, Jennifer & Orie Niedzviecki, Nusbaum Family Charitable Foundation, Connie Palozzi, Cathy & Richard Posluns, Deborah & David Propp, Lori & Marvin Rapp, Marci & Harold Rapp, Joyce & Aaron Rifkind, Cindy & Mike Rosen, Naomi & Zev Rosenblum, Shonna & Douglas Ross, Sarah & Harry Roz, Ruth & Joseph Rudner, Pearl & Ron Saban, Phyllis & Maier Sadwin, Sharona & David Safran, Marla & Jack Samuel, Caron & Reeve Serman, Joan & Bernard Shapiro, Mindy & Jay Shiel, Zahava & Mordie Shields, Susan & Albert Silverman, Susan & Murray Silverman, Andrea & Paul Skosowski, Tari Soiffer, Rosalie & Alan Steinfeld, Sari & Allan Stitt, Heather & Melech Tanen, Elaine & Sol Tanenzapf, Jacques Tjonasan, Rachel & Chuck Wagner, Miriam & Bill Webb, Leah & Sydney Wercberger, Irina & Alexander Werner, Alvina & Steven Wesfield, Mary Wolfe, Sylvia & Leo Wolynetz, Fran & David Woolf, Sharon & Zvi Woolf, Elsie Young, Sarah & Bram Zinman

# Committee

A very special thank you to the committee heads whose tireless devotion made this cookbook a reality.

*Dina Lebowitz:* P.R.
*Alina Mayer:* Photography
*Roberta Newman:* Recipe Collecting
*Sharona Safran:* Editing
*Marcia Shumacher:* Testing
*Laurie Teperman:* Launch
*Aryella Weisz:* Launch

To each volunteer and recipe contributor, thank you for sharing your family secrets, your own creations, favourite recipes and of course your time and expertise. Every volunteer contributed in their own way – typing, editing, testing, creating, P.R., sponsors, presentation and on the cookbook launch. Thank you all!

*Zehava Abramovitch*
*Kim Abrams*
*Michelle Anhang*
*Rebecca Ansel*
*Lauren Barrett*
*Preci Benyair*
*Anne Berger*
*Esther Bergman*
*Nina Bernstein*
*Susan Birnbaum*
*Vered Bitton*
*Miriam Bloch*
*Annette Breatross*
*Leigh Ann Brenman*
*Pam Brenman*
*Jill Cherniak*
*Esti Cohen*
*Helen Cohen*
*Sandy Cohen*
*Elite Collins*
*Linda Cymbalista*
*Frieda Davies*
*Carole Denver*

*David Diamond*
*Debbie Diamond*
*Patty Dolman*
*Vivian Dubrofsky*
*Sharon Durbach*
*Cheryl Einhorn*
*Randi Elituv*
*Honey Elmaleh*
*Lydia English*
*Oriane Falkenstein*
*Marla Figdor*
*Bess Fine*
*Bayla Fortinsky*
*Louis Franken*
*Michelle Frischman*
*Lea Frohwein*
*Baruch Frydman-Kohl*
*Cyma Gauze*
*Sigal Gelkop*
*Nadine Gesundheit*
*Rosalind Ginzburg*
*Terry Ginzburg*
*Barbara Glatt*
*GMB Catering*
*Robin Gofine*
*Moshe Goldstein*
*Lori Grafstein*
*Carol Green*
*Marjorie Green*
*Debbie Gross*
*Pam Gross*
*Tova Gutenberg*
*Clarissa Hahn*
*Monica Halberstadt*
*Iris Halbert*
*Nicky Halpert*
*Michele Herrmann*
*Brenda Herskovits*
*Vivi Hirchberg*
*Devorah Hoffman*
*Ilana Hollander*
*Esther Huberman*
*Cheryl Jenah*
*Lisa Jesin*
*Ahuva Karoly*
*Debbie Kates*
*Vivian Katz*
*Jeffrey & Serena Kay*
*Sharon Kerbel*
*Cheryl Klein*
*Simmi Kleinberg*

*Sarena Koschitzky*
*Joyce Krasman*
*Zeldie Kurtz*
*Marsha Lax*
*Shevi Lerner*
*Enid Lesser*
*Linda Levenstein*
*Dalya Lewis*
*Stacey Lofsky*
*Ruth Lockshin*
*Judy Magder*
*Ruthie Mammon*
*Rella Margolis*
*Sheryl Markus*
*Vivian Max*
*Karen Meyer*
*Leanne Meyerowitz*
*Barbara Miller-Schwartz*
*Vered Miroshnikov*
*Ruth Miskin*
*Yael Moran*
*Joyce Muller*
*Penina Nauenberg*
*Esther Ohana*
*Fern Orzech*
*Jennifer Paquette*
*Yael Pimontel*
*Nathalie Piwko*
*Cathy Posluns*
*Marci Rapp*
*Greta Reiss*
*Liliane Rende*
*Blima Rhodes*
*Joyce Rifkind*
*Elisa Rindenow*
*Karen Rom*
*Rose Lazar Catering*
*Arieh Rosenblum*
*Naomi Rosenblum*
*Sari Rosenblum*
*TK Rosenblum*
*Naomi Roskies*
*Shonna Ross*
*Sarah Roz*
*Nancy Rubenstein*
*Pearl Saban*
*Ron Saban*
*Perla Sabovich*
*Maier Sadwin*
*Phyllis Sadwin*
*Amanda Salem*

*Susana Sarfati*
*Wendy Scolnik*
*Alan Sebbag*
*Debbie Sedley*
*Karen Segal*
*Caron Serman*
*Leonie Serman*
*Crystal Seymour*
*Mindy Shiel*
*Zahava Shields*
*Sharon Shore*
*Margie Silver*
*Susan Silverman*
*Andrea Skosowski*
*Marilyn Sober*
*Tari Soiffer*
*Zev Steinfeld*
*Rochelle Strauss*
*Strub Brothers*
*Esther Sturm*
*Shaindy Sturm*
*Heather Tanen*
*Rosanne Tebbi*
*Francine Teller*
*Sandra Temes*
*Marci Tenenbaum*
*Rosanne Teplitsky*
*Valerie Toledano*
*Elizabeth Turk*
*Rachel Wagner*
*Nancy Wasserman*
*Miriam Webb*
*Cheryl Weinberger*
*Leah Wercberger*
*Alvina Wesfield*
*Elana Wolff*
*Lori Wolynetz*
*Dianna Zauderer*
*Ruth Zimmerman*
*Sarah Zinman*
*Wendy Zinner*

We received over 900 excellent contributions but due to limited space could not print each one as it was submitted. Every recipe was used in some way and you should be proud of the product you have created. We apologize if any names have inadvertently been omitted.

# Our Story

It started with a few mothers and their infant children on a Saturday afternoon in Toronto. Although school days were years away, these moms began to talk about educational choices. Few topics seem to stir passion, as do the issues and concerns of children's education. From a casual conversation, a group of families emerged bound together by a shared understanding of the important decision they were about to make.

The group grew and was able to articulate the values, goals and aspirations developed for their children's education. Someone verbalized the unspoken dream of many: "Let's start a school!" The initial responses dismissed the notion as fantasy and impracticality, but were replaced with excitement, vision and leadership along with a statement of philosophy and goals that identified the unique position that our school would occupy in the educational landscape of Toronto.

Netivot HaTorah Day School is based on values that inform a modern orthodox perspective. We believe the religious teachings of our Torah are the foundation for Jewish life and that life should be lived to its fullest extent. Therefore, we are required to embrace and explore the world through a meaningful general studies program. Modern Jewish life is not complete, however, without an appreciation for and identification with the State of Israel – its people, history and language.

On the opening day of classes, in September 1984, 42 students arrived. The viability and communal need of this fledgling school were proven when 160 students enrolled the following year. The growth of our student population to approximately 600 in 2003, the construction of a new school building and our expanding educational program all clearly demonstrate the vitality of Netivot's contribution to the Toronto Jewish community. Our dedicated staff and the Netivot Educational Support Services (N.E.S.S.) department provide support for students through enrichment programs as well as small group learning opportunities. From science experiments to Bible classes; from Talmudic analysis to championship basketball games; from early morning prayers to after-school clubs, Netivot is a thriving, growing school that embraces the whole Jewish child in today's modern world.

It began with a dream. We followed our hearts, our goals and our hopes for the future of our children.

Rabbi Elliott Diamond
Vice-Principal, Limudei Kodesh

# Foreword

"To know a community, eat its food." This folk saying rings particularly true for the Jewish community, where kosher cooking has long connected Jewish families to their heritage and to each other. These historical connections emerge most clearly in a kosher cookbook, where the recipes combine to tell a flavourful history of the Jewish experience: Eastern European garlics, Middle Eastern zatars, South African chutneys, North American meat loaves, and so forth. As Jews crossed continents and oceans over the past two thousand years, they accumulated a food heritage that reflected their many homes. These international food trends are even more apparent today, as "traditional" Jewish favourites – chopped liver, gefilte fish, and *kreplach* – are increasingly joined by new ones – Thai mango salad, teriyaki tofu, and quinoa pilaf.

Throughout these gastronomical journeys, the concept of Kashruth, or of "keeping kosher," has remained constant. One of the most central aspects of traditional Judaism, Kashruth is also one of its most misunderstood. For example, kosher food is not food that is blessed by a rabbi. Rather, the laws of Kashruth involve categories of foods that are and are not permissible according to traditional Jewish law, both as written explicitly in the Torah and as interpreted by rabbinical authorities. The Torah provides a long list of permitted and prohibited animals, with specific physical signs that demarcate each. Domesticated animals must have split hooves and must chew their cud. Fish must have identifiable fins and scales. Scavenger fish and birds of prey cannot be eaten. Even certain types of locusts and grasshoppers are permitted. (Most Jewish communities have lost the tradition of eating grasshoppers and locusts, although certain Yemenite communities still do. This cookbook – fortunately or not – follows the former tradition.)

In addition to the types of animals that can be eaten, the laws of Kashruth delineate how kosher food must be prepared. Meat and dairy products cannot be cooked or eaten together. (No cheeseburgers or chicken parmegian!) Even regular dairy products must be free of animal-based derivatives such as rennet. To ensure this separation, kosher kitchens contain separate utensils and dishes for meat and dairy food, separate meat and dairy sinks, and in many households even separate ovens. A third category of kosher food called *parve* includes all foods that contain neither meat nor dairy ingredients (such as fruits and vegetables) and can be prepared and eaten with either.

Because of modern food production, the millennia-old tradition of Kashruth remains central as ever. Whereas at one time, foods were made at home under direct personal supervision using few processed ingredients, modern foods are produced, manufactured, and packaged by anonymous companies using thousands of ingredients, additives, preservatives and flavourings – all of which require proper certification that they were derived from kosher sources and that no mixing of meat and dairy ingredients occurred. The result is that ingredients that few people pay attention to – monoglyceride, sodium caseinate, or stearic acid, for example – are of prime interest to kosher consumers. Yet to investigate every ingredient in every product is an impossible task. Instead, today's kosher consumers rely on a global network of kosher supervising agencies, such as the Orthodox Union (the "OU") or Toronto's Kashruth Council (COR), that certify that commercially prepared foods are permitted.

As "kosher" has become mainstream, the number of available products has increased exponentially and traditionalist Jews now comprise only a small fraction of kosher consumers. In fact, shoppers can walk down the aisles of any major grocery chain and fill their carts with readily available kosher products without even being aware that they are doing so!

Finally, it is fitting that this newest kosher cookbook emanates from Toronto. From the creation of Toronto's Kashruth Council in the late 1950s to the current array of local kosher restaurants, bakeries, caterers, and the one of the largest self-serve kosher departments in a North American grocery store, Toronto has witnessed the blossoming of the kosher experience over the past half century. The recipes provided herein, therefore, represent some of the finest expressions of kosher cooking as developed by some of the best kosher cooks around.


Etan Diamond is an historian and Netivot parent. He is author of several books and articles, including *And I Will Dwell in Their Midst: Orthodox Jews in Suburbia.*

# appetizers

*Everyone enjoys this recipe. Who can resist anything on a skewer?*

# Salmon Skewers with Pasta

MARINADE

| | |
|---|---|
| 2 | cloves of garlic, minced |
| ½ cup | ketchup |
| ¼ cup | pure maple syrup |
| 2 Tbsp | orange juice |
| 2 Tbsp | soy sauce |
| 2 tsp | sesame oil |
| 2 tsp | chili sauce |
| | |
| 1½ lbs. | salmon fillets, cut into 1-inch cubes |
| | wooden skewers, soaked for ½ hour in water |

PASTA SAUCE

| | |
|---|---|
| 2 (28-oz.) cans | tomatoes, diced |
| 6 | sun-dried tomatoes, chopped |
| 1 Tbsp | olive oil |
| 1 tsp | dried basil |
| 1 tsp | salt |
| | |
| 1 (450-g) pkg. | capellini pasta |

Preheat oven to broil.

In a small bowl, combine marinade ingredients. Mix well. Marinate salmon in the marinade for 15 minutes. Pierce 2 – 4 salmon pieces onto each skewer. Place each skewer onto a greased pan. Broil, uncovered, for approximately 3 minutes on each side, basting frequently. Lower oven to 350F and bake for an additional 10–15 minutes.

Meanwhile, combine tomatoes, sun-dried tomatoes, olive oil, basil and salt in a saucepan and bring to a boil. Simmer until sauce is thick, approximately 45 minutes. Stir constantly.

Prepare capellini noodles according to package directions.

For each serving, mix pasta with a little sauce and place on the centre of an appetizer-sized plate. Put a spoonful of the sauce in the centre of the pasta. Place a skewer on either side of the pasta. Looks and tastes fantastic.

Can be served warm or at room temperature.

Servings: 8-10
Prep time: 45 minutes

# Terrific Tilapia in Tortilla Wraps

MARINADE

| | |
|---|---|
| 3 Tbsp | barbecue sauce |
| 1 Tbsp | honey |
| 1 Tbsp | orange juice |
| 1 tsp, heaping | tarragon |
| ¾ tsp | lemon pepper |
| ¾ tsp | hickory seasoning |
| 6 pieces | tilapia divided in 3 or 4 slices |

WRAPS

| | |
|---|---|
| 6 | tortilla wraps |
| 2–3 | red peppers, halved |
| 1 | avocado, sliced |
| ⅓ cup | salsa, mild, equates to 2 tsp per roll |
| | chives, for ties |
| | ketchup for decorating |

Preheat oven to broil.

In a small bowl, combine marinade ingredients. Add fish to marinade. Cover. Refrigerate for a couple of hours or overnight.

Spray large skillet with cooking spray. Sauté fish until it flakes when prodded with a fork. Remove from heat. Set aside.

Place red peppers cut side down on a foil-covered baking tray. Broil until well roasted. Place them immediately into a paper bag. After they cool, the skin will peel easily.

Place fish (2 pieces per roll) in centre of a wrap. Discard marinade. Layer with peeled red pepper, avocado and 2 teaspoons of salsa. Roll tightly. Fasten with 2 chive ties, well spaced, leaving room to slice the roll in two.

PARVE

*Looks great. A little bit more work but well worth it.*

Tip: For a pretty look, sprinkle paprika around each plate.

Servings: 6-8
Prep time: 30–45 minutes

# Roasted Veggie Wrap

| | |
|---|---|
| 5 | Portobello mushrooms, sliced ½ inch thick |
| 1 | eggplant, large, peeled, sliced ½-inch circles |
| 1 | zucchini, large, peeled, cut in sticks |
| 1 | yellow pepper, sliced in strips |
| 1 | red pepper, sliced in strips |
| ¼ cup | olive oil |
| 1 Tbsp | fresh basil, chopped |
| 1 Tbsp | balsamic vinegar |
| | salt and pepper to taste |
| 1 (8-oz.) can | roasted red pepper hummus or plain hummus |
| 6–8 | wraps, regular or pesto for colour |
| | lettuce, for garnishing |

Preheat oven to 425F.

Place vegetables in a large bowl. Toss with oil, basil, balsamic vinegar, salt and pepper, to coat evenly.

In a roasting dish (or alternatively on a barbecue), place vegetables in a single layer and grill at until crispy and brown, turning them occasionally, approximately 10 minutes. Cool vegetables (can even leave in fridge until next day).

Spread hummus on wraps. Place a scoop of vegetables at top of the wrap and roll. Insert toothpicks on each side of wrap and cut it on a diagonal. Place lettuce on a serving platter and set wraps on it. Serve at room temperature.

Tips: Can easily be made into a main dish by adding barbecued chicken breasts. Slice the breasts into strips and roll with vegetables into the wrap.

Can be prepared a day ahead.

If not serving immediately wrap individually in plastic wrap.

Servings: 6–8
Prep time: 20–30 minutes

# Sushi Pizza

**SAUCE**

| | |
|---|---|
| 2 Tbsp | mayonnaise |
| 2 Tbsp | soy milk |
| 1 Tbsp | wasabi powder |

**SUSHI**

| | |
|---|---|
| 1¼ cups | water |
| 1 cup | sushi rice, rinsed, drained |
| ¼ cup | seasoned rice vinegar |
| 2 Tbsp | sesame seeds, toasted |
| 1 | avocado, thinly sliced |
| 1 sheet | roasted nori, cut in thin strips (with scissors) |
| ½ cup | English cucumber, thinly sliced |
| 2 Tbsp | pickled ginger |
| | soy sauce, to drizzle |

In a small bowl stir together sauce ingredients. Set aside.

In saucepan, combine water with rice. Bring to boil. Cover. Reduce heat. Cook for 20 minutes or until tender. With a fork, stir in vinegar and sesame seeds.

While rice is cooking, line a round or square 8-inch cake pan with plastic wrap. With a spatula, press the cooked rice firmly and evenly into pan. Let cool completely. Turn rice out onto a flat serving plate. Top with a layer of avocado slices. Sprinkle nori over avocado. Arrange cucumber and ginger on top. Drizzle sauce over top. Cut the rice into triangles or squares. Drizzle soy sauce on top.

Tips: Wasabi is also known as Japanese horseradish

You can cut nori into triangular shapes.

For variation: Add a layer of smoked salmon or imitation crab.

Serves: 6–8
Prep time: 30 minutes

# Three-Coloured Fish Loaf

| | |
|---|---|
| 1½ lbs. | frozen fish loaf, defrosted |
| 1 | egg, beaten |
| 1 Tbsp | sugar |
| 1 tsp | salt |
| ½ tsp | garlic powder |
| ½ tsp | onion powder |
| | pepper to taste |
| 1 (300-g) box | chopped spinach, defrosted and drained |
| 3 | medium-sized carrots, cooked, mashed |

Preheat oven to 350F.

In a large bowl, combine defrosted fish with egg, sugar, salt, garlic powder, onion powder and pepper. Divide mixture in half. Press one half into a 4½ x 8½-inch loaf pan. Divide remaining mixture in half. Mix spinach with one half of mixture and carrots with the other. Spread the spinach mixture over plain fish in loaf pan. Then spread carrot mixture over the spinach mixture.

Bake uncovered for 1 hour.

*This recipe looks gourmet but is very easy to prepare, and it is delicious.*

Tip: Serve horseradish in carved-out veggies like radishes, cucumber or zucchini.

Servings: 8–10
Prep time: 20 minutes

# Savory Pickled Salmon

| | |
|---|---|
| 2 | large onions, thinly sliced |
| 1 | red onion, thinly sliced |
| 1 Tbsp | olive oil |
| 1 cup | vinegar |
| 1 cup | water |
| 1 cup | ketchup |
| ½ cup | sugar |
| ¼ cup | chili sauce |
| 2 Tbsp | pickling spices, wrapped in gauze |
| 1 | whole bay leaf |
| ½ tsp | thyme |
| ¼ tsp | ginger |
| 1 tsp | salt |
| 8 | salmon fillets (1 inch thick) |

Preheat oven to 350F.

Sauté onions in saucepan with olive oil until softened. Add remaining ingredients, except for fish. Simmer for an additional 5 minutes.

Place fish, in a single layer, in ovenproof dish. Pour sauce over fish. Bake, uncovered, for 20 minutes, or until fish flakes when tested with a fork.

Refrigerate overnight before serving. Serve warm or cold.

Servings: 8
Prep Time: 25–30 minutes

# Easy Fish Starter

*"Very simple to make. This recipe is unique and delicious. As one of my friends said, 'A real keeper.'"*

| | |
|---|---|
| 1 (10-oz.) pkg. | spring mixed greens or other lettuce |
| 5 strips | imitation crab, cut into ½-inch slices |
| ½ | red onion, small, chopped |
| 1 | red pepper, diced |
| 1 (12-oz.) jar | artichoke hearts in marinade |

On a serving platter, arrange spring mixed greens. Place crab on top of greens. Sprinkle onion and pepper over crab. Pour contents of artichoke jar over salad. Can also be assembled on individual dishes.

Servings: 6-8
Prep time: 2 minutes

# Mushroom Filling with Chicken Sauce

MEAT

*A classic.*

SAUCE

| | |
|---|---|
| 1 lb. | fresh mushrooms, sliced or chopped |
| 1 | onion, finely chopped |
| 2-3 Tbsp | oil |
| ⅛ tsp | pepper |
| ¼ tsp | nutmeg, grated |
| ¼ cup | all purpose flour |
| 4 cups | boiling water combined with 4 tsp chicken soup mix |
| 6–8 | prepared crepes or pastry shells |

In a large skillet, over medium heat, sauté mushrooms and onion in oil until tender. Add pepper and nutmeg. Slowly stir in flour. The mixture may become lumpy but that's fine. Add chicken broth, one cup at a time, stirring quickly.

FILLING

| | |
|---|---|
| ½ lb. | fresh mushrooms, sliced |
| 2-3 Tbsp | oil |
| 2 | cloves of garlic, minced |
| 1 cup | mushroom sauce (from above) |

In a small skillet, over medium heat, sauté mushrooms and garlic in oil. Fill crepes or pastry shells with the mixture and pour warm sauce over top.

**Tip:** For a heartier dish, chop leftover chicken into 1-inch cubes and add to cooked filling!

Servings: 6-8
Prep time: 15–20 minutes

# Mushroom Rosettes

| | |
|---|---|
| 1 Tbsp | olive oil |
| 1 Tbsp | margarine |
| 6–8 | Portobello mushrooms, diced, or 3-4 cups button mushrooms, diced |
| 5-6 | cloves of garlic, minced |
| | salt and pepper to taste |
| 1 (17.3-oz.) pkg. | puff pastry |

Preheat oven to 350F.

In a skillet, heat oil and margarine on medium heat. Sauté mushrooms and garlic until tender. Add salt and pepper. Cool. Set aside.

Roll out puff pastry to ¼-inch thickness on a lightly floured surface. Cut pastry into 3-inch squares. Fill each square with mushroom mixture. Pinch corners together so it looks like a rose. Place rose in a greased muffin pan. Bake until brown, approximately ½ hour.

**Servings: 6–8**
**Prep time: 30 minutes**

*Have these ready in your freezer for when company drops by. Just heat and serve.*

**Tips:** Freezes well.
Cook small batches at a time. Place on a paper towel-lined dish to drain excess oil. Serve wontons with duck sauce.

# Somosas

| | |
|---|---|
| 4 | medium-large potatoes, peeled and finely diced |
| 4 | large onions, diced |
| 1-kg bag | frozen mixed vegetables |
| 2-3 Tbsp | oil, or enough for deep frying method |
| ½-¾ tsp | chili powder |
| | salt and pepper to taste |
| 100 | wonton wrappers |

In a large skillet over medium heat, sauté potatoes, onions and frozen vegetables in oil. Cook over low heat until potatoes are cooked through but not mushy. Add chili powder, salt and pepper. Remove from heat. Cool.

Place a teaspoon of filling on each wonton wrapper. Fold edges in to create a triangle. Seal the edges with a small amount of water. Cook somosas in a deep fryer or in hot oil, until golden brown.

**Servings: 100 pieces**
**Prep time: 30 minutes**

# Stuffed Zucchini

*Great for Sukkoth!*

SAUCE

| | |
|---|---|
| 1 | lemon, juiced |
| 1 (5.5-oz.) can | tomato paste |
| 1¼ cups | water |
| 3 Tbsp | oil |
| 1 Tbsp | chicken soup powder |
| ⅛ tsp | cinnamon |
| 8–10 | zucchini (vegetable marrow), washed, trimmed, cut in half lengthwise |
| ½ lb. | ground chicken, uncooked |
| 1½ cups | cooked rice |
| 5-6 | mint leaves, chopped |
| 1 | onion, chopped |
| ½ cup | fresh parsley, chopped |
| ¼-½ tsp | cinnamon |
| | salt and pepper to taste |

Preheat oven to 375F.

In a small mixing bowl, combine lemon, tomato paste, water, oil, chicken soup powder and cinnamon. Mix well. Pour half the sauce into a 9 x 13-inch dish. Set dish aside. Reserve remaining sauce.

Using a melon scooper, or instrument of your choice, scoop out the flesh of the zucchini, leaving the shell intact. Discard flesh. Set aside zucchini shell.

In a large mixing bowl, combine ground chicken and rice. Add mint leaves, onion and parsley. Add cinnamon, pepper and salt. Mix well. Fill zucchini shells with meat and rice mixture. You may have some mixture left over. Put the zucchini into sauce-filled dish. Pour remaining sauce on top. Cover. Bake until very well done, approximately 1 hour.

Tip: Vegetable marrow is small and yellow or green. It looks like a small zucchini.

Servings: 10–12
Prep time: 25 minutes

*Yummy!*

# Zucchini Sticks

---

| | |
|---|---|
| 2 | medium zucchini, cut into 2–3-inch sticks |
| ½ tsp | salt |
| ¾ cup | all purpose flour |
| ¼ tsp | fresh ground black pepper |
| 2 | eggs, beaten |
| 1 tsp | Dijon mustard |
| 2 pinches | hot pepper flakes |
| 1¾ cups | fine bread crumbs |
| | oil for frying |

Toss zucchini with salt and let sit for 10 minutes. Rinse and pat dry with towels.

Combine flour and pepper in a small bowl. Put the beaten eggs, mustard and pepper flakes into a second small bowl. Put the bread crumbs into a third small bowl. Roll zucchini sticks in flour mixture then dip them in egg mixture and finally coat them in the crumbs. Heat oil to a 1-inch depth in a frying pan and fry coated zucchini in small batches for approximately 2 minutes on each side until brown and crisp. Keep warm in 250F oven until serving.

Serve with Spicy Mustard Sauce (below.)

**Servings: 6–8**
**Prep time: 45 minutes**

# Spicy Mustard Sauce

---

| | |
|---|---|
| ½ cup | mayonnaise |
| ¼ cup | Dijon mustard |
| 3 Tbsp | sugar |
| 2 Tbsp | fresh lemon juice |
| 1 tsp | dry mustard |
| ⅛ tsp | hot pepper flakes |
| 2 Tbsp | chopped dill |

Whisk all ingredients together until blended.

**Servings: 6–8**
**Prep time: 5 minutes**

# Florentine Mushroom Caps

PARVE

| | |
|---|---|
| 20 | medium mushrooms |
| ¼ cup | margarine |
| 3 Tbsp | onions, minced |
| ¼ cup | frozen spinach, boiled, drained, finely chopped |
| ⅓ cup | pine nuts |
| ¼ cup | pistachio nuts, finely chopped |
| 1½ tsp | ground marjoram or (2 Tbsp fresh, chopped) |
| 2 Tbsp | dried parsley |
| | salt and pepper to taste |

Preheat oven to 350F.

Remove stems from mushroom caps. Wash mushroom caps and stems. Finely chop stems. Reserve caps.

In a skillet melt margarine; sauté stems and onions until onions are translucent. Add spinach, pine nuts, pistachios, marjoram, parsley, salt and pepper. Mix thoroughly.

Par-boil mushroom caps and drain. Spoon the mixture into mushroom caps. Set the mushrooms onto a baking sheet and bake for 2–5 minutes or until hot to the touch.

**Tips:** To make dairy, sprinkle some Parmesan cheese on the mushrooms prior to baking.

Parboil means to boil until partially cooked.

Servings: 8–10
Prep time: 40–45 minutes

# Avocado Pita Melts

| | |
|---|---|
| 6 | plain or whole wheat pitas |
| 1 | avocado, mashed |
| ¼ cup | green onion, finely chopped |
| 2 Tbsp | lime or lemon juice |
| 2 Tbsp | mayonnaise |
| ½ tsp | garlic, minced |
| dash | hot pepper sauce |
| 12 slices | tomato (2– 3 tomatoes) |
| 1 cup | alfalfa sprouts |
| 1½ cups | Colby or Monterey Jack cheese |

Preheat oven to 400F.

Cut pitas into quarters. Arrange them on a parchment-covered baking sheet. In a small bowl, combine avocado, green onion, lime or lemon juice, mayonnaise, garlic and hot pepper sauce. Spread the mixture evenly over pitas. Top pitas with tomato slices, alfalfa sprouts and cheese. Bake for 5–7 minutes or until cheese is melted.

Servings: 24 hors d'oeuvres
Prep time: 15–20 minutes

# Marinated Eggplant Salad

*This presents beautifully.*

MARINADE

| | |
|---|---|
| 3 | cloves of garlic, minced |
| ½ | lemon, juiced |
| ½ cup | vinegar |
| 2 Tbsp | dry red wine |
| 1½ tsp | dried basil |
| 1 tsp | dried thyme |

SALAD

| | |
|---|---|
| 3 | large eggplants, sliced 1 inch thick |
| | oil for frying |
| ½ | yellow pepper, diced |
| ½ | green pepper, diced |
| ½ | red pepper, diced |
| ¼–½ cup | fresh parsley, finely chopped |

In a large jar or cruet, combine marinade ingredients. Cover. Shake well. Set aside.

Salt both sides of eggplant slices and place them in a large shallow container. Place plates on top of the top layer of eggplant in order to press water out of eggplant. Let sit for ½ hour to 1 hour. Remove the plates. Rinse eggplant slices. Pat them dry.

Heat ¼ inch of oil in a large skillet on medium heat. Fry each side of the eggplant until just cooked, but not mushy. Drain eggplant on a paper towel lined plate. Once drained, arrange eggplant slices slightly overlapping onto a large platter. Drizzle dressing on top. Garnish with peppers and parsley. Allow to marinate for at least 24 hours in the refrigerator. Can be served chilled or at room temperature.

Tip: If oil is extremely hot, the eggplant will absorb less of it.

Servings: 6–8
Prep time: 45 minutes, marinate 24 hours

# Grapefruit, Avocado and Hazelnut Salad

*Exquisite and easy.*

**DRESSING**

| ½ cup | olive oil |
| 2 Tbsp | balsamic vinegar |
| 2 Tbsp | pink grapefruit juice |
| 1 Tbsp | honey |
| ½ tsp | Dijon mustard |

**SALAD**

| 2 cups | mixed greens |
| 2 | pink grapefruit, peeled and cut in slices or chunks |
| 1 | ripe avocado, peeled, thinly sliced |
| ¼ cup | roasted hazelnuts, lightly crushed |

**Tip:** To get more juice out of citrus fruits, knead them on a hard surface before cutting.

In a small jar or cruet, combine dressing ingredients. Cover. Shake well. Set aside.

On a large salad plate, arrange mixed greens, grapefruit sections and avocado. Sprinkle lightly with hazelnuts. Spoon dressing lightly over salad and serve. Use only enough dressing to lightly coat salad ingredients or serve separately.

Servings: 6–8
Prep time: 20 minutes

# Dijon Asparagus Salad

DRESSING

| ⅓ cup | coleslaw dressing, page 83 |
| 2 Tbsp | Dijon mustard |
| ¼ tsp | salt |
| ¼ tsp | fresh ground pepper |
| 2 oz. | linguini pasta, broken in half |
| ½ lb. | fresh asparagus, cut diagonally into 1-inch pieces |
| 9 | cherry tomatoes, quartered |
| 2 Tbsp | red onion, chopped |
| ¼ cup | pine nuts or toasted almonds |

In a cruet or small jar, combine dressing ingredients. Cover and shake well. Set aside.

Cook linguini according to package directions until al dente. Drain and rinse under cold water. Put some water in a medium-sized saucepan. Add the asparagus and bring the water to boil. Cook until slightly tender. Drain.

Combine linguini, asparagus, tomatoes, onion, and dressing. Refrigerate. Add pine nuts just before serving.

Servings: 4–6
Prep time: 25–30 minutes

# Thai Mango Salad

DRESSING

| | |
|---|---|
| 1 Tbsp | rice vinegar |
| 1 Tbsp | lime juice |
| 1 Tbsp | honey |
| 2 Tbsp | sugar |
| 1 tsp | lime zest, finely grated |
| ¼ tsp | hot pepper flakes |
| 3 Tbsp | vegetable oil |
| 1 Tbsp | sesame oil |
| ⅓ cup | fresh coriander, chopped (optional) |
| ¾ tsp | salt |
| ¾ tsp | pepper |

SALAD

| | |
|---|---|
| 2 | mangoes, just barely ripe, julienned |
| 1 | red pepper, julienned |
| 1 | green pepper, julienned |
| 1 | red onion, thinly sliced |
| 6 | Boston lettuce or radicchio leaves |

**Tip:** Julienne means to cut into long thin strips

In a large bowl, whisk together rice vinegar, lime juice, honey, sugar, lime zest and hot pepper flakes. Whisking constantly, drizzle in vegetable and sesame oils until well combined. Stir in coriander, salt and pepper. Add mangoes, peppers and onion. Gently toss until well combined.

Place a leaf of lettuce on a salad plate. Spoon a serving of the salad in the centre of the lettuce leaf.

Servings: 6
Prep time: 15–20 minutes

# Algerian Roasted Peppers & Tomatoes

| | |
|---|---|
| 2 | large red peppers, roasted, diced |
| 2 | large green peppers, roasted, diced |
| 1 | clove of garlic, minced |
| 1 (28-oz.) can | diced tomatoes, undrained |
| 5 Tbsp | olive oil |
| 1 Tbsp | sugar |
| ½–1 tsp | salt |
| | chili powder to taste (optional) |

In a medium-sized pot, combine all the ingredients. Bring to a boil. Reduce heat. Simmer until liquid is reduced, approximately 1–2 hours.

Alternatively, place ingredients in a microwaveable bowl, and cook on high for 15 minutes. Mix and check to see if most of the liquid has evaporated. If it has not, repeat for an additional 15 minutes. Repeat process until liquid has reduced. Mixture should have a paste consistency to indicate it has cooked. Cool. Add more spices, to taste.

PARVE

Tip: Roast peppers whole on a cookie sheet lined with foil. Broil or barbeque until the skin is uniformly blackened. Place them in a brown paper bag or covered bowl until slightly cooled. When cool enough to the touch remove the skins.

Servings: 4–6
Prep time: 45–60 minutes

# Turkish Salad

| | |
|---|---|
| ½ cup | oil |
| 1 | eggplant, round slices cut in quarters |
| 4 | cloves of garlic, cut in half |
| 1 | red pepper, diced |
| 1 | green pepper, diced |
| ¼ cup | fresh parsley, chopped |
| 4-5 Tbsp | tomato paste |
| 2 tsp | cumin |
| 1 tsp | salt |
| 1 tsp | paprika |

In a medium-sized skillet over medium-high heat, fry eggplant in oil until brown on both sides. Reduce heat. Add garlic, peppers, parsley, tomato paste, cumin, salt and paprika. Simmer for 15 minutes while occasionally stirring. Cool. Refrigerate in a sealed container.

PARVE

Tip: Can be served cold or at room temperature.

Servings: 4–6
Prep time: 25–30 minutes

# Spinach Pesto Dressing

*The walnuts and spinach
give this pesto a unique
flavor.*

**Tips:** This makes enough for
a crowd. You can halve the
recipe (4 cups of noodles) for
6–8 people. Serve cold.
Nuts stored in the freezer last
longer.

DRESSING

| | |
|---|---|
| ½ cup | oil or oil-free salad dressing |
| ½ cup | water |
| 1 tsp | salt |
| 1 tsp | dried basil |
| ½ cup | walnuts |
| 2 | cloves of garlic |
| 1 (300-g) pkg. | frozen, chopped spinach thawed, undrained |
| 1 (14-oz.) pkg. | ruffled pasta, cooked, drained |

Preheat oven to 375F.

In a large jar or cruet, combine oil, water, salt and basil. Cover. Shake well.
Set aside.

Process walnuts and garlic in a food processor, using a steel blade. Pulse until mixture becomes crumbly. Remove the mixture and spread it evenly on a cookie sheet. Toast it in oven for several minutes, until very crispy, keeping a close eye that it doesn't burn. Remove from oven. Cool.

Process spinach in a food processor, using a steel blade until pureed.

Combine with walnut/garlic mixture. Serve with pasta.

# Marvellous Mango Salsa

| | |
|---|---|
| 1 | ripe mango, peeled and diced |
| 1 | red pepper, roasted, seeded and diced |
| ¼ cup | red onion, finely diced |
| 2 Tbsp | fresh parsley, chopped |
| 1 Tbsp | fresh mint, chopped |
| 1 Tbsp | rice vinegar |
| ¼ tsp | cumin |

In a small bowl, gently mix together all the ingredients.

Serve with grilled chicken or fish.

# White Bean Salad

| | |
|---|---|
| 1 (19-oz.) can | white kidney beans, rinsed and drained |
| 1 | clove of garlic, minced |
| 1 Tbsp | olive oil |
| 4 tsp | lemon juice |
| ½ tsp | ground cumin |
| ½ tsp | pepper |
| ¼ tsp | salt |
| ⅛ tsp | hot pepper sauce |
| 2 Tbsp | fresh parsley, chopped (optional) |

Put the beans, garlic, oil, lemon juice, cumin, pepper, salt and hot pepper sauce in a blender or food processor. Process until smooth. Stir in parsley. Transfer to container. Refrigerate.

PARVE

*Tastes like hummus. It is an easy, quick protein.*

Tips: Serve with toasted pita, crackers or fresh vegetables. Doubles well.

Servings: 1⅓ cups
Prep time: 10 minutes

# Chopped Vegetarian Liver

| | |
|---|---|
| 2-3 Tbsp | oil |
| 2 | onions, chopped |
| 3 | eggs, hard cooked |
| 1 (14-oz.) can | green peas, drained |
| ¼ cup | almonds |
| | salt and pepper to taste |
| | lettuce leaves, for serving |
| | OR |
| | crackers, for serving |

In a large frying pan, sauté onions in oil over medium heat until soft, approximately 10 minutes.

In a food processor, blend onions, eggs and peas. Add almonds and process mixture until it becomes the consistency of chopped liver. Season with salt and pepper.

Serve as appetizer on a lettuce leaf or as hors d'oeuvres with crackers.

PARVE

*"This recipe has been in my family for years and is still a favourite."*

Tips: Sprinkle paprika on the edges of the lettuce, lining each individual cold appetizer plate.
Garnish with diced strips of yellow pepper, or cherry tomatoes; nice contrast of colours.

Servings: 6 as appetizer, more as hors d'oeuvres
Prep time: 20 minutes

# Guacamole

| | |
|---|---|
| 1 | avocado, ripe |
| 2 tsp | lemon juice, divided in half |
| 1 | clove of garlic, crushed |
| 2 tsp | onion, minced |
| ½ tsp | salt |
| ¼ tsp | chili pepper or hot pepper sauce |

Scoop avocado out of its skin and place it in a bowl. Toss with 1 teaspoon of lemon juice. Using a fork, mash it thoroughly until consistency is smooth. Combine mashed avocado with garlic, onion, remaining lemon juice, salt and chili pepper. Cover and refrigerate if not serving immediately. Mix again before serving.

Servings: 4–6
Prep time: 5–10 minutes

DAIRY

# Dressed-Up Guacamole

| | |
|---|---|
| 1 (10-oz.) pkg. | tortilla chips |
| 1 cup | grated Cheddar cheese |
| | guacamole (see recipe above) |
| 1 | red pepper, diced |
| 2 | large tomatoes, diced |
| 3 | green onions, diced |
| | olives or hot peppers, (optional) |
| 1 cup | sour cream |
| ½ cup | taco sauce or salsa |

Arrange chips on a large round oven-safe platter.

Sprinkle cheese over chips and broil in the oven until cheese melts, approximately 10 minutes.

Take dish out of the oven. Let cool 5-10 minutes.

Spoon the guacamole in the centre of the dish on top of the cheesy chips.

Sprinkle platter with diced peppers, tomatoes, green onions and olives. Serve with sour cream and salsa for dipping.

Servings: 6–8
Prep time: 10 minutes

# Spinach Feta Dip

DAIRY

*This dip is a healthier version of the famous spinach dip.*

DIP

| | |
|---|---|
| 1 (10-oz.) pkg. | chopped frozen spinach, thawed and well drained |
| 1 cup | non-fat plain yogurt |
| ½ cup | feta cheese |
| 1 | clove of garlic, minced |
| 1 tsp | oregano |
| ½ tsp | thyme |
| ¼ tsp | black pepper |
| 1 | round loaf of bread, e.g., pumpernickel |
| | assorted vegetables, sliced |

In a food processor combine dip ingredients. Process until chunky. Chill for 1 hour.

Hollow out the bread with a small paring knife, leaving a ½-inch shell. Cut the bread you have removed into 1-inch cubes. Set aside.

Spoon the dip mixture into the hollowed bread before serving. Serve with bread cubes and fresh vegetables for dipping.

Servings: approximately 2 cups
Prep time: 5–10 minutes

# Korozott/Cheese Spread

DAIRY

*Everyone loves it. Nice as a dip at a party.*

| | |
|---|---|
| 8 oz. | farmer's cheese, dry |
| 4 oz. | cream cheese, softened |
| ½ cup | butter, softened |
| 3 Tbsp | light sour cream |
| 3 | green onions, sliced, then halved (with green) |
| 1½ tsp | paprika |
| 1 tsp | caraway seeds or dill seeds |
| ½ tsp | salt |
| | parsley sprigs for garnish |

In a large bowl, combine ingredients in the order they are listed. Transfer the mixture to a serving dish. Gently shape it into a mound. Garnish with parsley. Serve with crackers, bread or raw vegetables.

Tips: Great with crackers or in hollowed-out bread.
Mix this in a blender for a smoother consistency. Stir in chopped scallions and sprinkle with chopped parsley.

Servings: 10–12
Prep time: 10 minutes

# Tchoutchouka (Moroccan Tomato Pepper Spread)

| | |
|---|---|
| 2 (28-oz.) cans | whole tomatoes, undrained |
| 1 | green pepper, diced |
| 1 | red pepper, diced |
| 6–8 | cloves of garlic, minced |
| 3–4 Tbsp | oil |
| 2 Tbsp | sugar |

In a large pot over medium-low heat, warm tomatoes, then mash them. Add peppers and garlic. Bring to a boil. Lower heat to medium setting. Simmer, uncovered, until liquid evaporates, approximately 6-8 hours, stirring every few hours. Add oil and sugar after 5 hours. Cool. Refrigerate. Serve cold.

Serve with crackers, bread, pita, or rice. This is especially good if you roast the peppers before dicing them.

Servings: 4–6
Prep time: 20 minutes

Tip: Frost the rims of the bowls by dipping the rims in water then in a pie plate of coloured sugar.

# Ceres Frozen Fruit Blizzards

| | |
|---|---|
| 3 cups | Ceres Medley of Fruits juice or orange juice |
| 1 (300-g) pkg. | frozen unsweetened raspberries |
| 1 cup | blueberries, fresh or frozen |
| 1 | banana, cut into chunks |
| ⅓ cup | maple syrup (optional) |

In a blender or food processor, blend together juice, raspberries, blueberries, banana and maple syrup until smooth, approximately 2 minutes. Pour into chilled glasses. Serve immediately.

Can only be refrigerated for up to 2 hours.

Servings: 6
Prep time: 5 minutes

# soups & sauces

# Chunky Vegetable Beef Soup

*Hearty soup for a cold winter day.*

| | |
|---|---|
| 1 lb. | boneless beef, chuck cut |
| 1 Tbsp | oil |
| 2 cups | beef broth |
| 1 tsp | salt |
| 1½ tsp | fresh marjoram leaves, chopped, or ½ tsp dried |
| 1½ tsp | fresh thyme, or ½ tsp dried |
| ⅛ tsp | fresh ground pepper |
| 1 | bay leaf |
| 3 cups | water |
| 1 cup | corn kernels, canned or frozen |
| 3 | medium carrots, sliced, approximately 1 cup |
| 1 | large stalk of celery, sliced, approximately ½ cup |
| 1 | medium onion, chopped |
| 1 (10-oz.) can | diced tomatoes, undrained |

In a large stockpot, brown beef in oil. Stir in broth, salt, marjoram, thyme, pepper, bay leaf and water. Bring soup to a boil. Reduce to low heat. Cover. Simmer for 1–1½ hours or until beef is tender. Add corn, carrots, celery, onion and tomatoes. Bring to a boil. Reduce to low heat. Cover. Simmer for an additional 35 minutes. Remove bay leaf before serving.

Tip: Use a pasta pot with the insert. When it is time to strain, simply lift out the basket and your soup is ready.

Servings: 5–6
Prep time: 15–20 minutes

# Sunday Barley Vegetable Soup

| | |
|---|---|
| 10–12 cups | boiling water |
| ¾ cup | pearl barley |
| 2–3 | large carrots, thinly sliced |
| 2–3 | outer celery stalks, thinly sliced |
| 2–3 | potatoes, diced |
| 2–3 | medium onions, diced |
| 1 cup | mushrooms, sliced |
| 2–3 | outer leaves of cabbage (optional) |
| 3 Tbsp | onion soup mix or onion and mushroom soup mix or alphabet soup mix |
| | salt and pepper to taste |

Pour 10 cups of boiling water into a large pot. Add barley. Cook uncovered, over high heat for 5 minutes. Skim off any white foam. Add vegetables, soup mix, salt and pepper. Cover. Simmer, stirring occasionally, for 1½ hours. Add 2 cups of boiling water to maintain volume.

**Tip:** For tomato soup, add 1 (28-oz.) can whole tomatoes, sliced.

To make the soup dairy, sprinkle grated cheese onto individual portions (¼ cup each).

Servings: 8–10
Prep time: 30 minutes

# Kitchen Sink Veggie Soup

| | |
|---|---|
| 6–8 cups | water |
| 6 | potatoes, peeled, cubed |
| 6 | carrots, peeled, cut in chunks |
| 3 | stalks of celery, chopped |
| 1 | onion, chopped |
| 1 cup | water (optional) |
| ¼ cup | parve chicken soup powder |
| 1 (28-oz.) can | diced tomatoes, drained |
| 1 (12-oz.) can | corn niblets, drained |
| 1 (19-oz.) can | red kidney beans, drained, rinsed |
| 1 (19-oz.) can | chickpeas, drained, rinsed |
| | salt and pepper to taste |
| | garlic to taste |

In a large pot, boil potatoes, carrots, celery and onion. Using a hand blender, purée the vegetables, adding 1 cup of water to the pot at the same time. Add chicken soup powder, tomatoes, corn, beans, chickpeas, salt, pepper and garlic. Cover. Cook on medium-high heat for 20–30 minutes. Stir occasionally.

# Carrot and Rice Soup

| | |
|---|---|
| ¼ cup | margarine |
| 1 | red onion, sliced |
| 1 | clove of garlic, minced (optional) |
| 5 | cups water |
| 2½ cups | carrots, peeled, sliced |
| ¼ cup | long-grain rice, uncooked |
| 2 Tbsp | parve chicken soup powder |
| ½ tsp | ginger powder |
| | salt to taste |
| | parsley to taste |

In an 8-quart saucepan, melt margarine. Sauté onion and garlic until tender. Add water, carrots, rice and chicken broth. Bring to a boil. Reduce heat. Cover. Simmer for 20–25 minutes. Remove from heat. Cool. Blend until smooth. Add ginger, salt and parsley.

# Minestrone

| | |
|---|---|
| 2–3 Tbsp | oil |
| ½ | green cabbage, shredded coarsely |
| 2 | celery stalks, sliced |
| 1 | clove of garlic, minced |
| 2 | large onions, chopped |
| 6 | carrots, peeled and diced |
| 2 | large tomatoes, peeled and chopped |
| 1 (14-oz.) can | kidney beans, drained |
| 8–10 cups | water (approximately, until pot is ¾ full) |
| 4 | vegetable soup cubes |
| 1 (12-oz.) can | tomato sauce |
| 2 | potatoes, peeled, chopped |
| | handful spaghetti, broken in half (optional) |
| 4 tsp | salt |
| ½ tsp | pepper |
| ½ tsp | dried basil |
| ½ tsp | dried oregano |

*Enough for a whole "gathering."*

In a large pot heat oil. Add cabbage, celery, garlic and onions. Sauté until softened.

Add carrots, tomatoes and beans. Fill pot with water until the pot is three quarters full (approximately 8–10 cups). Add soup cubes. Cover. Simmer for 1 hour.

Add tomato sauce, potatoes, spaghetti, salt, pepper, basil and oregano. Cook for an additional hour.

Adjust seasoning at the end if needed.

**Dairy soup:** Add grated cheese when ready to serve. Freezes well.

Servings: 8–10 servings
Prep time: 25–30 minutes

# Tortellini Turkey Soup

| | |
|---|---|
| 1 (680-g) pkg. | vegetable tortellini, cooked, drained |
| 12 cups | water |
| 3 | carrots, peeled and chopped |
| 2 | stalks of celery, chopped |
| 1 | onion, chopped |
| 1 | turkey leg or breast |
| 2 tsp | salt |
| ⅛ tsp | dried dill |
| ⅛ tsp | turmeric (optional) |
| ¾ cup | fresh spinach, washed, drained and chopped |
| 2 Tbsp | fresh parsley, chopped |
| 2 | eggs, whisked |

In a large stockpot, combine water, carrots, celery, onion, turkey leg or breast, salt, dill and turmeric. Bring to a boil. Reduce heat to medium. Cook for 20 minutes. Strain soup, removing and setting aside the vegetables and turkey leg or breast. Add spinach and parsley. Cook for an additional 10–20 minutes on medium to low heat.

Dice the vegetables and turkey. Add to soup. Add tortellini and eggs 5 minutes before serving.

Servings: 8–10
Prep time: 30 minutes

# Lemon Parsnip Soup

PARVE / MEAT

| | |
|---|---|
| 1 Tbsp | oil |
| 2 | onions, chopped |
| 2 Tbsp | fresh thyme leaves, chopped |
| 1 tsp | lemon zest, finely grated |
| 4 cups | parsnips, peeled, chopped |
| 2 cups | potatoes, peeled, chopped |
| 6 cups | chicken or vegetable broth |
| 1 Tbsp | lemon juice |
| ½ tsp | salt |
| | pepper to taste |
| | thyme sprigs |

In a large saucepan, heat oil. Add onion, thyme leaves, and lemon zest. Sauté on low heat for 5 minutes, stirring often. Add parsnips and potatoes. Simmer for 10 minutes over medium-low heat, stirring occasionally. Stir in broth. Bring to a boil. Cover. Reduce heat and simmer, stirring occasionally, for 1 hour or until parsnips and potatoes are very soft. Remove from heat. Cool.

Transfer soup to a blender, or use a hand blender and blend until smooth. Stir in lemon juice, salt and pepper. Adjust seasonings. Garnish with thyme sprigs before serving.

Tip: Lemons provide a tart accent to this soup and in many dishes.

Slices, wedges or bits of peel add both flavour and colour to garnishes

Servings: 4–6
Prep time: 15–20 minutes

# Squash & Fennel (Anise) Soup

| | |
|---|---|
| 1 | fennel (anise) bulb |
| 1 Tbsp | margarine |
| 1 | celery stalk, chopped |
| 1 | onion, chopped |
| 1 | butternut squash, peeled, seeded, and cubed |
| | broth: 2 cups water with 1 Tbsp vegetable or parve chicken soup mix |
| 2 cups | water |
| ½ tsp | salt (optional) |

Take greenery off fennel bulb. Reserve greenery for garnishing. Chop fennel bulb into thick pieces. Reserve.

Melt margarine in an 8 quart pot over medium heat. Add celery and onion stirring regularly until vegetables are translucent but not golden. Stir in fennel, squash, broth, and additional water. Bring to a boil. Reduce heat. Cover and simmer until vegetables are tender, approximately 15–30 minutes. Add salt to taste.

Allow soup to cool down before puréeing with a hand blender or in a food processor. Reheat prior to serving.

**Tips:** Freezes well.
Other types of squash may be substituted in lieu of butternut.

Servings: 6–8
Prep time: 10 minutes

# Moroccan Peanut and Tomato Soup

PARVE

| | |
|---|---|
| 1 | onion, finely chopped |
| 4 | cloves of garlic, minced |
| 2 Tbsp | margarine |
| 1 (28-oz.) can | tomatoes, crushed or diced |
| 1 cup | peanut butter |
| ¼ cup | ketchup |
| ¼ cup | vinegar |
| 2 Tbsp | chili powder |
| 1 tsp | cumin |
| 1 tsp | black pepper |
| 1 tsp | hot pepper sauce |
| 1 tsp | mustard powder |
| 1 tsp | parsley flakes (optional) |
| 2 cups | water |

In a large pot, sauté onion and garlic in margarine until translucent. Add remaining ingredients, except water. Bring to a boil, stirring constantly, being careful not to burn the mixture. Add water slowly. Reduce heat to simmer and cook uncovered for 10–15 minutes. Stir occasionally.

*"Whenever I serve this dish, the tasters are amazed to discover that the magic ingredient is peanut butter. A friend, who is also a restaurateur, was so impressed with the dish, he wanted to add it to his restaurant's menu. But please, before serving such a dish, check that your guests have no allergies to peanuts!"*

**Tips:** Serve with croutons or garlic bread.
Can also make the soup dairy by sprinkling shredded Parmesan cheese on top of each serving or using dairy margarine.

Servings: 8
Prep time: 15–20 minutes

# Red Pepper Bisque

| | |
|---|---|
| 1 Tbsp | olive oil |
| ½ Tbsp | margarine |
| 3 | onions, diced |
| 8 | red peppers, diced |
| 3 | potatoes, diced |
| 3 | cloves of garlic |
| 3 Tbsp | tomato paste |
| 2 | chicken flavoured soup cubes, parve |
| 1–2 tsp | sugar |
| | fresh ground pepper to taste |
| | sea salt to taste |
| | fresh basil, chopped, to taste |
| ⅛ tsp | cayenne pepper |
| ½ cup | parve sour cream |

Heat oil and margarine in a large skillet. On medium heat sauté onions until translucent. Add peppers, potatoes and garlic. Sauté on low heat until soft. Remove from heat and purée with a hand blender. Add tomato paste, chicken cubes and sugar. Add pepper, salt, basil and cayenne pepper to taste. Mix well. Add sour cream just before serving. Serve hot or at room temperature.

**Tip:** The sour cream can be added in a dollop to individual bowls for a beautiful presentation.

Servings: 6–8
Prep time: 30 minutes

# Red Pepper and Fennel Soup

| | |
|---|---|
| 3 | red peppers, seeded, chopped |
| 1 | bulb fennel, chopped |
| 1 | medium onion chopped |
| 2 Tbsp | oil |
| 1 | hot pickled red cherry pepper, seeded, chopped |
| 4 cups | parve chicken broth |
| 1 cup | parve sour cream |
| | salt to taste |
| | parve sour cream, to garnish |
| | fresh basil, chopped, to garnish |
| | croutons, to garnish |

In a large pot, sauté red peppers, fennel and onion in oil until tender, approximately 15–25 minutes. Add hot pepper and chicken broth. Bring to a boil. Simmer, covered, for 35–45 minutes. Cool.

Purée with an electric hand blender. Add parve sour cream and salt. Heat the soup being careful, not to boil. Garnish with sour cream, basil and croutons. Serve warm or at room temperature.

Tip For a less spicy version, use half the cherry pepper.

Servings: 4–6
Prep time: 15 minutes

*This is a great staple to serve before or after a fast.*

Tips: Freezes well.

You can use an electric hand blender and process it directly in the pot.

# Zucchini Potato Soup

| | |
|---|---|
| 2 Tbsp | margarine |
| 2 | potatoes, diced |
| 2 | zucchinis, unpeeled, sliced |
| 1 | onion, diced |
| 3 cups | parve chicken broth (2 Tbsp chicken soup mix/ 3 cups water) |
| | salt and pepper to taste |

In a large pot, sauté potatoes, zucchinis, and onion in margarine until tender. Stir in broth, salt, and pepper. Bring soup to a boil. Reduce heat. Cover. Simmer for 30 minutes. Cool. Transfer the soup in batches to a blender or food processor. Process until smooth.

Servings: 4–6
Prep time: 10–15 minutes

# Potato Leek Soup

| | |
|---|---|
| 1 | onion, chopped |
| 6–8 | leeks, washed well, chopped |
| 3 Tbsp | oil or margarine |
| 5 lbs. | red potatoes, peeled, sliced |
| 10–12 cups | water |
| 3 Tbsp | parve chicken soup powder |
| 1–2 Tbsp | fresh chives, chopped |
| | salt and pepper to taste |

In a large pot, sauté onion and leeks in oil for 3 minutes or until tender. Add potatoes, water and soup powder. Bring to a boil. Cover. Reduce heat. Simmer until vegetables are soft. Remove from heat. Cool.

Transfer soup to a blender or use a hand blender and process until smooth. Stir in chives. Add salt and pepper to taste.

Serve cold or hot. Garnish with extra chives.

Freezes well!

**Tips:** For a creamier, dairy soup, add 1 cup milk to ingredients.

Garnish with soup mandel.

To avoid "crying" when peeling onions, hold them under cold water while peeling them or refrigerate the onions before peeling them.

Servings: 6–8
Prep time: 15–20 minutes

# Sweet Potato, Chickpea & Corn Chowder with Roasted Red Pepper

PARVE

*Exquisite! A real down to earth and homey soup.*

| 1 Tbsp | oil |
| 1 | large onion, diced |
| 2 | cloves of garlic, minced |
| 2 | medium sweet potatoes, peeled, cut into ½-inch cubes |
| 1 Tbsp | paprika |
| 3–4 cups | vegetable stock |
| 1 (19-oz.) can | chickpeas, drained |
| 1 (12-oz.) can | corn niblets, drained |
| 1 tsp | salt |
| | fresh ground black pepper to taste |
| | cayenne pepper to taste |
| 2–3 Tbsp | fresh parsley or cilantro, chopped or 2–3 tsp dried |

RED PEPPER PURÉE

| 1 | large red pepper, roasted |
| 1 | clove of garlic |
| 1 Tbsp | olive oil |
| ⅛ tsp | coarse salt |
| few drops | balsamic vinegar |
| | fresh ground pepper, to taste |

In a large pot, heat oil and sauté onion until translucent. Add garlic and sauté until savory. Add sweet potatoes and paprika, tossing to coat the potatoes. Pour in vegetable stock and bring to a boil. Lower heat. Simmer, covered, for 10 minutes or until potatoes are soft. Add chickpeas, corn, salt, pepper and cayenne. Gently stir the soup until it becomes slightly thick. Add parsley and season to taste. Soup may be eaten chunky or puréed with a hand blender.

**RED PEPPER PURÉE:** Place all ingredients in a blender and purée. Season to taste.

Serve soup in shallow, wide bowls and garnish with a spoonful of red pepper purée and a sprig of fresh parsley or cilantro.

Servings: 6–8
Prep time: 20–30 minutes

# Roasted Tomato Bisque

*This is a real heart-warming soup!*

| | |
|---|---|
| 2 | onions, peeled, quartered |
| 6 | ripe tomatoes, halved |
| 1 Tbsp | olive oil |
| 1 bulb | garlic, roasted (see tip) |
| 2 Tbsp | brown sugar |
| 1 (28-oz.) can | chopped tomatoes |
| ½ cup | parve chicken broth |
| | salt and pepper to taste |
| ¼ cup | fresh basil leaves, chopped, for garnish (optional) |

Preheat oven to broil.

Spray a large baking pan with non-stick cooking spray. Place onions and tomatoes in the pan. Broil until onions are golden and slightly blackened around the edges and tomato skins are blackened. Remove tomato skins from tomatoes.

In a skillet, heat olive oil. Add onions, tomatoes and roasted garlic cloves. Sauté for 2 minutes. Add brown sugar, canned tomatoes and broth. Simmer on medium heat till reduced by half. Using a hand blender, purée soup. Season with salt and pepper to taste. Before serving, garnish with fresh basil.

**Tip:** To roast garlic, leave the bulb whole. Trim top, brush with a little oil and bake at 350F for 45–60 minutes. The cloves should push easily out of their skin.

Servings: 4–6
Prep time: 15–20 minutes

# Asparagus Soup

| ¾ cup | onion, chopped |
| 2 Tbsp | oil |
| 1 lb. | asparagus, cut in 1-inch pieces |
| 1½ stalks | celery, cut in 1-inch pieces |
| 1 | baking potato, peeled, chopped |
| 4 cups | vegetable stock or water |
| 1 cup | dry white wine |
| ¼ cup | fresh dill, chopped or 1 Tbsp dried dill |
| | salt and pepper to taste |
| | fresh dill, to garnish |

In a heavy pot, sauté onions in oil for approximately 10 minutes. Stir in asparagus, celery and potato. Add stock, wine, dill, salt and pepper. Simmer, partly covered, for 30 minutes, until vegetables become tender. Cool. Purée with an electric hand blender or put the soup through a sieve, pouring it back into the pot.

To serve, reheat soup and season. Garnish with dill.

PARVE

Tip: Broccoli or cauliflower can be substituted for asparagus.

Servings: 6
Prep time: 15 minutes

# Chilled Gazpacho

| 1 (28-oz.) can | tomatoes, undrained |
| 1 | green pepper, seeded and cubed |
| 1 | English cucumber, peeled |
| 1 | onion, diced |
| 2 cloves | garlic |
| ¼ cup | cider vinegar |
| 1 tsp | salt, optional |
| ¼ tsp | fresh ground pepper |
| 2–3 drops | Tabasco sauce |
| 1 (28-oz.) can | vegetable juice |

Combine all ingredients (except for vegetable juice) in a large bowl. Blend, using a counter-top or hand blender, until desired consistency is reached. Add vegetable juice and mix well. Refrigerate overnight. Serve cold with croutons.

PARVE

Gazpacho is delicious smooth or chunky. Make your signature soup by adding different vegetables.

Servings: 6–8
Prep time: 15 minutes

Tips: You can also use a hand blender to process ingredients.
If you like a sweeter taste, add more honey or sugar to taste.
Garnish with mint.

Servings: 4–6
Prep time: 20 minutes

PARVE

*Great served as an appetizer, drink or dessert.*

Tips: May be frozen.
To keep berries longer, wash right before serving.

Servings: 8–10
Prep Time: 20–30 minutes

# Ceres Peach Melon Soup

| | |
|---|---|
| 6 | fresh peaches, halved, with pit removed |
| ⅓ cup | lemon juice |
| ¼ cup | dry white wine |
| 1 Tbsp | honey |
| ¼ tsp | cinnamon |
| ⅛ tsp | nutmeg |
| 1 | cantaloupe, peeled and cut into chunks |
| 1 cup | The Ceres Apple, Berry and Cherry juice (Secrets of the Valley) or orange juice |

Dip peaches in boiling water for 30 seconds to 1 minute then in ice water. Remove skin. Place peaches, lemon juice, wine, honey, cinnamon and nutmeg in a blender or food processor. Process until smooth. Transfer to a container. Set aside.

Process cantaloupe and fruit juice. Combine both mixtures. Refrigerate.

# Refreshing Fruit Soup

| | |
|---|---|
| 2 (14-oz.) cans | Bing cherries, pitted, undrained |
| 2 quarts | strawberries |
| 2 cups | blueberries |
| 2 cups | raspberries |
| ¼ cup | sweet wine |
| 2 Tbsp | sugar |
| 1 Tbsp | lemon juice |
| 1 (85-g) pkg. | strawberry gelatin mix |
| 1 Tbsp | cornstarch dissolved in 2 Tbsp cold water |

In a medium-sized saucepan, bring the cherries, strawberries, blueberries, raspberries, wine, sugar and lemon juice to a boil. Reduce to medium-low heat. Add strawberry gelatin and dissolved cornstarch to the fruit mixture. Simmer, covered, for 20 minutes. Additional sugar, lemon juice or wine may be added to taste at this time. Chill. Serve cold. Soup can be puréed or served as is.

# Chilled Strawberry Soup

| | |
|---|---|
| 3 quarts | strawberries, washed and hulled |
| 1–2 Tbsp | lemon juice |
| ¼ cup | sweet red wine or to taste |
| ¼ cup | sugar, to taste |
| 4 oz. | whipped cream topping (optional) |

Put the strawberries in blender or food processor. Add lemon juice, red wine and sugar. Process until smooth. Soup should be sweet and tangy. You can add more lemon juice, wine or sugar according to your taste.

Strain mixture through a sieve to remove seeds. Stir in whipped cream topping to thicken. Transfer to container. Cover. Refrigerate. Serve cold.

PARVE

Tip:The whipped topping adds a creamy thickness to the soup, giving it a soft pink colour.
Portions do not have to be big. Small ice-cream bowls or wide glasses make nice serving dishes.

Servings: 4–6
Prep time: 10–15 minutes

# Worcestershire Sauce

| | |
|---|---|
| ¼ cup | balsamic vinegar |
| ¼ cup | soy sauce |
| ¼ tsp | freshly ground black pepper |
| ¼ tsp | corn syrup |
| ¼ tsp | vegetable oil |
| ¼ tsp | garlic powder |
| ¼ tsp | onion powder |

In a large jar or cruet, combine all ingredients. Cover. Shake well. You can adjust seasonings according to your individual taste. Refrigerate.

PARVE

*Worcestershire sauce is often called for in meat recipes, yet it is very difficult to find without fish in it. This recipe should be a quick easy solution for you to use.*

Servings: ½ cup
Prep time: 5 minutes

# Cranberry Sauce

| | |
|---|---|
| 1 (16-oz.) can | pineapple tidbits, drained. Reserve juice. |
| | orange juice, sufficient to make 1½ cups liquid when added to pineapple juice, |
| 1 (12-oz.) pkg. | cranberries |
| 1¼ cups | sugar |
| ½ tsp | cinnamon |
| ½ tsp | ground ginger |
| ¼ tsp | allspice |
| 1 cup | raisins |

Put the pineapple tidbits in a small bowl. Put the reserved juice in a separate bowl. Add enough orange juice to pineapple juice to make 1½ cups liquid.

In a medium-sized saucepan, combine juices, cranberries, sugar, cinnamon, ginger, allspice and raisins. Stir over medium heat. Cook mixture until berries pop. Cool. Add pineapple tidbits. Transfer the mixture to a bowl and refrigerate, covered, for several hours.

Servings: 6–8
Prep time: 10 minutes

# Ceres Cranberry Sauce

| | |
|---|---|
| 1 (12-oz.) pkg. | fresh cranberries |
| ½ cup | Ceres Pineapple juice or orange juice |
| ½ cup | sugar |

In a large saucepan, combine cranberries, juice and sugar. Bring to a boil. Simmer, uncovered, for 15–20 minutes until liquid becomes jelly-like in texture. Cool. Cover. Refrigerate.

Servings: 6
Prep time: 5 minutes

3

# salads & dressings

# Summer Sweet Salad

DRESSING

| | |
|---|---|
| ½ | red onion, chopped |
| 1 cup | oil |
| ½ cup | sugar |
| ⅓ cup | cider vinegar |
| 1 tsp | salt |
| 1 tsp | dry mustard |

SALAD

| | |
|---|---|
| 1 | Romaine lettuce, torn into bite-sized pieces |
| 1 (10-oz.) pkg. | baby spinach |
| ½ pint | strawberries, hulled and sliced thickly |
| 1 | mango, cut in cubes |
| ½ pint | blueberries |
| ½ pint | raspberries |
| ½ | red onion, sliced |
| ¾ cup | candied almonds (see recipe below) |

In a small jar or cruet, combine dressing ingredients. Cover. Shake well. Set aside.

Put the lettuce and spinach in a serving bowl. Add fruit, onion and candied almonds on top. Add dressing just before serving. Toss well.

*Candied Almonds*

| | |
|---|---|
| ¾ cup | slivered almonds |
| 2–3 Tbsp | sugar or sufficient to cover almonds |

Put the almonds in a skillet on medium-high heat. As they start to get hot, sprinkle sugar over top and keep stirring until sugar dissolves and caramelizes the almonds. Transfer them onto a piece of foil, separating the pieces so they don't stick together and form clumps.

Servings: 6–8
Prep time: 15–20 minutes

# Mango Salad

**DRESSING**

| ½ cup | oil |
| ¼ cup | wine vinegar |
| 2 Tbsp | honey |
| 2 Tbsp | brown sugar |
| ½ tsp | dry mustard |
| ¼ tsp | salt |

**SALAD**

| 3–4 | ripe mangoes, peeled and thinly sliced |
| 4 | avocados, peeled and thinly sliced |
| 1 cup | coconut flakes, toasted, (optional) |
| ½ (12-oz.) can | pineapple chunks, drained |
| 1 cup | any mix of caramelized nuts |

In a small jar or cruet, combine dressing ingredients. Cover. Shake well. Set aside.

Lay mango slices on a serving platter. Arrange the avocado slices over mango. Add coconut and pineapple. Pour dressing over salad. Add nuts right before serving.

Tip: Pour dressing at room temperature to prevent brown sugar from clumping.

---

**To Caramelize Nuts**

| 1 cup | nuts, chopped |
| 1 cup | sugar |

In a small saucepan, over a low heat, stir sugar and nuts until sugar caramelizes. Stir constantly being careful not to let the mixture burn. Remove from heat.

Servings: 4–6
Prep time: 15–20 minutes

# Avocado and Hearts of Palm Salad

*Simple and healthy.*

DRESSING

| | |
|---|---|
| 1 | clove of garlic, minced |
| ½ cup | vinegar |
| ½ cup | olive oil |
| 2 Tbsp | Dijon mustard |
| ½–1 tsp | sugar |
| ½ tsp | pepper |

SALAD

| | |
|---|---|
| 10–12 | cherry tomatoes, halved, or to taste |
| 1–1½ lbs. | asparagus, steamed, cut into 1–2-inch chunks |
| 1 (14-oz.) can | hearts of palm, drained, sliced into 1-inch chunks |
| 2–3 | green onions, sliced |
| 1–2 | avocados, peeled and cubed |
| 2–3 Tbsp | pine nuts |

In a large jar or cruet, combine dressing ingredients. Cover. Shake well. Set aside.

Place tomatoes, asparagus, hearts of palm and green onions in a serving dish. Add dressing. Toss gently. Add avocados and pine nuts just before serving.

**Tips:** Dressing can be served on leafy salads as well.

Avocados should be cut and added right before serving to avoid discoloration otherwise toss them in lemon juice.

---

*If you are in a rush, try a simpler version of this recipe:*

| | |
|---|---|
| 2 | avocados, peeled and cubed |
| 1 (14-oz.) can | hearts of palm, drained, cut into chunks |
| 1 Tbsp | lime juice |
| 1 Tbsp | fresh parsley |
| ⅛ tsp | cayenne pepper |
| | freshly ground black pepper to taste |

In a serving bowl, combine all ingredients. Serve.

Servings: 4–6
Prep time: 5 minutes

---

Servings: 6–8
Prep time: 20 minutes

# Sesame Pea Shoot Salad

PARVE

*These unique ingredients make for a tasty salad.*

DRESSING

| | |
|---|---|
| 2 Tbsp | rice vinegar |
| 2 Tbsp | sesame oil |
| 1½ Tbsp | brown sugar |
| 4 tsp | soy sauce |
| 4 tsp | sesame seeds, toasted |

SALAD

| | |
|---|---|
| 1 cup | sugar snap peas |
| ½ cup | snow peas |
| ½ cup | fresh green peas, shelled |
| 1 cup | pea shoots or pea sprouts |
| | red peppers, sliced, to garnish |
| | carrots, slivered, to garnish |

In a small jar or cruet, combine dressing ingredients. Cover. Shake well, until sugar dissolves. Set aside.

Blanch sugar snap peas in water for 2 minutes. Add snow peas and green peas and blanch for an additional minute. Drain. Rinse immediately under cold water. Pat peas dry between paper towels.

Put the pea shoots and peas in a serving bowl. Toss with dressing. Garnish with red peppers and carrots. Serve immediately.

Servings: 4–6
Prep time: 10–15 minutes

# Green Papaya Salad

DRESSING

| | |
|---|---|
| 1 | lime, juiced |
| 1 Tbsp | brown sugar |
| 2 tsp | soy sauce |

SALAD

| | |
|---|---|
| 6 | cherry tomatoes, chopped |
| 2 | cloves of garlic, minced |
| 1 | chili, fresh, finely chopped |
| 2 cups | firm green papaya, peeled, seeded and chopped |
| ¾ cup | green beans, blanched |
| ¼ cup | unsalted peanuts, without skins, coarsely chopped, to garnish |

In a small jar or cruet, combine dressing ingredients. Cover. Shake well. Set aside.

In a serving bowl, combine salad ingredients. Mix. Drizzle with dressing. Toss gently. Garnish with peanuts.

**Tips:** To blanch green beans: Put beans in a large pot of boiling water just until they turn a deep green, approximately one minute. Remove immediately. Drain in a colander. Place colander in a large bowl of cold water for one minute. Remove. Place on dishcloth to dry.

It is advisable to wear gloves to protect your hands when cutting the chili peppers.

Serve with pasta to make this a pasta salad.

Servings: 4–6
Prep time: 20–25 minutes

# Sweet Cabbage Salad

DRESSING

| | |
|---|---|
| ¼ cup | olive oil |
| ¼ cup | soy sauce |
| ¼ cup | brown sugar |
| ¼ cup | vinegar |
| ¼ cup | pecans, chopped |
| 2 Tbsp | pine nuts |
| 2 Tbsp | sesame seeds |
| ¼ cup | golden raisins |

SALAD

| | |
|---|---|
| 2 (10-oz.) pkgs. | coleslaw mix |

In a large jar or cruet, combine dressing ingredients. Cover. Shake well. Set aside.

Preheat oven to 350F.

On a baking dish, roast pecans for 2 minutes. Remove from oven and add pine nuts, sesame seeds and raisins. Return to oven for an additional 5 minutes.

Put the coleslaw mix into a large serving bowl. One to two hours before serving, add dressing and nuts. Cover. Refrigerate. Serve chilled.

Servings: 8–10
Prep time: 10–15 minutes

# Sweet Lover's Coleslaw

DRESSING

| | |
|---|---|
| ½ cup | sugar |
| ½ cup | oil |
| ⅓ cup | vinegar |
| 1 pouch | flavour package from soup mix below OR 1 tsp chicken soup mix powder |

GARNISH

| | |
|---|---|
| ¾ cup | almonds, slivered |
| ½ cup | sunflower seeds, roasted and salted |
| 1 (2.8-oz.) pkg. | ramen noodle soup mix or ⅓ cup (3 oz.) ramen noodles, crushed |

SALAD

| | |
|---|---|
| 2 cups | coleslaw mix |
| ½ | green pepper, diced |
| ½ | red pepper, diced |

Combine dressing ingredients in a jar. Cover. Shake well. Set aside.

Preheat oven to 350F.

Toast the almonds, sunflower seeds and noodles until golden, approximately 3–5 minutes.

In a serving bowl combine the coleslaw mix and peppers. Add dressing and nut mixture when ready to serve.

**Tip:** For variation substitute broccoli-slaw for coleslaw. Dressing also works well with rice vinegar.

Servings: 6–8
Prep time: 15 minutes

# Broccoli-slaw

PARVE

*A modern version of an old favourite.*

DRESSING

| 1 pouch | flavour package from ramen noodles or |
| | 1 tsp chicken soup mix powder |
| ½ cup | oil |
| ½ cup | rice vinegar |
| 6 Tbsp | sugar |
| 2 Tbsp | sesame oil |
| 1 tsp | salt |

SALAD

| 4 cups | broccoli slaw or grated broccoli stems |
| ½ cup | slivered almonds, toasted |
| ½ cup | ramen noodles, toasted |

In a small jar or cruet, combine dressing ingredients. Cover. Shake well. Set aside.

In a serving bowl, combine broccoli slaw with almonds and ramen noodles. Just before serving, pour dressing over slaw. Toss gently.

Servings: 6–8
Prep time: 5–10 minutes

# Baby Spinach Salad with Asian Dressing

DRESSING

| | |
|---|---|
| ⅓ cup | olive oil |
| 3 Tbsp | soy sauce |
| 3 Tbsp | rice vinegar |
| 3 Tbsp | sugar |
| 1 | clove of garlic, crushed |
| | salt and pepper to taste |

SALAD

| | |
|---|---|
| 1 Tbsp | olive oil |
| 1 (3-oz.) pkg. | ramen noodles, broken into pieces |
| ½ cup | slivered almonds |
| 2 Tbsp | sesame seeds |
| 1 (10-oz.) bag | baby spinach leaves |
| ½ cup | chives, chopped |
| ½ cup | cherry tomatoes, halved |

In a small bowl, combine dressing ingredients. Mix. Set aside.

Heat olive oil in a non-stick pan over medium heat. Add noodles and almonds. Stir for 3 minutes, being careful not to burn the ingredients. Add sesame seeds and stir until all ingredients are golden. Cool.

In a serving bowl, combine spinach, chives and tomatoes. Add ingredients from pan. Toss with dressing.

Serving: 6–8
Prep time: 15 minutes

# Layered Spinach Salad

DRESSING

| | |
|---|---|
| 2 | cloves of garlic, minced |
| ¼ cup | ketchup |
| ¼ cup | white grape juice |
| ¼ cup | vinegar |
| ¼ cup | olive oil |
| ¼ cup | sugar |
| ¼ Tbsp | paprika |
| ¼ tsp | dry mustard |
| ¼ tsp | salt |
| ¼ tsp | dried basil |
| ¼ tsp | oregano |
| ⅛ tsp | pepper |

SALAD

| | |
|---|---|
| 1 (10-oz.) pkg. | baby spinach |
| 1 pint | cherry tomatoes |
| ½–1 pint | alfalfa sprouts |
| 1½–2 cups | bean sprouts |
| 1 cup | cashews, roasted, salted |
| 1 | mango, peeled and diced |
| 1 | avocado, peeled and diced |

In a small bowl, combine dressing ingredients. Set aside.

In a tall serving bowl or dish, layer the salad ingredients. Add avocado and dressing just before serving. Do not toss!

Servings: 6–8
Prep time: 20–25 minutes

# Spinach Salad Supreme

*Delicious and different!*

DRESSING

| | |
|---|---|
| 2 Tbsp | Dijon mustard |
| 2 Tbsp | wine vinegar |
| 2 tsp | honey |
| | salt to taste |
| | fresh ground black pepper to taste |

SALAD

| | |
|---|---|
| 1 Tbsp | oil, for sautéing |
| 1 lb. | beef fry strips, or any cold cuts, cut into strips |
| 1 cup | shallots, thinly sliced |
| 6 | fresh mushrooms, sliced or 3–4 Portobello mushrooms, sliced |
| 1 lb. | spinach or 1 (10-oz.) bag baby spinach |
| 4 | hard-cooked eggs, sliced |

In a small jar or cruet, combine dressing ingredients. Cover. Shake well. Set aside.

In a small skillet, sauté beef fry strips until crispy, approximately 6–8 minutes. Remove from heat. Set aside.

In the same skillet, sauté shallots. Remove from heat. Set aside.

In the same skillet, sauté mushrooms. Remove from heat. Transfer to a dish. Set aside.

Put the spinach into a large serving bowl. Add shallots and mushrooms. Drizzle the dressing on top. Toss to coat. Garnish with eggs and beef fry strips.

Servings: 6–8
Prep time: 20–30 minutes

# Spinach Salad With Spiced Pecans

DRESSING

| | |
|---|---|
| 1 cup | olive oil |
| ⅓ cup | cider vinegar |
| ¼ cup | sugar |
| 2 Tbsp | corn syrup |
| 1 Tbsp | poppy seeds |
| 1 tsp | salt |
| 1 tsp | dry mustard |
| 1 tsp | celery seed |

SALAD

| | |
|---|---|
| 6 cups | spinach, washed, dried |
| 2 cups | strawberries, hulled and sliced |
| 1 cup | mushrooms, sliced |
| ¾ cup | red onion, sliced |
| | spiced pecans (see recipe below) |

In a large jar, combine dressing ingredients. Shake well. Set aside.

In a large serving bowl, combine salad ingredients except for the spiced pecans. Just before serving, add dressing. Toss gently. Sprinkle with spiced pecans.

---

*Spiced Pecans*

| | |
|---|---|
| 1 | egg white |
| ¾ tsp | vanilla |
| 1 cup | sugar |
| 1 Tbsp | water |
| 1 cup | pecans, whole |

Preheat oven to 200F.

In a large mixing bowl, beat egg white until very frothy, but not stiff. Add vanilla, sugar and water. Add pecans. Mix to coat. Place pecans evenly on a baking sheet covered with parchment paper. Bake them for 45 minutes, turning every 15 minutes.

---

Servings: 6
Prep time: 15–20 minutes

# Nutty Bok Choy Salad

**DRESSING**

| | |
|---|---|
| 3 Tbsp | balsamic vinegar |
| 3 Tbsp | soy sauce |
| 2 Tbsp | honey |
| 2 tsp | peanut butter |

**TOPPING**

| | |
|---|---|
| ½ cup | dry roasted peanuts |
| 1 (2.8-oz.) pkg. | ramen noodles, crushed |

**SALAD**

| | |
|---|---|
| 5 cups | bok choy, sliced |
| 2 | green onions, sliced on the diagonal |
| 1 | red pepper, thinly sliced |
| ½ cup | cherry tomatoes |

In a small bowl, whisk together vinegar, soy sauce, honey and peanut butter until well combined. Set aside.

In a medium sized non-stick skillet, sauté peanuts and noodles until golden. Remove from heat.

Put the salad ingredients in a large shallow bowl. Right before serving, sprinkle the noodles and nuts over the salad. Drizzle with dressing.

*"This recipe has been a hit at every party I have been invited to."*

Servings: 10
Prep time: 15 minutes

# Oriental Pepper Salad

**DRESSING**

| | |
|---|---|
| ¾ cup | rice vinegar |
| ½ cup | oil |
| ¼ cup | sugar or Splenda |
| ½ tsp | salt |
| ½ tsp | pepper |

**SALAD**

| | |
|---|---|
| 1 | red pepper, cut in strips |
| 1 | green pepper, cut in strips |
| 1 | zucchini, thinly sliced |
| ½ cup | snow peas |
| 1 lb. | fresh mushrooms, sliced |
| 2 | large carrots, peeled and grated |
| 1 (14 oz.) can | baby corn, drained |
| ¼ cup | cashews, to garnish |
| ½ cup | cherry tomatoes, to garnish |

In a large jar or cruet, combine dressing ingredients. Cover. Shake well. Set aside.

Put the salad ingredients in a large serving bowl. Toss with dressing, to coat. Cover. Marinate for a few hours. Garnish with cashews and cherry tomatoes before serving.

Servings: 6–8
Prep time: 10–15 minutes

# Antipasti Salad

DRESSING

| | |
|---|---|
| 3–4 | cloves of garlic, minced |
| ¼ cup | olive oil |
| ¼ cup | red wine vinegar |
| | salt and pepper to taste |

SALAD

| | |
|---|---|
| 3 Tbsp | olive oil |
| 3 | medium zucchini, unpeeled, julienned |
| 1 (10-oz.) pkg. | mixed baby greens |
| 2 | medium tomatoes, diced |
| 1 | small red onion, finely chopped |
| ¼ cup | fresh parsley, chopped |
| ½ cup | feta cheese, crumbled |
| ¼ cup | sunflower seeds |
| ¼ cup | toasted almonds, sliced |
| ¼ cup | pistachio nuts |
| ¼ cup | pine nuts |
| | garlic croutons, to garnish |

In a small jar or cruet, combine dressing ingredients. Cover. Shake well. Set aside.

Heat oil in a large skillet and sauté zucchini until browned and crispy. Set aside.

In a large serving bowl, arrange mixed greens; add tomatoes, onion, parsley and feta cheese. Sprinkle seeds and nuts on top. Top with zucchini strips. Drizzle dressing on top. Garnish with croutons. Toss.

Tip: This looks nice served in a wide shallow bowl.

Servings: 8–10
Prep time: 15 minutes

# Gingered Sushi Salad

*This modern salad will
impress even your pickiest
guest.*

| | |
|---|---|
| 1½ cups | sushi rice, uncooked |
| 1¾ cups | cold water |

DRESSING

| | |
|---|---|
| ½ cup | rice vinegar |
| 1 Tbsp | oil |
| 1 Tbsp | toasted sesame oil |
| 1 Tbsp | soy sauce |
| 1 tsp | fresh ginger, grated |
| ½ tsp | garlic, minced |
| ¼ tsp | wasabi powder |

SALAD

| | |
|---|---|
| 1 | carrot, peeled and grated |
| ½ | red pepper, julienned |
| ¼ cup | red onion, minced |
| 2 Tbsp | sesame seeds, toasted |
| 2 Tbsp | pickled ginger, diced |
| 1 sheet | toasted nori cut into 2- inch julienne strips (may be broken into pieces), reserve ¼ sheet for garnish |

Cook sushi rice as directed on package.

In a small bowl, combine dressing ingredients. Slowly add the dressing to hot rice, tossing gently. Add carrot, pepper, onion, sesame seeds, ginger and nori. Toss and sprinkle with reserved nori.

**Tip:** Cooking Sushi rice is not like cooking ordinary rice. Rinse rice under water until the water runs clear. Put the rice in a saucepan and add cold water. Cover. Bring to a boil. Do not mix. Cook for 5 minutes. Reduce heat and continue cooking for an additional 5 minutes, until the water has been absorbed. Remove from heat. Uncover. Cool for 10 minutes.

Servings: 6–8
Prep time: 30 minutes

# Greek Rice Salad

DRESSING

| | |
|---|---|
| ½ cup | olive oil |
| ⅓ cup | vinegar |
| 1½ Tbsp | lemon juice |
| | salt and pepper to taste |

SALAD

| | |
|---|---|
| 1 cup | rice, uncooked |
| 1 cup | black pitted olives, drained |
| ½ cup | grape or cherry tomatoes |
| ½ | cucumber, cubed |
| ½ | small red pepper, diced |
| ½ | small green pepper, diced |
| ½ cup | feta cheese, crumbled (can be omitted if making parve) |
| | avocado, peeled and cubed |

Prepare rice according to package directions. Cool.

In a small jar, combine dressing ingredients. Shake well. Set aside.

In a large serving bowl, combine rice, black olives, tomatoes, cucumber, red and green peppers and feta cheese. Unless serving the salad right away, refrigerate it. Add dressing and avocado right before serving. Toss gently.

Tip: Squeeze lemon over cut-up apples, avocados, mushrooms, bananas or pears so they don't turn brown.

Serving: 8–10
Prep time: 20 minutes

*"No matter how many times I double or triple this recipe, there is never a bite left."*

Tip: Stays fresh for 2 days.

Serving: 6–8
Prep time: 20 minutes

Tip: May be served warm or cold.
Variation: Add green olives with pimento.

Servings: 4–6
Prep time: 15–20 minutes

# Chow Mein Rice Salad

DRESSING

| ½ cup | oil |
| ¼ cup | soy sauce |
| 1–2 | cloves of garlic, minced |

SALAD

| 2 cups | cooked rice, cooled |
| 1 cup | pine nuts |
| 1 cup | mushrooms, sliced |
| ½ cup | bean sprouts |
| ½ cup | golden raisins |
| 2–4 | shallots, chopped |
| 1 Tbsp | parsley, chopped, to taste |
| ½ cup | thin chow mein noodles |

In a small container, combine dressing ingredients. Cover. Shake well. Set aside. In a serving bowl, combine rice, pine nuts, mushrooms, bean sprouts, raisins, shallots and parsley. Right before serving, add dressing and noodles. Toss.

# Spicy Zucchini Salad

| 2 Tbsp | oil |
| 3 | zucchini, cubed |
| 1 | green pepper, chopped |
| 1 | onion, chopped |
| 3 | cloves of garlic, minced |
| 1 cup | tomato paste |
| 1 cup | water |
| 1 Tbsp | parve chicken soup powder |
| ½ tsp | cumin |
| | salt and pepper to taste |

In a large skillet, heat oil and sauté zucchini, green pepper and onion until tender. Add remaining ingredients. Reduce heat. Cook for additional 10 minutes.

# Wheat Berry Salad

SALAD

| | |
|---|---|
| 1 cup | soft wheat berries |
| 3 | green onions, chopped |
| ½ cup | parsley or coriander |
| ½ cup | dried cranberries |
| 2 | tart apples, cored and chopped |
| ½ cup | thinly sliced fennel bulb |
| | mixed greens |

DRESSING

| | |
|---|---|
| ⅓ cup | raspberries (frozen or fresh) |
| ⅓ cup | olive oil |
| 1 Tbsp | Dijon mustard |
| 1 ½ Tbsp | balsamic vinegar |
| 1 ½ Tbsp | honey |
| | salt & fresh ground pepper to taste |

Rinse wheat berries in cold water. Soak them overnight. Drain well.

Put the wheat berries in saucepan with cold water to cover by a couple of inches.

Bring to a boil, reduce heat, and cook for approximately 30–45 minutes. The berries should be tender but not too soft. Drain and rinse.

In a bowl, combine wheat berries, onions, parsley, cranberries, apples and fennel.

In separate bowl or blender, purée raspberries, oil, mustard, vinegar, honey, salt and pepper.

Pour the dressing over salad and toss well.

Marinate at least 1 hour. Serve over a bed of the mixed greens.

Servings: 10–12
Prep time: 1 hour

# Couscous Salad with Mandarins

DRESSING

| | |
|---|---|
| 2 | cloves of garlic, minced |
| 2 Tbsp | olive oil |
| ¼ cup | orange juice |
| ⅓ cup | reserved mandarin juice – see salad ingredients below |
| 1 tsp | cumin |
| 1 tsp | salt |
| 1 tsp | fresh ground black pepper |
| ⅛ tsp | cayenne |

SALAD

| | |
|---|---|
| 2 cups | couscous |
| 1 tsp | olive oil |
| ¼ tsp | turmeric |
| 1 (11-oz.) can | mandarin segments, drained – reserve juice |
| 1 (19-oz.) can | chickpeas, drained and rinsed |
| 1 cup | green onions, chopped |
| ½ cup | parsley, chopped |
| ¼ cup | dried cranberries |
| ¼ cup | currants |

In a medium bowl, whisk together dressing ingredients. Set aside.

Prepare couscous according to package instructions. Transfer the couscous to a large serving bowl. Cool. Mix in olive oil and turmeric. Add mandarins, chickpeas, onions, parsley, cranberries and currants. Mix well. Drizzle dressing over couscous salad, being careful not to over-saturate it.

Servings: 8–10
Prep time: 45 minutes

# Israeli Couscous Salad

**DRESSING**

| | |
|---|---|
| ⅛ cup | oil |
| ¼ cup | sugar |
| 2 Tbsp | lemon juice |
| 2 Tbsp | vinegar |
| ½ tsp | salt |
| ⅛ tsp | pepper |

**SALAD**

| | |
|---|---|
| 1¼ cups | Israeli style toasted couscous |
| 1 (12-oz.) can | corn kernels, drained |
| ¼ cup | red onion, chopped |
| ½ | red pepper, chopped |
| ½ | green pepper, chopped |

In a small jar or cruet, combine dressing ingredients. Cover. Shake well. Set aside.

Boil couscous in water for 5–7 minutes until just tender. Drain. Rinse with cold water.

In a serving bowl, mix couscous with corn, onion and peppers. Pour dressing over couscous mixture. Mix well.

**Tip:** Decorate the finished salad with peppers and/or red onion rings.

Servings: 8–10
Prep time: 10–15 minutes

# Pasta Salad with Feta

**DRESSING**

| | |
|---|---|
| ⅔ cup | olive oil |
| 3 Tbsp | vinegar |
| 2 Tbsp | green onion, chopped |
| 2 Tbsp | Parmesan cheese |
| 2 tsp | dried basil |
| ½ tsp | salt |
| ¼ tsp | freshly ground black pepper |
| ¼ tsp | oregano |
| 1 lb. | feta cheese |

**SALAD**

| | |
|---|---|
| 1 (450-g) pkg. | tri-colour spiral pasta |
| 1 | green pepper, chopped |
| 1 | red pepper, chopped |
| 2 | tomatoes, cut in wedges |
| 10 | black olives (optional) |
| 2 Tbsp | Parmesan cheese |

Put the olive oil, vinegar, green onion, Parmesan cheese, basil, salt, pepper and oregano into a food processor. Blend well. Add feta cheese for a few quick pulses. Set aside.

Cook pasta. Drain. Set aside.

In a serving bowl, combine pasta, peppers, tomatoes and olives. Toss with dressing and chill for ½–1 hour before serving. Just before serving add remaining Parmesan cheese.

Servings: 6–8
Prep time: 30 minutes

# Tortellini Salad

*Tortellini is always a favourite with the kids.*

DRESSING

| | |
|---|---|
| ½ cup | olive oil |
| 2 Tbsp | red wine vinegar |
| 2 | large cloves of garlic, minced |
| 1 tsp | dried thyme |

SALAD

| | |
|---|---|
| 1 (500-g) pkg. | cheese-filled tortellini, cooked, rinsed and drained in cold water |
| 1 cup | stuffed green olives, sliced thinly |
| 3 | ripe plum tomatoes, cut in half, seeds removed, finely chopped |

In a small jar or cruet, combine dressing ingredients. Cover. Shake well. Set aside.

In a medium-sized serving bowl, combine tortellini, olives and tomatoes. Cover. Refrigerate for 30–60 minutes before serving. Add dressing, and toss to coat.

Servings: 6
Prep time: 20 minutes

*Fresh tuna...yum!*

# Grilled Tuna Nicoise

DRESSING

| | |
|---|---|
| ½ cup | parve chicken broth |
| ¼ cup | shallots, chopped |
| ¼ cup | red wine vinegar |
| 2 Tbsp | balsamic vinegar |
| 2 Tbsp | extra virgin olive oil |
| 1 Tbsp | parsley, minced |

SALAD

| | |
|---|---|
| ½ | medium onion, thinly sliced |
| 1 | small red pepper, sliced |
| ½ lb. | fresh green beans, cooked tender crisp |
| 8 | small red potatoes, unpeeled, quartered and cooked |
| 8 | cherry tomatoes, halved |
| 4 | tuna fillets, fresh (4–6 oz. each) |
| 4 cups | mesclun or mixed salad greens |

In a small jar or cruet, combine dressing ingredients. Cover tightly. Shake well. Set aside.

Spray a skillet with cooking spray and put on medium heat. Add the onion and pepper. Cook until slightly tender but crisp. Remove from heat. Transfer onion and pepper to bowl with green beans and potatoes. Add tomatoes. Add ½ cup of dressing. Mix well. Refrigerate, covered, for about 15 minutes.

Place tuna fillets on a baking dish. Grill or broil tuna for approximately 3 minutes per side, until slightly browned. Remove from oven. Break tuna into chunks.

Arrange mixed greens on a platter. Pile potato/vegetable mixture in the centre and top with grilled tuna. Drizzle salad with remaining dressing and serve!

Servings: 4
Prep time: 15–30 minutes

# Mock Crab Salad

DRESSING

| | |
|---|---|
| ¼–½ cup | mayonnaise |
| 2–3 Tbsp | honey mustard |
| ¼ tsp | garlic, crushed |
| 1–2 Tbsp | sugar |
| | salt and pepper to taste |
| 1 | lemon, juiced |

SALAD

| | |
|---|---|
| 1–2 | endives, sliced |
| 1 | stalk celery, sliced |
| 1 (2.8-oz.) pkg. | imitation crab meat, broken into pieces |

In a small bowl, mix mayonnaise, mustard, garlic, sugar, salt and pepper. Thin out, as needed, with lemon juice.

In a serving dish, combine endive, celery and mock crab with dressing. Mix well. Chill and serve.

Servings: 4–6
Prep time: 5–10 minutes

# Asian Grilled Beef Salad

MARINADE

| | |
|---|---|
| 4 | cloves of garlic, crushed |
| ¼ cup | soy sauce |
| 2 Tbsp | hoisin sauce |
| 2 Tbsp | honey |
| 1 Tbsp | fresh ginger, chopped |
| 2 tsp | lemon juice |
| 1 lb. | London broil (1-inch thick) or beef flat irons |

DRESSING

| | |
|---|---|
| ⅓ cup | sugar |
| ⅓ cup | orange juice |
| 2 | cloves of garlic, chopped |
| 2 Tbsp | cider vinegar |
| 1 Tbsp | soy sauce |
| 1 Tbsp | lime juice |
| | salt to taste |

SALAD

| | |
|---|---|
| 1 (10-oz.) bag | mixed greens |
| 1 | carrot, peeled and grated |
| ½ cup | green onions, chopped |
| ½ | red pepper, sliced |

Combine marinade ingredients. Coat steak with marinade. Transfer to a glass dish, cover and refrigerate for a minimum 4 hours (or overnight).

Meanwhile, combine dressing ingredients in a jar and shake well. Add salt to taste. Set aside.

Grill beef for 3–4 minutes per side or until medium-rare, basting occasionally. Cool for 10 minutes. Slice thinly on diagonal.

On a large platter, arrange mixed greens. Place carrots, onions and pepper on top of the greens. Drizzle half the dressing over salad. Place beef on top and drizzle with remaining dressing.

Servings: 6–8
Prep time: 30 minutes, marinated 4 hours or overnight

# Chicken Fajita Salad

MARINADE

| | |
|---|---|
| 2 | cloves of garlic, minced |
| ¼ cup | olive oil |
| 2 Tbsp | lime juice |
| 2 Tbsp | honey |
| 1 Tbsp | lemon rind, grated |
| 2 tsp | chili powder |
| | salt to taste |

SALAD

| | |
|---|---|
| 2 | chicken breasts, boneless, skinless |
| 4 cups | lettuce, shredded |
| 1 cup | cherry tomatoes, halved |
| 1 | avocado, peeled, sliced |
| 1 | green onion, chopped |
| | olives to taste |

In a small jar or cruet, combine marinade ingredients. Cover. Shake well. Set aside. Reserve 3 tablespoons of marinade.

Put the chicken breasts in a glass dish. Pour marinade over chicken. Cover. Refrigerate for a minimum of 2 hours or overnight.

Preheat oven 375F.

Transfer chicken to a baking dish. Bake uncovered for 1 hour. Alternatively, grill chicken on barbecue over medium heat for 20 minutes or until done. Brush with marinade while baking or grilling. Cool. Cut chicken into 1-inch strips.

On large platter, arrange the lettuce, tomatoes, avocado, green onions and olives. Place sliced chicken on top. Drizzle with reserved marinade.

Servings: 6–8
Prep time: 15 minutes

# Chicken Salad with Avocado Dressing

| | |
|---|---|
| 4 (4–6-oz. each) | chicken breasts, boneless, skinless |
| 1 cup | Italian salad dressing, page 80 |

DRESSING

| | |
|---|---|
| ½ cup | olive oil |
| ½ | ripe avocado, peeled |
| 2 Tbsp | fresh lemon juice |
| | salt and pepper to taste |

SALAD

| | |
|---|---|
| 1 (10-oz.) pkg. | mixed greens |
| 1 pint | cherry tomatoes |
| 2 | avocados, cut in small chunks |
| 1 (8-oz.) can | canned corn, drained |

Put the chicken in a shallow glass dish. Pour Italian dressing over chicken. Cover. Marinate in the refrigerator 3–4 hours or overnight.

Preheat oven to broil.

Put the chicken in an ovenproof dish. Broil the chicken breasts 6 minutes on each side or until fully cooked. Cool. Refrigerate. This can be done a day ahead.

Using a hand blender or food processor, purée the olive oil, avocado, lemon juice, salt and pepper. Transfer to a small jar or cruet. Cover. Refrigerate.

Prior to serving, slice chicken breasts into 1-inch strips. On a serving platter, or bowl, place mixed greens, chicken, tomatoes, avocados and corn. Pour dressing over the salad. Toss gently.

Serves: 4–6
Prep time: 15–20 minutes

# Chicken Salad with Basil and Sun-dried Tomatoes

| | |
|---|---|
| 1 | small onion, chopped |
| 5 Tbsp | olive oil, divided 1 Tbsp, 1 Tbsp, 3 Tbsp |
| 1 Tbsp | water |
| 12 | sun-dried tomatoes, in oil, thinly sliced, reserve 1 Tbsp of the tomatoes |
| 4 | large chicken breasts, boneless, skinless, pounded to ¼-inch thickness |
| 1 bunch | fresh basil |
| 3 Tbsp | red wine vinegar |
| 1¼ tsp | freshly ground black pepper |
| ¾ tsp | sugar |
| 1 tsp | salt |
| 2 | small tomatoes, sliced |
| 1 | head lettuce, washed |

In a medium-sized skillet, sauté onion in 1 tablespoon oil until lightly browned. Add water. Cook until onions become tender. Stir in sun-dried tomatoes, reserving 1 tablespoon.

Spread onion mixture on top of chicken. Place one whole basil leaf on top of onion mixture on each chicken breast and roll breasts like a jelly roll. Secure with toothpicks. Chop remaining basil leaves. Set aside.

In a large skillet, cook chicken in 1 tablespoon oil over medium heat until lightly browned on both sides. Reduce heat to low. Cover. Cook approximately 10 minutes, turning after 5 minutes. Remove from heat. Cool. Remove toothpicks from chicken and slice into ½-inch thick pinwheels.

In a small bowl, combine wine vinegar, pepper, sugar, salt, reserved chopped basil, remaining 3 tablespoon oil, and remaining sun-dried tomatoes. Mix well.

Divide lettuce and tomatoes among 4 plates. Arrange chicken pinwheels on top. Drizzle with dressing.

Serve hot or at room temperature.

*This recipe is a lot easier than it looks and it presents beautifully.*

Servings: 4–6
Prep time: 1 hour

# Dijon Deli Salad

*This recipe is also great
served as an appetizer.*

DRESSING

| | |
|---|---|
| 1 cup | mayonnaise |
| 2 Tbsp | lemon juice |
| 1½ Tbsp | Dijonnaise mustard |
| 2 tsp | dried dill or 2 Tbsp fresh dill, chopped |
| ½ tsp | salt |
| ⅛ tsp | pepper |

SALAD

| | |
|---|---|
| 4 cups | spiral or penne pasta, cooked |
| 2 cups | asparagus cut into 1-inch pieces, cooked |
| 1 | red pepper, sliced |
| ½ | red onion, sliced |
| 1½ inch | turkey roll cut in strips or squares |
| 1½ inch | pastrami or corned beef, cut in strips or squares |
| 1½ inch | salami, cut in strips or squares |

Combine dressing ingredients and blend. well Set aside.

In a large serving, bowl combine pasta, vegetables, and cold cuts. Add dressing. Toss.

**Tips:** If preparing pasta in advance, run the cooked pasta under cold water to loosen it before adding the dressing and other ingredients.

When cooking pasta, add 1 to 2 tablespoons of oil to the boiling water to prevent clumping.

For those watching their carbohydrates, substitute 1 (10-oz.) pkg. of European salad mix instead of the pasta.

Servings: 6–8
Prep time: 10–15 minutes

# Bartender's Chickpea Salad

PARVE

| | |
|---|---|
| 1 (19-oz.) can | chickpeas, washed, and drained |
| 3 | small stalks of celery, with leaves, chopped |
| 1½ | carrots, peeled and chopped |
| ½ | red pepper, chopped |
| 2 | cloves of garlic, minced |
| 1 Tbsp | red onion, chopped |
| 1 Tbsp | sesame seeds |
| 1 | medium-sized lemon, cut in pieces |
| ½ | medium-sized lime, cut in pieces |
| 3 Tbsp | fresh parsley, finely chopped |
| ⅓ cup | olive oil |
| ⅓ cup | lemon juice |
| ⅛ tsp | Tabasco |
| | salt and pepper to taste |
| | oregano to taste |
| | basil to taste |

In a large serving bowl, combine chickpeas, celery, carrots, red pepper, garlic and red onion. Sprinkle in sesame seeds. Add lemon, lime (these are not intended to be eaten, although some people do) and parsley. Drizzle oil and lemon juice over salad. Add Tabasco, salt, pepper, oregano and basil to taste. Combine well. If you like it moister, add more lemon juice and oil.

**Tips:** Bartenders play with the proportions – however, the flavour from the celery leaves, lemon, lime and sesame are all-important.

May be prepared a day ahead to impart a clean fresh flavour from the lemon and lime chunks.

Servings: 6–8
Prep time: 20 minutes

Tip: Serve inside a cut out
cucumber.

Servings: 6–8
Prep time: 10 minutes

*A flavourful twist to basic
potato salad.*

Tip: Cool potatoes only
enough to be able to handle
them. Adding dressing to
warm potatoes helps potatoes
absorb dressing, providing
more flavour.

Servings: 6
Prep time: 15–20 minutes

# Corn Salad

DRESSING

| | |
|---|---|
| 2 | cloves of garlic, minced |
| ¼ cup | oil |
| 2 Tbsp | vinegar |
| 2 tsp | lime or lemon juice |
| ½ tsp | honey mustard |
| ½ tsp | cumin |
| ¼ tsp | salt and pepper each |

SALAD

| | |
|---|---|
| 1 (12-oz.) can | corn niblets, drained |
| 1 | small red pepper, cubed |
| 1 | small green pepper, cubed |
| ½ | Spanish onion, chopped |
| ½ cup | fresh parsley, chopped |

Combine dressing ingredients. Cover. Shake well. Set aside. In a serving bowl, combine salad ingredients. Add dressing 1 hour before serving.

# Creamy Dijon Potatoes

DRESSING

| | |
|---|---|
| ⅓ cup | olive or vegetable oil |
| 3 Tbsp | Dijon mustard |
| 2 Tbsp | vinegar |
| 1 tsp | dried basil |
| ½ tsp | salt |
| ¼ tsp | pepper |
| 7 | medium red potatoes, unpeeled, boiled, cut into cubes |
| 3 | green onions, sliced |
| ¾ cup | celery, sliced |

Combine dressing ingredients. Cover. Shake well. Set aside.

In a large serving bowl, combine potatoes, onions and celery. Toss dressing to coat. Cover. Refrigerate for 1 hour minimum .

# Black Bean and Corn Salad

DRESSING

| ¼ cup | oil |
| ¼ cup | red wine vinegar |
| ½ tsp | cumin |
| ½ tsp | sugar |
| ½ tsp | salt |
| | fresh ground black pepper to taste |
| | minced garlic to taste |

SALAD

| 1 (19-oz.) can | black beans, drained, rinsed |
| 1 (19-oz.) can | red kidney beans, drained, rinsed |
| 1½ cups | frozen corn, thawed |
| 1 | small sweet pepper, diced |
| 1 | small jalapeno pepper, diced |
| ⅓ cup | fresh parsley, chopped |
| ¼ cup | red onion, diced |

In a small jar or cruet, combine dressing ingredients. Cover. Shake well. Set aside.

In a serving bowl, combine beans, corn, peppers, parsley and onion. Add dressing. Toss.

TIp: Try browning the corn in a skillet to add a smokey flavour to the salad.

Serves: 8
Prep time: 15 minutes

# Italian Dressing

| | |
|---|---|
| ¾ cup | olive oil |
| ¼ cup | vinegar |
| 2 tsp | sugar |
| 1 | clove of garlic, minced |
| ½ tsp | dry mustard |
| ½ tsp | paprika |
| ½ tsp | salt |
| ¼–½ tsp | oregano |
| ¼–½ tsp | dried basil |
| ¼ tsp | cayenne pepper |

In a medium-sized jar or cruet, combine ingredients. Cover. Shake well.

# Honey-Lemon Dressing

| | |
|---|---|
| ¼ cup | oil |
| ¼ cup | lemon juice |
| 3 Tbsp | honey |
| 2 | cloves of garlic, minced |
| 1½ tsp | salt |
| | pepper to taste |

In a small jar or cruet, combine ingredients. Cover. Shake well.

# Balsamic Vinaigrette

| | |
|---|---|
| 1 | clove of garlic, minced |
| 1½ cups | olive oil |
| ½ cup | balsamic vinegar |
| 1 Tbsp | Dijon mustard |
| 1–2 tsp | fresh basil, finely chopped |
| 1–2 tsp | fresh marjoram, finely chopped |
| 1–2 tsp | fresh rosemary, finely chopped |
| 1–2 tsp | fresh thyme, finely chopped |
| ¼ tsp | salt |
| | pepper to taste |

In a large jar or cruet, combine all the ingredients. Cover. Shake well.

Refrigerate for 30 minutes before serving.

# Spinach Salad Dressing

| | |
|---|---|
| 1 cup | canola oil |
| ½ cup | sugar |
| ⅓ cup | ketchup |
| ¼ cup | red wine vinegar |
| 2 Tbsp | minced dry onion |
| 1 tsp | salt |

In a large jar or cruet, combine ingredients. Cover. Shake well. Refrigerate if not using immediately.

PARVE

Tip: Some herbs and vegetables give off certain smells and oils that remain on your cutting board even after being washed and can affect other foods. To solve this problem, mark one side of your cutting board with indelible ink FRUIT and cut fruit only on that side. Mark the other side VEGETABLES and cut your veggies and herbs on that side only.

Servings: 2 cups
Prep time: 5–10 minutes

PARVE

Servings: approximately
2 cups
Prep time: 10 minutes

*For the mustard lovers out there.*

# Low-Cal Mustard Dressing

| | |
|---|---|
| 3 | green onions, finely chopped |
| ¼ cup | water |
| 1½ Tbsp | cider vinegar |
| 1 Tbsp | fresh parsley, chopped |
| 1 Tbsp | oil |
| 2½ tsp | Dijon mustard |
| 1½ tsp | honey |
| ½ tsp | dried thyme |
| ¼ tsp | pepper |

In a small jar or cruet, combine ingredients. Cover. Shake well. Refrigerate.

Servings: ¾ cup
Prep time: 5–10 minutes

# Strub's Basil and Pickled Pepper Dressing

| | |
|---|---|
| ¼ cup | olive oil |
| ¼ cup | fresh basil, chopped |
| 1 | clove of garlic, minced |
| 1½ Tbsp | Parmesan cheese |
| 2 Tbsp | Strub's Sweet Pimento Peppers, finely chopped |

In a medium bowl, using a wire whisk, blend together oil, basil, garlic, cheese and pickled peppers. Transfer to a cruet. Cover. Refrigerate until ready to serve.

Servings: ⅓ cup
Prep time: 10–15 minutes

# Caesar Salad Dressing

| | |
|---|---|
| ½ cup | mayonnaise |
| ¼ cup | milk |
| ¼ cup | Parmesan cheese, grated |
| 2 Tbsp | lemon juice |
| 2 Tbsp | Dijon mustard |
| 1 | clove of garlic, minced |
| 1 | anchovy fillet, crushed (optional) |
| ¼ tsp | pepper |
| | salt to taste |

In a large jar or cruet, combine ingredients. Cover. Shake. Refrigerate.

# Coleslaw Dressing

| | |
|---|---|
| ⅓ cup | sugar |
| ¾ cup | mayonnaise |
| ⅓ cup | lemon juice or white vinegar |
| 1 tsp | dry mustard |
| 1 tsp | salt |
| ⅛ tsp | pepper |

In a large jar or cruet, combine all the dressing ingredients. Cover. Shake well.

Tips: Keeps up to one week. Enough for two or three heads of romaine lettuce. Serve with croutons. Serve with salad and breadsticks.

Servings: 10–12
Prep time: 5 minutes

Tip: This is enough for two (10-oz.) packages of shredded cabbage or coleslaw mix.

Servings: 8–10
Prep time: 10 minutes

# Mango Vinaigrette

| | |
|---|---|
| 1½ cups | mangoes, peeled and diced |
| ¼ cup | rice vinegar |
| 1 tsp | Dijon mustard |
| ½ tsp | dry mustard |
| ½ tsp | paprika |
| 1 tsp | fresh parsley, chopped |
| 1 | clove of garlic, chopped |
| ¼ tsp | salt |
| ⅓ cup | olive oil |

Put mangoes, vinegar, mustards, paprika, parsley, garlic, and salt in a blender.
Blend while adding oil slowly in a thin stream.

*As an alternative serve with*

| | |
|---|---|
| 5 cups | mixed greens |
| ⅓ cup | cashews or sliced almonds |
| ½ cup | croutons |

Put mixed greens in a large serving bowl. Drizzle dressing over them. Toss to coat.
Add nuts and croutons just before serving.

Servings: 6–8
Prep time: 5 minutes

Servings: 6–8
Prep time: 15 minutes

# dairy, brunch & breads

# Spring Rolls with Tuna Cheese Filling

| | |
|---|---|
| 4 (7-oz.) cans | tuna, drained and flaked |
| ¼ (10-oz.) can | mushroom soup |
| ½ cup | mayonnaise |
| ½ cup | pressed dry cottage cheese |
| ¼ cup | Cheddar cheese, grated |
| 2 Tbsp | milk |
| 2 Tbsp | onion, minced |
| | salt and pepper to taste |
| 22 | spring roll wrappers |
| | oil to deep fry |

In a large mixing bowl, combine tuna, mushroom soup, mayonnaise, cottage and Cheddar cheeses, milk, onion, salt and pepper. Mix well. Place 2–3 tablespoons of the mixture in one corner of a spring roll wrapper. Fold the opposite corner up over mixture. Fold sides in and roll from center. Place on a platter and cover to prevent them from drying until ready to fry.

In a large deep skillet, heat oil. Fry on medium heat until wrapper is golden brown. Remove from skillet onto a paper-lined dish.

**Tips:** Substitute salmon for tuna.

May be frozen. Reheat in oven at 350F until hot.

---

### Alternative filling for Spring Rolls

| | |
|---|---|
| ½ lb. | mushrooms, cut in thick slices |
| 1 | clove of garlic, minced |
| 3 Tbsp | butter |
| ¼ cup | brandy |
| ½ tsp | salt |
| | pepper to taste |
| ½ cup | sour cream |
| 1 (7-oz.) can | tuna |

In a large skillet, sauté mushrooms and garlic in butter until tender. Pour in brandy. Cook on high until brandy has evaporated. Season with salt and pepper. Remove from heat. Add sour cream and tuna. Proceed as above with filling the spring rolls and frying.

Servings: 4–6
Prep Time: 5 minutes

Servings: 20–22 rolls
Prep time: 30–45 minutes

# Phyllo Filled with Spinach and Cheese

| | |
|---|---|
| 1 | onion, chopped |
| ½ tsp | garlic, minced |
| 3 Tbsp | butter |
| 1 (10-oz.) pkg. | frozen chopped spinach, thawed |
| 2 Tbsp | fresh parsley, chopped |
| 2 | green onions, chopped |
| ½ lb. | pressed cottage cheese |
| ½ tsp | salt |
| | pepper, to taste |
| 2 | eggs, beaten |
| 6 sheets | phyllo pastry |
| | melted butter, to brush on phyllo |
| ½ cup | dried bread crumbs |

Preheat oven to 350F.

In a large skillet, sauté onion and garlic in butter until tender. Add spinach. Cook until liquid evaporates. Remove from heat. Add parsley, green onions, cottage cheese, salt, pepper and eggs. Mix well. Set aside.

On a board, lay out one sheet of phyllo pastry and brush it with the melted butter. Add remaining layers of phyllo, brushing with butter between each layer. On final sheet of phyllo, sprinkle dried bread crumbs. Spoon filling mixture along the long edge, leaving a 2-inch border along the bottom and on each end. Fold over the excess border on each short side and then roll the long side up jelly-roll fashion. Press together to fully encase the filling. Place seam side down on a greased parchment-lined cookie sheet. Cut slits in top 1 inch apart. Bake for 20 minutes or until golden.

**Tip:** This dish can be frozen before or after baking. When working with phyllo dough, make sure to keep unused phyllo covered as it dries out quickly.

Servings: 6–8
Prep time: 20 minutes

# Pizza Variations

*A store-bought pizza crust is easy to find but what to put on it is the question. Try these three easy and elegant pizza toppings.*

DAIRY

FOR ALL THREE

On a lightly floured surface, roll out pizza dough. Place dough on a greased pizza pan. Brush with 1–2 tablespoons olive oil. Follow topping directions. Then put the pan in a cold oven and turn it on to 500F. Bake for 10–15 minutes or until sauce and/or cheese begins to bubble.

## Bruschetta Pizza

| | |
|---|---|
| 2 | tomatoes, seeded, diced |
| 1 cup | mozzarella cheese, grated |
| ½ cup | mayonnaise |
| ¼ cup | Parmesan cheese |
| 1 | clove of garlic, minced |
| ½ tsp | dried basil |

In a large bowl, combine tomatoes, mozzarella cheese, mayonnaise, Parmesan cheese, garlic and basil.

Spread over dough, leaving a 1-inch crust.

Servings: 8–10
Prep time: 10–15 minutes

# Pesto Pizza

| | |
|---|---|
| 1 cup | pesto sauce (see recipe page 20) |
| 2 | tomatoes, thinly sliced |
| 2 | onions, thinly sliced |
| 1 | red pepper, thinly sliced |
| 1 | green pepper, thinly sliced |
| 1 cup | mozzarella cheese, grated |
| ¼ cup | Parmesan cheese, grated |

Spread pesto sauce over pizza dough. Sprinkle tomatoes, onions and peppers on top of pesto. Sprinkle mozzarella and Parmesan cheeses on top.

DAIRY

Tip: To be sure that every slice (even appetizer size) has all the vegetables in it, layer the tomatoes, onions and peppers.

Servings: 8–10
Prep time: 15–20 minutes

# Greek Pizza

| | |
|---|---|
| 1 (7.5-oz.) can | pizza sauce |
| ½ cup | mozzarella cheese, grated |
| 3–4 oz. | feta cheese, crumbled |
| 5 | sun-dried tomatoes, sliced |
| 1 (5-oz.) pkg. | spinach, cooked, squeezed, drained |
| 5–6 | fresh basil leaves, sliced |
| | black olives, sliced (optional) |
| | green olives, sliced (optional) |

Spread pizza sauce over dough. Sprinkle with mozzarella and feta cheeses, tomatoes, spinach, basil and black and green olives.

DAIRY

Servings: 8–10
Prep time: 20 minutes

# Pizza Turnovers

| | |
|---|---|
| 2 Tbsp | margarine |
| ⅓ cup | mushrooms, chopped |
| ¼ cup | peppers, various colours, chopped |
| ¼ cup | onion, chopped |
| 1 (6-oz.) can | tomato paste |
| ¼ cup | water |
| 1 tsp | oregano |
| ½ tsp | salt |
| ¼ tsp | garlic powder |
| 1 cup | Cheddar cheese, shredded |
| 16 | puff pastry squares, (4½ x 4½ inches each) |

Preheat oven to 400F.

In a large skillet, sauté mushrooms, peppers and onions in margarine until tender. Gently stir in tomato paste, water and seasonings. Simmer for 15 minutes. Remove from heat and stir in cheese. Set aside.

Meanwhile, cut each puff pastry square in half diagonally, to make 2 triangles.

Place 1 teaspoon of mixture in the centre of each triangle and fold it over, to make smaller triangles. Pinch the edges together with a fork. Place them on a lightly greased baking sheet. Bake for 10–12 minutes, or until lightly browned.

*"I cannot make these fast enough for my kids. They eat them as I make them."*

**Tip:** Just leave out the vegetables if your kids don't like them.

**Servings:** 32 turnovers
**Prep time:** 30 minutes

# Spinach Boureka Pie

| | |
|---|---|
| ¼ cup | olive oil |
| ½ cup | onions, finely chopped |
| 2 (10-oz.) bags | spinach or 2 lbs., washed, drained, finely chopped |
| | salt and pepper to taste |
| ⅓ cup | milk |
| ½ lb. | feta cheese, crumbled |
| 3 | eggs |
| 1 (17.3-oz.) pkg. | puff pastry, thawed |
| 1 tsp | water |

Preheat oven to 325F.

In a large heavy saucepan, heat olive oil and sauté the onions until tender and translucent, approximately 5 minutes. Stir in spinach, salt and pepper. Cook, uncovered, for about 10 minutes, until most of the liquid has evaporated. If there is some liquid left in the pan, drain in a colander. Transfer the mixture to a deep bowl. Blend in milk. Cool. Add cheese and blend. Separate the white from one egg and set it aside. Beat the yolk from this egg with the other two whole eggs and slowly blend the eggs into the spinach mixture. Set aside.

Cut the puff pastry in half. On a floured board, roll first half to approximately 13 x 16 inches. Place the pastry in a greased 9 x 13-inch ovenproof dish and let it hang over edge of dish. Spread spinach mixture evenly over dough in dish. Roll second half to 9 x 13-inch size and place it over spinach mixture. Fold the overlapping dough over. Beat reserved egg white with 1 teaspoon of water. Brush it on top of the pie. Bake in the middle rack for 50–60 minutes, or until the pastry is crisp and delicately browned. Cut into squares and serve hot or at room temperature.

Servings: 8–10
Prep time: 40 minutes

# Zoglo's™ Zucchini Pastry Pie

| 4 cups | zucchini, thinly sliced, approximately |
| | 3 medium zucchini |
| 1 cup | onion, chopped |
| 1 Tbsp | margarine |
| ½ cup | fresh parsley, finely chopped |
| | salt and pepper to taste |
| ¼ tsp | garlic powder |
| ½ tsp | dried basil |
| ¼ tsp | dried oregano |
| 2 | eggs, well beaten |
| 8 oz. | mozzarella cheese, shredded (2 cups) |
| 1 (17.3-oz.) pkg. | Zoglo's™ puff pastry dough, thawed |
| 2 tsp | mustard |

Preheat oven to 375F.

In a large non-stick skillet over medium heat, sauté zucchini and onion in melted margarine for approximately 10 minutes until soft and tender. Stir in parsley and seasonings. Set aside.

In large bowl, blend eggs with cheese. Stir in vegetable mixture.

On a floured surface, roll out the pastry until thin. Place a large pie plate, preferably a fluted-edge type, under dough and trim off excess dough. Press dough into pie plate. Flute edges with a fork if desired. Prick bottom with a fork. Spread mustard on the bottom of the pastry. Fill pastry shell and bake until well browned, approximately 40 minutes or more.

Bake earlier in the day so filling sets. Reheat. Cut into wedges.

**Tip:** To decorate the pie, use extra trimmed-off pastry to cut three small leaves. Use a sharp knife to make veins in the leaf. Arrange the leaves in the centre of the pie, overlapping slightly.

Servings: 6–8
Prep time: 20 minutes

# Broccoli and Cheddar Quiche

*Kids love this. You can also make it in mini muffin tins without the crust.*

| | |
|---|---|
| 1 | 9-inch pie shell |
| 1 Tbsp | Dijon mustard |
| 1 | onion, finely chopped |
| 2 Tbsp | butter |
| 2–3 Tbsp | fresh dill or 1 tsp dried dill |
| 1 bunch | broccoli, chopped |
| 1½ cups | old Cheddar cheese, grated |
| 3 | eggs |
| 1½ cups | milk |
| 1 tsp | salt |
| ¼ tsp | pepper |
| pinch | nutmeg (optional) |
| pinch | cayenne pepper (optional) |

Preheat oven to 375F.

Brush pie shell with Dijon mustard.

In a skillet, sauté onion in butter until it becomes translucent. In a medium-sized bowl, combine onion, dill, broccoli and cheese. Spoon mixture into pie shell. In another bowl, beat together eggs, milk, salt, pepper, nutmeg and cayenne. Pour the mixture into the pie shell. Bake for 45–60 minutes until cheese is melted and a golden colour.

Servings: 6–8
Prep time: 15 minutes

# Broccoli Soufflé

| | |
|---|---|
| 1 cup | sour cream |
| 1 cup | low-fat pressed cottage cheese |
| ½ cup | pancake mix |
| 2 | eggs |
| 2 Tbsp | butter, melted |
| 1 | onion, chopped |
| 1 (10-oz.) can | mushrooms, drained |
| 1 Tbsp | oil |
| 1 head | broccoli flowerets, steamed |
| ½ cup | Mozzarella cheese, grated |
| 2–3 | firm tomatoes cut into thin rings |
| ¼ cup | Parmesan cheese |

Preheat oven to 350F.

In a blender, combine sour cream, cottage cheese, pancake mix, eggs and butter. Set aside.

In a small skillet, sauté onion and mushrooms in oil until golden brown.

Put the broccoli on the bottom of a greased lasagna pan. Pour half the blender mixture over top of broccoli. Add mushrooms and onion mixture. Then add the other half of the blender mixture. Sprinkle mozzarella cheese over the top. Cover mixture completely with tomatoes. Sprinkle with Parmesan cheese. Bake for 40 minutes or until browned.

**Tip:** Bake the soufflé ahead of time and let it sit. It tastes better when "firmed up." Reheat when serving. Cut into squares.

**Variations:** asparagus instead of broccoli

green onion instead of onions

leeks (minced finely) instead of green or regular onion

Servings: 10–12
Prep time: 20 minutes

# Summer Cheese Strata

| | |
|---|---|
| 1 (7.5-oz.) can | salmon |
| 4 | eggs, beaten |
| 2 cups | milk |
| 1 tsp | dry mustard |
| 1 tsp | Worcestershire sauce |
| ½ tsp | curry powder |
| ½ tsp | salt |
| 5 slices | bread, buttered, cubed |
| ¼ cup | sharp Cheddar cheese, grated |

Preheat oven to 350F.

In a medium-sized bowl, combine salmon, eggs, milk, mustard, Worcestershire sauce, curry powder and salt. Mix well. Set aside.

In a 1-quart casserole dish, combine bread and cheese. Pour the egg mixture over bread and cheese. DO NOT MIX. Cover and refrigerate. It can stay refrigerated for up to 2 days. The longer it sits, the more the flavour is enhanced.

Bake for 1 hour. Serve immediately.

Servings: 4–6
Prep time: 20 minutes

# Salmon Leek Quiche

*This is a quick dinner idea.*

| | |
|---|---|
| 1 | 9-inch-deep dish pie crust, defrosted |
| 2 | large leeks, cleaned thoroughly, sliced in half lengthwise, sliced thinly |
| 1 Tbsp | butter |
| 1 (16-oz.) can | salmon, drained, and flaked |
| 1 cup | Cheddar cheese, grated |
| 3 | eggs |
| ¾ cup | milk |
| | salt and pepper to taste |

Preheat oven to 400F.

Bake pie shell for 5 minutes. Remove from oven. Cool. Lower oven to 375F.

In a large skillet, sauté leeks in butter until tender. Remove from heat. Set aside.

Put the salmon in bottom of pie shell. Add leeks and cheese.

In a medium bowl, beat the eggs with the milk, salt and pepper. Pour evenly over mixture in pie shell. Bake for 25–35 minutes, or until set and golden. Let stand 5 minutes, and then serve.

Servings: 6–8
Prep time: 15–20 minutes

# Broccoli-Cheese Stuffed Potatoes

| | |
|---|---|
| 6 | large baking potatoes, washed, pierced a few times with a fork |
| ½–1 cup | sour cream |
| | salt and pepper to taste |
| 1 bunch | broccoli, steamed until tender, finely chopped |
| 1½ cups | Cheddar cheese, orange coloured, grated and divided into 1 cup and ½ cup |

Preheat oven to 450F.

Place potatoes on a parchment-lined baking sheet. Bake for 30 minutes or until soft. Lower oven to 350F.

Cut off tops and hollow out potato, reserving the potato shells/skins and the potato.

In a large bowl, mash potato with sour cream, salt and pepper until smooth. Mix in broccoli and 1 cup of cheese. Spoon mixture back into the potato shell (skins). Overfill them. Sprinkle the remainder of the cheese over the top of each potato. Return potatoes to the oven. Bake until cheese is bubbly, about 15 minutes.

Servings: 8–10
Prep time: 10 minutes

# Dilled Scalloped Potatoes

| | |
|---|---|
| ¼ cup | cornstarch |
| 2 tsp | salt |
| 10 | medium potatoes, peeled, cut into ¼-inch thick slices |
| 1 bunch | green onions, thinly sliced, diagonally |
| 1 cup | fresh dill, chopped |
| 1 cup | Parmesan cheese, grated |
| 2 cups | 35% whipping cream |
| 1 cup | milk |
| 1 cup | Swiss cheese, grated |

Preheat oven to 350F.

In a small bowl, combine cornstarch and salt. Set aside.

Put the potatoes in a large bowl. Add cornstarch and toss until evenly coated. Add onions, dill and Parmesan. Set aside.

In a large bowl, combine the cream with the milk. Set aside.

In a greased baking dish, layer half of potatoes. Pour half the cream mixture over top. Repeat the process. Sprinkle Swiss cheese on top. Cover. Bake for 1¼ hours. Uncover. Bake for an additional 20–30 minutes. Pierce with a fork to test for readiness. Potatoes should be soft.

Servings: 8–10
Prep time: 20 minutes

# Savory Vegetable Lasagna

*You won't have any left.*

| | |
|---|---|
| 9 | lasagna noodles, cooked al dente, rinsed, drained |
| 1–2 Tbsp | oil |
| 1 | eggplant, medium, sliced |
| 2 | zucchinis, peeled, diced |
| 2 cups | mushrooms, diced |
| 1 | green pepper, diced |
| 2 | onions, diced |
| 2 stalks | celery, diced |
| 1½ (24-oz. cans) | tomato sauce, flavoured if desired |
| 1 cup | mozzarella cheese, shredded |
| 1 cup | cottage cheese |

Preheat oven to 400F.

In a large skillet, sauté vegetables until tender. Remove from heat. Set aside.

Cover bottom of a 9 x 13-inch baking pan with a thin layer of tomato sauce. Layer lasagna noodles, tomato sauce, vegetables and cheeses. Repeat 3 times, leaving cheese layer on top. Bake covered for 40 minutes. Uncover. Bake for additional 10–15 minutes.

**Tip:** Make in advance and freeze. Defrost completely and bake covered at 400F until heated through, then uncover and bake for 10 minutes.

Servings: 8
Prep time: 45 minutes

# Blueberry Pancakes

| | |
|---|---|
| 2 cups | all purpose flour |
| ½ cup | sugar |
| 4 tsp | baking powder |
| ½ tsp | salt |
| 2 | eggs |
| 2 cups | milk |
| 2½ tsp | oil |
| ½ cup | blueberries |
| | oil for frying (or non-stick pan) |

In a medium-sized bowl, combine flour, sugar, baking powder and salt. Set aside.

In a separate bowl, beat the eggs lightly. Slowly add milk and oil. Fold the dry ingredients into the egg mixture and continue mixing with a fork until batter is slightly lumpy. Gently fold in blueberries.

Using a large spoon, drop batter onto a hot, lightly greased skillet. Fry on one side until bubbles appear on the top side of the pancake. Flip it over and fry on the other side. Repeat until batter is used up.

The batter may be covered and stored in refrigerator until ready to use.

Tip: Variation to blueberry pancakes – Add to batter ½ cup thinly sliced apples, or 1 diced banana or leave out fruit for basic pancakes.

Serve on a platter sprinkled with icing (confectioner's) sugar and decorated with sliced fanned-out strawberries and blueberries.

Servings: 6–8
Prep time: ½ hour

# Raspberry Scones

| | |
|---|---|
| 2 cups | all purpose flour |
| ¼ cup | sugar |
| 1 Tbsp | baking powder |
| ½ tsp | baking soda |
| ⅛ tsp | salt |
| ¼ cup | butter, cold |
| ½ cup | buttermilk (or ½ Tbsp lemon juice or vinegar and add milk to equal ½ cup) |
| 1 | egg, lightly beaten |
| 2 tsp | vanilla |
| 1 cup | fresh or frozen raspberries (or blueberries); firm are best |

ORANGE DRIZZLE ICING

| | |
|---|---|
| ¾ cup | icing (confectioner's) sugar |
| 3–4 tsp | orange juice |

Preheat oven to 400F.

In a large mixing bowl, combine flour, sugar, baking powder, baking soda and salt. Cut in butter until mixture is crumbly. In a separate bowl, combine buttermilk, egg and vanilla. Add to flour mixture. Stir until just combined. Turn out dough onto a lightly floured surface. Knead dough by folding and pressing it gently for 10 strokes.

Press dough into a 7-inch circle. Spread a third of the berries over the dough. Fold dough in half. Press it into a 7-inch circle again and spread a third of the berries over it and fold in half. Repeat process with last third of the berries. Pat dough into a 7-inch circle and place on a cookie sheet lined with parchment paper. Cut dough into 10–12 wedges. Bake for 15–20 minutes until golden.

Meanwhile, prepare icing by combining the ingredients in a small bowl, and stirring until smooth, adding enough juice to make a drizzle consistency. Drizzle scones with icing when slightly warm. Serve warm.

Servings: 10–12
Prep time: 20 minutes

# Banana Craisins Muffins

PARVE

| | |
|---|---|
| 3 | bananas, mashed |
| 2 | eggs |
| ½ cup | oil |
| ½ cup | apple or orange juice |
| 2 cups | all purpose flour |
| 1½ cups | brown sugar |
| 1 tsp | baking soda |
| 1 tsp | baking powder |
| ¼ cup | dried cranberries |
| ¼ cup | walnuts, crushed |
| ¼ cup | raisins (optional) |

Preheat oven to 350F.

With an electric mixer, combine bananas, eggs, oil and juice. Mix well.

In another bowl, combine flour, sugar, baking soda and powder. Add liquid ingredients to dry ingredients. Mix well. Fold in cranberries, walnuts and raisins. Spoon batter into greased or paper-lined mini muffin tins. Bake for 20 minutes.

Servings: 4 dozen mini muffins
Prep time: 15 minutes

# Blueberry Muffins

PARVE

| | |
|---|---|
| ½ cup | margarine, softened |
| ½ cup | oil |
| 1 cup | sugar |
| 3 | eggs |
| 1 tsp | vanilla |
| 1 tsp | baking powder |
| 2 cups | all purpose flour |
| 1½ cups | blueberries |

Preheat oven to 350F.

With an electric mixer, cream margarine, oil and sugar. Add eggs and vanilla. Add baking powder and flour. Mix until just blended. Fold the blueberries in by hand. Spoon the batter into paper-lined muffin tins. Bake mini muffins for 20 minutes; regular muffins for 30–35 minutes.

Servings: 12 regular or 24 mini muffins
Prep time: 10 minutes

# Oatmeal Chocolate Chip Muffins

*Easy, delicious and healthy!*

| 1 cup | boiling water |
| ⅔ cup | oatmeal |
| ¼ cup | margarine, softened |
| 1½ cups | all purpose flour |
| ½ cup | brown sugar |
| 1 tsp | baking powder |
| 1 tsp | baking soda |
| ½ tsp | salt |
| 2 | eggs |
| 1 tsp | vanilla |
| 1 cup | chocolate chips |

Preheat oven to 400F.

In a medium-sized mixing bowl, combine boiling water, oatmeal and margarine. Let stand for 20 minutes or until cooled.

Meanwhile combine flour, sugar, baking powder, baking soda and salt. Set aside.

Add eggs and vanilla to flour mixture. Mix well.

Using a wooden spoon, stir in oatmeal mixture. Mix until moistened. Stir in chocolate chips. Pour into 12 lightly greased muffin tins. Alternatively, paper cups can be placed in muffin tins. Bake for 20 minutes.

Servings: 12
Prep time: 10–15 minutes

# Challah

| | |
|---|---|
| 2¼ tsp | quick rise yeast or 18-g sachet |
| 3 cups + 2 Tbsp | all purpose flour (can use 1 cup whole wheat flour in place of 1 cup all purpose) |
| 1 tsp | salt |
| 1 cup | very warm water, 120F (50C) |
| ¼–½ cup | honey |
| ¼ cup | oil |
| 1 | egg |
| 1 | egg yolk + 1 Tbsp water for egg wash |
| | poppy or sesame seeds, to garnish |

In a large bowl, combine quick rise yeast with 1 cup + 2 teaspoons flour and salt. Add warm water, honey, oil, egg and enough flour to make a soft dough. Knead. Cover bowl. Set aside for 15 minutes.

On a lightly floured surface, shape dough into challah. Place on a lightly greased baking sheet (or in 2 4 x 8-inch loaf pans). Let rise until doubled in size, approximately 2 hours.

Preheat oven to 350F.

Brush challah with egg wash. Sprinkle with sesame or poppy seeds. Bake for 25 minutes or until golden brown.

It can be placed in fridge overnight once it is shaped, but rising time would be at least 4 hours.

If making the dough in a bread machine, put ingredients in machine in the following order: egg, water, oil, honey, salt, flour, yeast or according to manufacturer's direction.

---

*For a nice sweet topping put this on after brushing with egg wash*

**STREUSEL TOPPING**

| | |
|---|---|
| ¾ cup | all purpose flour |
| ½ cup | raisins with flour coating (optional) |
| ¼ cup | margarine |
| ¼ cup | sugar |

Mix in processor until crumbly, approximately 8–10 seconds

Servings: 1 large or 2 small
Prep time: 15 minutes

# Greek Braided Bread with Feta and Spinach

| | |
|---|---|
| 1 | bread recipe (see page 107) |
| 1 (7½-oz.) can | pizza sauce |
| ½ (400-g) pkg. | frozen spinach, thawed, squeezed dry |
| 6–8 | fresh basil leaves, chopped |
| 5–6 | sun-dried tomatoes, sliced |
| 10 | black olives, sliced (optional) |
| 10 | green olives, sliced (optional) |
| 3–4 oz. | feta cheese, crumbled |
| ½ cup | grated mozzarella cheese |
| 1 egg yolk + 1 Tbsp | water for egg wash (optional) |
| | sesame seeds (optional) |

Tips: Can freeze before baking and then bake when defrosted. Freezes well.

Preheat oven to 350F.

Prepare bread dough (facing page) but do not bake.

Divide bread dough in half. Roll out each half into a narrow long rectangle, approximately 8 x 12 inches.

Spread pizza sauce down the middle of each rectangle, leaving a 2-inch border on each side.

Make slits on a diagonal, 1 inch apart, down each dough border. Spread spinach, basil, sun-dried tomatoes, olives, feta and mozzarella cheeses on top of pizza sauce. Fold the "tabs" created by the slits over the sauce area, starting at the top and alternating sides so it looks like a braid. Brush top of braid with egg wash or spray top with cooking spray. Sprinkle with sesame seeds if desired. Cover. Let rise for 30 minutes. It can be frozen at this point.

Bake for 20–25 minutes until golden brown on top.

## Bread recipe

| | |
|---|---|
| 1 Tbsp | yeast |
| ½ cup | warm water (100F) |
| 1 tsp | sugar |
| 3 Tbsp | oil |
| 2¾ cups | all purpose flour |
| 3 Tbsp | sugar |
| 1 tsp | salt |
| ½ cup | warm water (100F) |

Sprinkle yeast into ½ cup warm water in a small bowl. Sprinkle 1 teaspoon sugar on top. Stir. Let stand for 10 minutes until it doubles in size. Add oil.

In processor bowl, mix flour, 3 tablespoons sugar and salt. Pour yeast mixture into processor bowl through feed tube while processor is on. Add warm water slowly until a ball is formed and cleans side of bowl. Add more flour (1 tablespoon at a time) if too sticky, more water (1 tablespoon at a time) if too dry. Place into a large bowl. Cover. Let rise until double in bulk, approximately 1 hour.

Preheat oven to 400F.

Shape the risen dough as desired.

Bake for 15–18 minutes for 8–12 rolls, 20 minutes for a bread loaf.

Tips: Buy pre-made bread dough and incorporate it into the recipe.

Use any combination of the fillings (spinach, basil, cheeses, tomatoes and olives). It is not necessary to use them all. Just use what you love most.

Servings: 2 loaves
Prep time: 1 hour

# Lavash Crackers

| 1¾ cups | all purpose flour |
| ½ cup | cornmeal |
| ½ cup | sesame seeds |
| ¼ cup | poppy seeds |
| 2 Tbsp | dill seeds |
| 1 Tbsp | sugar |
| 1 tsp | garlic powder |
| 1 tsp | onion powder |
| ½ tsp | salt |
| ½ tsp | baking soda |
| ½ cup | margarine, softened |
| ½ cup | water |
| 2 Tbsp | vinegar |

Preheat oven to 350F.

In a large mixing bowl, combine flour, cornmeal, sesame seeds, poppy seeds, dill seeds, sugar, garlic and onion powders, salt and baking soda. Mix well. Add margarine, water and vinegar. Mix well.

On a lightly floured surface, roll dough out really thin and cut it into squares. It doesn't have to be exactly square shaped. Place the squares onto a greased cookie sheet. Bake for 10–15 minutes, or until crisp and golden.

Servings: 6–8
Prep time: 15 minutes

5

**fish**

# Lemon and Soy Steaks

| ½ cup | olive oil |
|---|---|
| ¼ cup | soy sauce |
| ¼ cup | fresh lemon juice |
| 1 | clove of garlic, minced or ½ tsp garlic powder |
| 1 Tbsp | fresh parsley, chopped |
| 6-8 | salmon or trout steaks (4–6 oz. each) |

Preheat oven to 325F.

In a small bowl, combine olive oil, soy sauce, lemon juice, garlic and parsley. Set aside.

Place fish in a single layer in a greased shallow baking dish. Pour sauce over fish.

Turn 1–2 times to coat the fish with the sauce. Bake for 20 minutes or until fish flakes easily when prodded with a fork.

OR

Brush the barbecue with oil and grill 5–10 minutes each side (until ready). Serve with lemon wedges on a bed of rice.

Servings: 6–8
Prep time: 10 minutes

# Salmon with Brown Sugar Glaze

PARVE

GLAZE

| | |
|---|---|
| 1 Tbsp | brown sugar |
| 1 Tbsp | honey |
| 2 tsp | margarine |
| 3 Tbsp | Dijon mustard |
| 1 Tbsp | soy sauce |
| 1 tsp | olive oil |
| 4 | salmon fillets (4–6 oz. each) |

Preheat oven to 425F.

In a small saucepan, on low heat, melt brown sugar, honey and margarine. Remove from heat. Whisk in mustard, soy sauce and olive oil. Set aside.

In a greased pan, place salmon skin side down. Brush it with glaze and bake for 10–15 minutes until cooked. Fish is opaque and flakes easily when tested.

Servings: 4
Prep time: 15 minutes

# Melt in Your Mouth Salmon

DAIRY

| | |
|---|---|
| 1 Tbsp | butter |
| 2–4 | salmon steaks or fillets (2–4 oz. each) |
| 1 cup | dry white wine, divided in half |
| 2 Tbsp | fresh parsley, chopped |
| 2 | green onions, chopped |
| ½ | lemon, juiced |
| 1 Tbsp | honey |
| | salt and pepper to taste |
| ¼ cup | yogurt or light sour cream |
| 2 Tbsp | Dijon mustard |
| ½ tsp | tarragon |

**Tip:** If you have ever wondered whether the fish you are buying at the market is fresh try this: Fish is fresh if your thumbprint pops up and is not fresh if the impression stays indented.

In a large skillet over medium heat, melt butter and sear salmon for 2 minutes on each side. Add ½ cup wine, parsley and onions. Cover. Cook for 10–15 minutes.

Remove salmon to a warm plate. Increase heat and add remaining ingredients to pan. Simmer, stirring 2 minutes or until sauce is thick. Remove from heat. Pour over salmon.

Servings: 2–4
Prep time: 15 minutes

# Baked Dijon Salmon

| | |
|---|---|
| ¼ cup | honey |
| ¼ cup | margarine, melted |
| 3 Tbsp | Dijon mustard |
| ¼ cup | dry bread crumbs |
| ¼ cup | pecans, crushed |
| 1 Tbsp | dried parsley flakes |
| 1 | large fillet of salmon (approximatly 2 – 2.5 lbs.) |
| | lemon wedges (optional) |
| | salt and pepper to taste |

**Tip:** Use remaining honey mustard sauce for dipping.

Preheat oven to 400F.

In a small bowl, mix honey, margarine and mustard. Reserve.

In another small bowl, combine bread crumbs, pecans and parsley. Reserve.

Place salmon on a foil-lined sheet, and brush top with honey-mustard mixture. Sprinkle bread crumb-pecan mixture, covering the fish completely. Bake uncovered for 25 minutes. Salmon should flake when prodded with a fork.

Serve with lemon wedges, salt and pepper to taste.

Servings: 6
Prep time: 10–15 minutes

# Oriental Salmon Salad Dinner

| | |
|---|---|
| 3 Tbsp | sherry or white wine |
| 2 Tbsp | water |
| 2 Tbsp | soy sauce |
| 2 Tbsp | brown sugar |
| 2 Tbsp | oil |
| 1 Tbsp | honey |
| 2 tsp | garlic, crushed |
| 1 tsp | fresh ginger, minced |
| 4 | salmon fillets (4–6 oz. each) |
| 2 tsp | cornstarch dissolved in a little cold water |
| 1 head | romaine lettuce, cut into pieces |
| | tomatoes, in wedges, for garnish |
| | mushrooms, halved, for garnish |
| | coloured peppers, sliced, for garnish |
| | chow mein noodles, for garnish |

In a small bowl, combine sherry, water, soy sauce, brown sugar, oil, honey, garlic and ginger. Divide the sauce in half. Place salmon in a glass dish and pour half of the mixture on top. Cover and marinate in refrigerator for 2–4 hours.

Preheat oven to broil.

Add cornstarch to remaining marinade. In a small saucepan, bring marinade to a boil for a few minutes, stirring constantly, until sauce begins to thicken. Remove from heat and let cool.

Remove salmon from glass dish and place it in an oven-proof baking dish. Broil fish for 5–10 minutes on each side or until the centre is no longer pink and the salmon flakes easily.

Meanwhile, arrange lettuce over 4 dinner plates. Place 1 fillet on each plate on top of the lettuce. Garnish with tomato wedges, mushroom halves and slices of coloured peppers. Sprinkle crispy chow mein noodles on top. Drizzle sauce over salmon and salad.

Tip: Ideal served with pasta.

Servings: 4
Prep time: 20 minutes

# Salmon with Stir-Fry Veggies and Mango Sauce

### SALMON

| | |
|---|---|
| 4 | salmon fillets (4–6 oz. each) |
| ⅛ tsp | salt |
| ⅛ tsp | pepper |
| 1 Tbsp | sesame oil, divided in half |
| 1½ | red pepper, julienned |
| 1½ | green or orange pepper, julienned |
| 2 cups | asparagus, sliced |
| 1 cup | carrots, julienned |

### MANGO SAUCE

| | |
|---|---|
| 2 | mangoes, peeled, chopped |
| ⅔ cup | chicken broth |
| 2 tsp | lime juice |
| 1½ tsp | fresh ginger, peeled, grated |
| 1 tsp | hot chili pepper, minced, seeded |

Preheat oven to 425F.

**SALMON:** Place salmon in a baking dish. Sprinkle with salt, pepper and half the sesame oil. Bake uncovered for 15 minutes.

Meanwhile, in a small skillet, add remaining sesame oil and sauté the peppers, asparagus and carrots for 5 minutes. Reserve.

**MANGO SAUCE:** In a small saucepan over medium heat, combine mangoes, chicken broth, lime juice, ginger and chili. Stir occasionally and continue to cook for 10 minutes. Cool. Pour into a blender and process until smooth.

Place each fillet on a plate. Top with veggies and spoon on mango sauce.

Servings: 4 servings
Prep time: 15–20 minutes

*"Make sure you prepare enough. My guests all ate double portions."*

Tip: **Serve with couscous.**

# Steamed Halibut with Simmering Vegetables and Feta Cheese

| | |
|---|---|
| 2 Tbsp | olive oil |
| 2 | red onions, thinly sliced (approximately 2 cups) |
| 1 | red pepper, in 1-inch cubes |
| 2 | cloves of garlic, minced |
| 1 (14-oz.) can | diced tomatoes with juice |
| 1 cup | orange juice |
| 1 tsp | dried oregano |
| | salt to taste |
| | freshly ground pepper to taste |
| ¼ cup | black olives, sliced |
| 4 | halibut fillets (4–6 oz. each) |
| 2 Tbsp | fresh parsley, chopped |
| 3 oz. | feta cheese, cubed |

In a large skillet, heat the oil. Sauté onions, red pepper and garlic for a few minutes. Add tomatoes, orange juice and oregano. Bring to a boil, then reduce heat and simmer for a few more minutes. Season with salt and pepper. Add olives. Arrange halibut fillets over vegetables. Cover and simmer gently until fish is just cooked through, about 10 minutes depending on the thickness of the fillets. Add parsley and feta cheese in the last few minutes of cooking.

Servings: 4
Prep time: 25–30 minutes

# Sole Fillets Meridian

| | |
|---|---|
| 8 pieces | frozen sole fillets, thawed |
| | salt and pepper to taste |
| 1 | large tomato, thinly sliced |
| ¼ cup | white wine |
| ½ tsp | dried basil |
| ½ cup | Swiss cheese, grated |

Preheat oven to 375F.

In a shallow, greased, 9 x 13-inch ovenproof dish, place fish in a single layer. Sprinkle with salt and pepper. Arrange tomato slices on top. Pour wine over fish, and then sprinkle with basil. Bake for 10 minutes. Remove from oven and sprinkle cheese on fish. Return it to oven. Bake for an additional 5 minutes. Carefully transfer the fish to a serving platter.

DAIRY

Tip: If you like a milder cheese taste, use mozzarella or Cheddar instead of Swiss.

Servings: 6–8
Prep time: 5 minutes

Servings: 4–6
Prep time: 20 minutes

Tip: Tie each lemon half in a cheesecloth bag to trap seeds when lemon is squeezed.

Servings: 4–6
Prep time: 15–20 minutes

# Moroccan Coriander Fish

| | |
|---|---|
| 1 | red pepper, diced |
| 4 | cloves of garlic, cut in half |
| ⅓ cup | oil |
| 1½ tsp | paprika |
| 4–6 pieces | white fish, halibut or salmon (4–6 oz. each) |
| 1 tsp | salt |
| ½ cup | fresh coriander, chopped |
| ⅓ cup | water |

Put the red pepper and garlic in a large skillet.

In a small dish, mix oil and paprika. Dip fish in mixture then place pieces next to each other in the skillet. Sprinkle with salt and coriander. Pour water over fish and add remaining oil mixture. Bring to a boil then reduce heat to low and cover. Baste occasionally. Cook for ½ hour, or until fish is cooked. Do not turn fish.

# Tilapia

| | |
|---|---|
| 2 Tbsp | olive oil |
| 1 | green pepper, cubed |
| 1 | red pepper, cubed |
| 1 | tomato, cubed |
| 4 | cloves of garlic, minced |
| ½ (5½-oz.) can | tomato paste |
| | salt and pepper to taste |
| 4 | tilapia fillets |
| ½ | lemon, juiced |

Preheat oven to 350F.

In a large skillet, sauté vegetables and garlic in oil until tender. Add tomato paste, salt and pepper. Mix well.

Place fish in a 9 x 13-inch baking dish in a single layer. Squeeze lemon over fish. Add vegetable mixture. Bake for 20 minutes.

# "Seafood" Stir Fry

| 3 | cloves of garlic, minced |
| 1 Tbsp | fresh ginger, minced |
| 1 Tbsp | oil |
| 1 lb. | frozen veggies, stir fry mix |
| 1 lb. | mock port lock crab |
| 1 tsp | hot chili-garlic sauce |
| 1 Tbsp | cornstarch |
| ½ cup | teriyaki sauce |
| 1 Tbsp | sesame oil |

In a large skillet, sauté garlic and ginger in oil for approximately 2 minutes.

Add frozen veggies. Continue to sauté until vegetables have partially thawed.

Add port lock crab and chili-garlic sauce. Mix. Cook, covered, stirring often, for about 7 minutes.

Meanwhile, in a small bowl, whisk cornstarch into teriyaki sauce until dissolved. Add to skillet. Stir until mixture thickens, approximately 2–3 minutes. Remove from heat. Drizzle sesame oil over stir fry just before serving.

**Tip:** Nice served over rice.

Servings: 4–6
Prep time: 15–20 minutes

## Sole with Mustard Caper Butter Sauce

| | |
|---|---|
| 4 (4 oz. each) | fillets of sole |
| ½ cup | butter or margarine, softened |
| 1 tsp | dry mustard |
| 1 Tbsp | finely chopped parsley or 1 tsp dry parsley |
| 1 Tbsp | lemon juice |
| 1 Tbsp | capers |

Preheat oven to 350F.

Grease a shallow ovenproof 9 x 13-inch dish and place sole in a single layer.

In a small saucepan, melt butter or margarine. Add dry mustard, parsley, lemon juice and capers. Mix. Pour over sole. Bake uncovered for 20 minutes or until fish flakes at the touch of a fork.

Servings: 4
Prep time: 10 minutes

# poultry

# Double Mushroom Chicken

This chicken is superb. Your guests will not be able to guess what the great topping is made of.

SAUCE

| | |
|---|---|
| 1 | clove of garlic, minced |
| 1 tsp | olive oil |
| 6–7 | mushrooms, sliced |
| 1 Tbsp | cornstarch dissolved in 1 cup chicken broth |
| | salt and pepper to taste |
| 2 (3 lb. each) | chicken cut into eighths or boneless and skinless chicken breasts or thighs, |
| 1 (1.4-oz.) pkg. | porcini mushrooms, dried |
| ½ cup | dry bread crumbs |
| ½ cup | mayonnaise |
| 2 tsp | Dijon mustard |
| 1½ tsp | paprika |
| ¼–½ tsp | curry powder (optional) |
| 1 tsp | paprika |

Preheat oven to 375F.

In a non-stick saucepan over medium heat, sauté garlic in olive oil. Add mushrooms. Add cornstarch-chicken broth, salt and pepper and bring to a boil, stirring constantly. Remove from heat. Set aside.

Rinse chicken pieces. Pat dry. Set aside on parchment paper placed in a large pan.

Lightly run cold water through porcini mushrooms and drain well. Place them on paper towels and pat until absolutely dry. (Air-dry for a while.) Cut any large pieces by hand. Put them in a food processor. Process well. Add bread crumbs. Process until mixture becomes crumb-like.

Combine mayonnaise, mustard, curry powder and paprika and coat chicken pieces, returning the coated pieces to the pan. Sprinkle with mushroom crumbs and paprika to give colour.

Place chicken, uncovered, in oven. After 20–25 minutes, baste with half the mushroom sauce. After another 30 minutes add remaining sauce. Do not overcook chicken. Depending on the size of the chicken pieces, chicken should be cooked for about an hour and then checked. To reheat, cover pan with foil.

Servings: 10–12
Prep time: 25–30 minutes

# Portobello Chicken

| | |
|---|---|
| 4 | Portobello mushrooms, sliced thinly |
| 1 | onion, sliced thinly |
| 6 | chicken breasts, boneless, skinless |
| 2 | cloves of garlic, minced |
| 1 Tbsp | basil, fresh, chopped |
| | salt and pepper to taste |
| ½ cup | olive oil |
| 4 | plum tomatoes, sliced thinly |

Preheat oven to 350F.

Lightly grease a large roasting pan. Place mushrooms and onion on the bottom of the pan. Top with a row of chicken breasts. Sprinkle garlic, basil, salt and pepper on top of chicken. Drizzle oil over the chicken. Place sliced tomatoes on top and bake, covered, for 30 minutes. Uncover. Baste. Bake for additional 15–20 minutes.

Servings: 6
Prep time: 20 minutes

# Maple Mustard Grilled Chicken

MARINADE

| | |
|---|---|
| ½ cup | oil |
| ½ cup | 100% pure maple syrup |
| 3 Tbsp | balsamic vinegar |
| 2 Tbsp | Dijon mustard |
| 1 tsp | pepper |
| 1 tsp | garlic, chopped |
| 6 | chicken breasts, boneless, skinless (4–6 oz. each) |

In small jar or cruet, combine marinade ingredients. Cover. Shake well. Set aside.

Arrange chicken in shallow glass dish. Add marinade. Toss to coat.

Cover and refrigerate at least 4–6 hours, preferably overnight.

Preheat oven to 400F. Bake for 30 minutes, basting periodically. Broil for a few minutes to brown. Or if preferred, chicken can be grilled, basting periodically.

*Prepare this chicken for the best barbecue you have ever tasted.*

Servings: 6
Prep time: 10 minutes

# Sliced Chicken with Lemon-Basil Vinaigrette

*This chicken looks and tastes spectacular. The contrast of red tomatoes in this recipe really highlights the chicken.*

VINAIGRETTE

| | |
|---|---|
| ¼ cup | lemon juice, fresh |
| ¼ cup | olive oil |
| 2 | cloves of garlic, minced |
| 2 tsp | dried basil |
| 2 tsp | lemon zest |
| ½ tsp | thyme |
| 4 | chicken breasts, skinless, boneless (4–6 oz. each) |
| 4 | medium vine-ripe tomatoes cut into chunks or wedges |

In a small jar or cruet, combine vinaigrette ingredients. Cover. Shake well.

Place chicken in a shallow glass dish. Coat chicken breasts with 3 tablespoons of vinaigrette. Let marinate for 10–30 minutes.

Put tomatoes in a small bowl. Add 3 tablespoons of vinaigrette. Marinate for 1 hour.

Preheat oven to broil setting.

Transfer chicken to an ovenproof dish. Broil in oven for 5 minutes on each side or barbecue until cooked. Slice each chicken breast into 6 slices.

On a platter place sliced chicken in the centre and marinated tomatoes around the outside. Drizzle with remainder of marinade.

Good served warm or at room temperature.

Servings: 4
Prep time: 1 hour

# Chicken with Lemon and Artichoke

MARINADE FOR CHICKEN AND POTATOES

| | |
|---|---|
| 2–3 | large lemons, squeezed to make ½ cup juice, keep remains for artichoke preparation |
| 3 Tbsp | olive oil |
| 4–5 | cloves of garlic, thinly sliced |
| 1 tsp | dried oregano |
| | salt and pepper to taste |
| 2 | medium-size-chickens, cut into eighths |
| 8–10 | small red potatoes, cut into halves or quarters |

ARTICHOKE

| | |
|---|---|
| 4–5 | large, fresh artichokes or 12–16 small artichokes |
| 2–3 | large lemon skins reserved from marinade |
| 2 Tbsp | lemon juice |
| 8–10 cups | cold water |

Preheat oven to 450F.

In a small bowl, mix lemon juice, oil, garlic, oregano, salt and pepper. Coat chicken and potatoes with marinade. Put them in a roasting pan. Bake uncovered for 20–30 minutes.

**ARTICHOKE PREPARATION:** Remove outer dark leaves. Small ones should be cut in half and the fuzzy choke removed from the centre. Large ones should be cut into quarters.

Put lemon skins and lemon juice in a large pot. Add water. Bring to a boil. Cook artichokes in boiling water for 10 minutes or until just tender. Drain.

Remove chicken from oven, and add artichokes. Return chicken to oven. Continue baking for an additional 20–30 minutes until juice from chicken runs clear.

*This looks great served on a large oval platter garnished with fresh lemon wedges.*

**Tips:** It is best to cook artichokes in a pot large enough for them to move around while cooking.

The best flavour and the most juice can be found in small, round or oval lemons with smooth, unblemished skins.

When lemons are stored at room temperature, you will obtain more juice from them.

Servings: 10–12
Prep time: 1 hour

# Lemon Ginger Chicken

| | |
|---|---|
| 2 Tbsp | honey, slightly warmed |
| 1 (6-oz.) box | potato pancake flakes |
| 2 | eggs, beaten |
| 4–6 | chicken breasts, boneless, skinless |
| 3 Tbsp | oil for frying |

SAUCE

| | |
|---|---|
| 2–3 | onions, sliced |
| 2 inches | fresh ginger, peeled and sliced thinly |
| 1½ cups | water |
| 3 Tbsp | sugar |
| 2 Tbsp | lemon juice |
| 1 Tbsp | margarine |
| 2 tsp | cornstarch, dissolved in 2 Tbsp cold water |
| | garnish: fresh parsley |
| | lemon slices |
| | green onions |

Preheat oven to 350F.

Put honey, potato flakes and eggs into three separate shallow dishes. Dip chicken breasts first in honey, then coat in potato pancake flakes, followed by dipping into beaten eggs. Place breasts on a dish.

Heat oil in a large skillet over medium heat and fry the chicken quickly to set coating. Place chicken on a baking sheet in a single layer.

Mix ingredients for sauce in a small saucepan. Bring to a boil and continue stirring until sauce thickens slightly. Remove from heat. Pour over chicken and bake, uncovered, for 20–25 minutes, until chicken is no longer pink on the inside.

Garnish with fresh parsley, lemon slices and fresh green onions.

**Tips:** If preparing ahead of time, do not bake chicken – freeze chicken after sauce is poured over it and bake when you defrost it.

Can be used for Passover.

**Interesting fact:** Ginger has a potent yet refreshing kick. Grate it fresh into salsas and sautés. Use ground ginger in baked goods.

Servings: 4–6
Prep time: 15–20 minutes

# Sweet Chicken Cutlets

| | |
|---|---|
| 2 Tbsp | oil |
| 2 | onions, diced |
| 1 | red pepper, sliced |
| 1 | yellow pepper, sliced |
| 8 | single boneless chicken breasts |
| 15–20 | Parisienne potatoes (optional) |
| 1 cup | ketchup |
| ½ cup | duck sauce |
| ½ cup | apricot jam |
| 2 Tbsp | honey |

Preheat oven to 350F.

In a small skillet, sauté onions and peppers in oil until soft. Put them in a roasting pan. Rinse chicken cutlets. Pat dry. Put in pan. Add potatoes, at this point, if desired.

In a small saucepan bring ketchup, duck sauce, apricot jam and honey to a boil. Pour over chicken. Cover pan. Bake for 2 hours.

**Tip:** If you need to flatten cutlets, first wrap in Saran Wrap and then pound them, so the juices will stay inside meat.

Servings: 8–10
Prep time: 25 minutes

# Chicken on a Skewer

MARINADE

| | |
|---|---|
| 3 Tbsp | ketchup |
| 3 Tbsp | soy sauce |
| 2 Tbsp | brown sugar |
| 2 Tbsp | oil |
| 1 Tbsp | vinegar |
| 1½ Tbsp | dry onion soup mix |
| | garlic powder to taste |
| 1½ lbs. | boneless dark or white meat chicken, cut into pieces for skewers (approximately 50 pieces) |
| 10–12 | large wooden skewers, soaked in cold water for 1 hour |

**Tips:** Marinade is great for barbecuing any meat.

Chicken skewers may be barbecued as well.

Delicious warm or at room temperature the next day.

In a small dish, combine marinade ingredients. Mix well.

In large glass bowl, add marinade to chicken. Cover. Refrigerate for 1 hour or overnight.

Preheat oven to broil setting.

Thread chicken onto soaked skewers. Place 5 chicken pieces on each skewer and place on a large baking sheet. Broil in oven for 5 minutes on each side or until cooked through.

Servings: 4–6
Prep time: 10 minutes

# Chicken Picatta

| | |
|---|---|
| ¾ cup | all purpose flour |
| 1 tsp | pepper |
| 1 tsp | paprika |
| 1 tsp | salt |
| 4 | chicken breasts, skinless, boneless, pounded flat |
| 3 Tbsp | olive oil |
| 2 Tbsp | margarine |
| 2 | cloves of garlic, minced |
| ¼ cup | white wine |
| ¼ cup | chicken broth |
| ½ | fresh lemon, juiced or 3 Tbsp lemon juice |
| 3 Tbsp | fresh parsley, chopped |

In a small bowl, combine flour, pepper, paprika and salt. Dredge the chicken in the flour mixture. Place on a dish. Set aside.

In a large skillet, heat oil and margarine. Brown the chicken breasts. When the chicken is no longer pink on the inside, approximately 3–5 minutes on each side, remove from skillet. Place in a covered dish to keep chicken warm. Set aside.

Add garlic to the skillet and sauté. Add wine and chicken broth. Cook over high heat, until the liquid is reduced by half. Stir lemon juice into mixture. Add browned chicken breasts to skillet. Warm with the liquid mixture, over low heat, for 5 minutes. Remove from heat.

Remove the chicken breasts onto a serving platter and top with liquid mixture. Garnish with parsley.

Servings: 4
Prep time: 15 minutes

# Sizzling Cajun Chicken

| | |
|---|---|
| ½ cup | all purpose flour |
| 2 tsp | paprika |
| ¼ tsp | pepper |
| | salt to taste |
| 1 | chicken, cut into eighths, rinsed, patted dry |
| 1 | medium onion, chopped |
| 2 | cloves of garlic, minced |
| 1 Tbsp | white horseradish, fresh or jarred |
| 1 Tbsp | oil |
| ½ tsp | dried oregano |
| ⅛ tsp | cayenne pepper |
| 1 cup | ketchup |
| ½ cup | chicken stock |

In a small bowl, mix together flour, paprika, pepper and salt. Coat chicken thoroughly with flour mixture. Place chicken in a shallow glass dish. Cover and refrigerate for 30 minutes.

In a large skillet, sauté onion and garlic in oil for 3–5 minutes. Add horseradish, oregano and cayenne pepper. Stir until sauce reduces a little. Add ketchup and stock. Bring to a gentle simmer, stirring constantly. Remove from heat. Transfer to a bowl. Reserve.

Grill chicken on barbecue for 20 minutes until golden brown. Lower heat to medium and baste with sauce. Keep basting until chicken is done, approximately 20 minutes.

Servings: 4–6
Prep time: 45 minutes

# Marinated Grilled Chicken

MARINADE

| | |
|---|---|
| 2 | lemons, juiced |
| 1 | chicken cube or 1 tsp chicken soup powder |
| ¼ cup | oil |
| 1 Tbsp | dried parsley |
| 1 tsp | oregano or mixed herbs |
| 1 tsp | salt |
| 1 tsp | dry mustard |
| 1 tsp | pepper |
| ½ tsp | dried thyme |
| 1 (4–5 lbs.) | whole chicken, washed, patted dry |

In a small jar or cruet, combine marinade ingredients. Cover. Mix well. Set aside.

Put chicken in a large glass container. Pour marinade over chicken, to coat. Cover. Refrigerate overnight.

The next day, preheat oven to 350F.

Transfer chicken to an ovenproof pan. Bake, uncovered, for 45–60 minutes. Alternatively, grill, rotisserie or barbecue chicken until tender, basting occasionally.

Servings: 6–8
Prep time: 10 minutes, marinate overnight

# Broiled Butterflied Chicken

*Your local butcher will be happy to butterfly the chicken for you.*

| | |
|---|---|
| 2 | onions, cut into thick slices |
| 3 | carrots, peeled and cut into 2-inch pieces |
| 3 | stalks of celery, cut into 2-inch pieces |
| 1½ tsp | black peppercorns, crushed |
| 4 | cloves of garlic, minced |
| ½ tsp | kosher salt |
| 1 | lemon peel, zested |
| 1 tsp | lemon juice |
| 1 (3–4 lbs.) | chicken, butterflied |
| | olive oil |
| 1 cup | red wine |
| 1 cup | chicken broth |
| 2–3 | sprigs of thyme |

**Tip:** Use the vegetables to garnish, or discard them.

Preheat oven to broil.

Place onions, carrots and celery on bottom of a roasting pan.

In a small bowl, combine peppercorns, garlic, salt, zest and lemon juice. Mix well, until it forms a thick paste. Rub paste under skin and in cavity of chicken. Place chicken, skin side down, on top of vegetables. Drizzle olive oil on top. Broil for 15–20 minutes with oven door open. Turn chicken over. Broil for an additional 15–20 minutes. Remove chicken and cover to keep warm. Siphon off fat.

In a small saucepan, combine wine, chicken broth and thyme. Bring to a boil to reduce quantity by one-third. Pour wine sauce over chicken to serve.

Servings: 6–8
Prep time: 10 minutes

# Rosemary Grilled Chicken

| 6 | chicken breasts, skinless, boneless |
| 3 | fresh sprigs rosemary |
| 1 cup | white wine |
| ¼ cup | olive oil |
| 3 Tbsp | lemon juice |
| 1 tsp | freshly ground pepper |
| 1 | clove of garlic, chopped |
| 1 | lemon, thinly sliced, for garnish |

Place chicken in a re-sealable bag.

In a small bowl, combine rosemary, wine, oil, lemon juice, pepper and garlic. Pour into bag over chicken. Place in refrigerator and marinate up to 6 hours.

Preheat your grill or if using an oven broil on high.

Remove chicken from bag and place on a roasting pan. Grill both sides until centre of breast is no longer pink, approximately 6–8 minutes per side. Garnish with lemon.

Servings: 4–6
Prep time: 10 minutes, marinate up to 6 hours in advance

# Terra Chip Chicken

| | |
|---|---|
| ½ cup | all purpose flour |
| 1 Tbsp | garlic powder |
| ½ tsp | salt |
| ½ tsp | pepper |
| 6 | chicken breasts, boneless, skinless |
| 1 | egg |
| 1 Tbsp | Dijon mustard |
| 1 tsp | lemon juice |
| 1 tsp | lemon and herb spice |
| 1 (170 g) bag | Terra chips, crushed |
| ⅓ cup | margarine |

Preheat oven to 350F.

In a small bowl, combine flour, garlic powder, salt and pepper. Dredge chicken breasts in mixture. Set aside.

In another small bowl, beat egg, mustard, lemon juice and lemon and herb spice together. Set aside.

Place crushed chips in a large bowl. Dip chicken first in egg mixture then in crushed Terra chips. Place chicken breasts in roasting pan.

In a small saucepan, melt margarine. Drizzle on top of chicken. Place roasting pan, uncovered, in oven. Bake for 30–45 minutes.

*Colourful and unique.*

**Tips:** To crush chips and still maintain texture, put them into a sealable plastic bag and use a rolling pin for crushing. For a finer texture, crush chips in a food processor.

For Passover, adapt this recipe by using any type of potato chips.

Terra chips come in a variety of flavours and colours.

Servings: 6
Prep time: 15 minutes

# Mediterranean Chicken with Dried Fruit

| ½ cup | dried apricots |
| ½ cup | pitted prunes |
| 6 | cloves of garlic, unpeeled |
| 1 | onion, sliced |
| 1 | carrot, cut in small chunks |
| 1 tsp | cumin |
| 1 tsp | garlic powder |
| 1 tsp | paprika |
| 1 tsp | curry powder |
| 1 Tbsp | sesame seeds |
| 1–2 Tbsp | olive oil |
| 1 (3–4 lb.) | chicken cut in eighths, washed, patted dry |
| 2 Tbsp | honey |
| ⅓ cup | water |
| ¼ cup | toasted almonds, sliced |

**Tips:** Nice to serve over cous-cous.

Serve fruit and vegetables alongside chicken.

Preheat oven to 375F.

Place apricots, prunes, garlic, onion and carrot on the bottom of a medium-sized roasting pan. Set aside.

In a small bowl, combine cumin, garlic powder, paprika, curry powder, sesame seeds and oil. Mix well. Rub over chicken. Place chicken on top of the fruits and vegetables in the roasting pan. Drizzle honey on top. Pour water into the bottom of the pan. Sprinkle with almonds. Bake, uncovered for 30 minutes. Remove from oven. Cover. Bake additional 45–60 minutes.

Servings: 6–8
Prep time: 20 minutes

# Cornmeal Coated Chicken

| | |
|---|---|
| 4–5 | boned chicken pieces, rinsed, patted dry |
| COATING | |
| ¼ cup | cornmeal |
| 2 tsp | paprika |
| 1 tsp | salt |
| 1 tsp | garlic powder |
| ½ tsp | pepper |
| ½ tsp | cumin |

Preheat oven to 350F.

In a small bowl, combine cornmeal, paprika, salt, garlic powder, pepper and cumin. Dip chicken in mixture to coat. Place in an ovenproof baking dish. Cover. Bake for 1 hour.

MEAT

**Tip:** Cut chicken into finger-sized pieces and proceed with rest of recipe. Presents nicely in small baskets lined with a napkin. Serve with french fries.

Servings: 4
Prep time: 5–10 minutes

# Zatar Chicken

| | |
|---|---|
| 1 (3–4 lb.) | chicken, cut into eighths |
| 2 Tbsp | olive oil |
| ¼ cup | zatar (hyssop) |

Preheat oven to 350F.

In a small bowl, combine oil and zatar.

Place chicken in baking dish. Rub mixture over chicken. Bake, uncovered for 45 minutes or until slightly brown and cooked through.

MEAT

*Zatar is a unique and tasty Middle-Eastern spice. Don't be fooled by how easy this recipe is to make. It tastes delicious.*

Servings: 6
Prep time: 5 minutes

# Spinach Stuffed Chicken Breasts

| | |
|---|---|
| ½ lb. | fresh mushrooms, diced |
| 6-oz. | fresh spinach, chopped |
| ½ tsp | salt |
| ⅛ tsp | pepper |
| 6 | chicken breasts, boneless, skinless |
| 1 cup | all purpose flour |
| 2 | eggs |
| 8 oz. | seasoned bread crumbs |
| 2 Tbsp | oil |

Preheat oven to 350F.

In a skillet, sauté mushrooms and spinach. Add salt and pepper. Cool.

Meanwhile, create a pocket in each breast by slicing into the thick side of the breast but not cutting right through. Stuff chicken pockets with mixture, being careful not to overfill. Set aside.

Put flour in a shallow dish. In a small bowl, whisk eggs. Spread seasoned bread crumbs on a flat plate. Dredge chicken breasts in flour. Dip breasts in egg mixture followed by bread crumbs. It is messy but try to form a tight pocket.

Heat oil in a large skillet. Sear the chicken in hot oil for 3–5 minutes on each side. Place chicken in an ovenproof dish. Bake, uncovered, for 40–50 minutes or until cooked through.

Servings: 6
Prep time: 30 minutes

# Pastrami Stuffed Chicken Breasts with Dipping Sauce

| | |
|---|---|
| 4 | chicken breasts, skinless, boneless |
| 4 | slices pastrami |
| 1 | egg |
| 1 Tbsp | lemon juice |
| 1 tsp | honey Dijon mustard |
| ½ cup | pecans, coarsely chopped |
| ½ cup | cornflake crumbs |
| 1 tsp | garlic powder |
| | salt and pepper to taste |

DIPPING SAUCE

| | |
|---|---|
| ¼ cup | Dijon mustard |
| 3–4 Tbsp | honey |
| 2 tsp | soy sauce |

Preheat oven to 375F.

Make a horizontal slice in each chicken breast to form a pocket, making sure not to cut straight through. Insert a slice of pastrami.

In a shallow bowl, whisk together egg, lemon juice and mustard. In a separate shallow bowl, combine pecans, cornflake crumbs, garlic powder, salt and pepper.

Coat chicken pieces in egg mixture, then in pecan mixture. Place on a lightly greased or parchment-lined baking sheet. Let stand 15 minutes. Bake for 30–35 minutes, or until cooked through.

In a small dish, whisk together sauce ingredients. Serve chicken with dipping sauce on side.

Servings: 4
Prep time: 30 minutes

# Rolled Chicken Breast with Roasted Red Pepper Stuffing

| | |
|---|---|
| 1 Tbsp | olive oil |
| 1 | small onion, chopped |
| 4 | cloves of garlic, minced |
| 2 cups | fresh parsley, chopped |
| 2 | large red peppers, roasted, chopped |
| 1 Tbsp | lemon juice |
| 2 tsp | fresh thyme, chopped, or ½ tsp dried thyme |
| ¼ tsp | salt |
| ¼ tsp | pepper |
| ⅛ tsp | hot pepper flakes |
| 2 Tbsp | all purpose flour |
| 6 | chicken breasts, boneless, skinless, pounded flat |
| ½ cup | white wine |
| ½ cup | chicken stock |
| 4 tsp | potato starch, dissolved in 2 Tbsp cold water |

Preheat oven to 325F.

In a large skillet, over medium heat, add onion and garlic to oil. Sauté for 3 minutes. Stir in parsley, red pepper, lemon juice, thyme, salt, pepper and hot pepper flakes. Cook until parsley is wilted, approximately 3 minutes. Remove from heat. Stir in flour. Cool.

Lay chicken breasts on a flat surface. Spread filling over top. Roll the chicken into rolls. Secure with string. Sprinkle with additional salt and pepper. Place chicken in a heated skillet, and brown chicken on all sides. Transfer chicken to a roasting pan. Pour wine and stock into skillet. Bring to a boil, scraping up brown bits. Pour over chicken. Cover pan tightly. Bake for 15–20 minutes, or until centres are no longer pink. Let chicken cool slightly. Remove chicken from pan and remove string. Cut each roll into slices. Transfer to serving platter.

Pour remaining sauce from the roasting pan, to a saucepan. Bring to a boil. Add potato starch. Boil, whisking constantly until sauce thickens. Pour over chicken.

Servings: 6
Prep time: 1 hour

# Honey-Garlic Wings

| | |
|---|---|
| 2–3 lbs. | chicken wings |
| | pepper to taste |
| | garlic powder to taste |
| SAUCE | |
| ½ cup | honey |
| ¼ cup | soy sauce |
| ½ cup | ketchup |
| ¼ cup | brown sugar |
| 1–2 | cloves of garlic, chopped |

*Cooking these wings for so long makes the sauce nice and gooey.*

Preheat oven to 375F.

Spread wings in a roasting pan and season with pepper and garlic powder. Put in oven. Bake, covered, for 45 minutes.

Meanwhile, whisk together honey, soy sauce, ketchup, sugar and garlic. Set aside.

Remove wings from oven and pour off liquid in roasting pan. Pour sauce over wings. Return to oven and turn up heat to 400F. Bake uncovered for an additional 20 minutes. Turn wings over and bake another 20 minutes.

**Tip:** When preparing poultry that has sugar in the sauce, cook the chicken first and then add the sauce and continue cooking.

Servings: 6–8
Prep time: 30 minutes

# Spicy Sesame Apricot Ginger Wings

MARINADE

| | |
|---|---|
| 1 cup | apricot jam, melted |
| 3–4 tsp | soy sauce |
| 2–3 tsp | sesame oil |
| 1 tsp | ground ginger |
| ½–1 tsp | red pepper flakes |
| 15–20 | wings |
| | OR |
| 10-12 | drumsticks |

Preheat oven to 350F.

In a small bowl, combine jam, soy sauce, sesame oil, ginger and red pepper flakes. Whisk well. Set aside.

Place chicken in a baking dish. Brush sauce over chicken pieces. Cover. Bake for 30–60 minutes. Uncover. Turn chicken over. Bake, uncovered, additional 30 minutes. Baste frequently. You can broil the chicken for a few minutes if you like it to be crisp.

Tip: Chicken can be barbecued as well.

Servings: 8–10
Prep time: 10 minutes

# Hoisin Chicken Wraps

| | |
|---|---|
| ½ cup | soy sauce |
| ¼ cup | hoisin sauce |
| ¼ cup | light brown sugar |
| 1 Tbsp | cornstarch |
| | cooking spray |
| 4 | chicken breasts, boneless, skinless, cut into 1-inch pieces |
| 2 | cloves of garlic, minced |
| ½ (10-oz.) pkg. | coleslaw mix |
| 6 | tortillas or wraps |

In a small bowl, mix soy sauce, hoisin sauce, brown sugar and cornstarch. Set aside.

Spray a large deep skillet with cooking spray. Add chicken and garlic. Cook on medium temperature until chicken is cooked through (opaque and no longer pink).

Stir in coleslaw mixture. Continue to cook an additional 5 minutes until mixture wilts. Add sauce to skillet. Stir occasionally. Cook until heated through.

Meanwhile, heat tortillas according to package instructions. There is no need to heat if using wraps.

Serve by spooning chicken mixture over tortillas or wraps and rolling burrito-style.

**Tip:** To add colour and freshness, replace coleslaw with fresh veggies sliced thinly to equal 1½ cups.

Servings: 5–6
Prep time: 30 minutes

# Sautéed Vegetable and Chicken Lasagna

*Don't count on any left-overs.*

| | |
|---|---|
| 12 | lasagna noodles, cooked, rinsed, drained |

MEAT SAUCE

| | |
|---|---|
| 2 tsp | olive oil |
| 1 | onion, chopped |
| 3 | cloves of garlic, minced |
| 2 lbs. | lean ground chicken |
| 1 (24-oz.) can | garlic pasta sauce, reserve 3 Tbsp |
| ½ cup | water |
| 4 | bay leaves |

Preheat oven to 350F.

In a large skillet, heat oil. Add onion and garlic. Sauté for a few minutes. Add chicken. Stir to break up into small pieces. Continue cooking until meat is no longer pink. If you are not using lean ground chicken you will want to pour off any fat that has accumulated before continuing. Add pasta sauce, water and bay leaves. Simmer for a few minutes. Remove from heat. Set aside.

CHEESELESS SAUCE

| | |
|---|---|
| 1 | onion, chopped |
| 3 Tbsp | margarine |
| ¼ cup | all purpose flour |
| 3 cups | chicken broth |
| 2 Tbsp | non-dairy cream |
| 4 | egg yolks, beaten |

In a large skillet, sauté onion in margarine. Add flour. Cook for additional minute. Whisk in broth. Stir until mixture becomes smooth. Add cream. Stir. Remove a cup of the sauce into a bowl. Add egg yolks to the sauce in the bowl and gently mix. Return egg yolk mixture to the saucepan. Combine. Remove from heat. Set aside.

## SAUTÉED VEGETABLES

| | |
|---|---|
| 2 tsp | olive oil |
| 2 | zucchini, diced (approximately 3 cups) |
| 1 | red pepper, diced |
| 1 cup | mushrooms, sliced |
| 2 Tbsp | balsamic vinegar |
| 1 tsp | dried rosemary |
| 1 tsp | dried thyme |
| | salt and pepper to taste |
| ¼ cup | fine bread crumbs, for sprinkling |

In a large skillet, heat oil. Add zucchini. Cook for 5 minutes. Stir in red pepper and mushrooms. Cook until liquid has evaporated. Add vinegar, herbs and salt and pepper. Cook on high until vinegar evaporates.

Preheat oven to 350F.

In lasagna pan, spread reserved pasta sauce over bottom. Arrange 3 lasagna noodles over sauce. Spread one-third of meat sauce, followed by one-third of cheeseless sauce and vegetables. Repeat process twice; ending with noodles and topping off with cheeseless sauce. Sprinkle bread crumbs on top. Bake, uncovered, for 35 minutes or until bubbling. Allow to stand for 10 minutes before serving.

Tip: Freezes well.

Servings: 10–12
Prep time: 30 minutes

# Turkey Breast

| | |
|---|---|
| 1 | turkey breast on bone |

MARINADE

| | |
|---|---|
| 4 | cloves of garlic, minced |
| ⅓ cup | honey |
| 2 Tbsp | Dijonnaise mustard |
| 2 Tbsp | olive oil |
| 2 Tbsp | lemon juice |
| 1 tsp | dried rosemary |

Rinse turkey breast. Pat dry. Combine marinade ingredients and rub over turkey breast. Refrigerate for 8 hours or overnight.

Preheat oven to 350F.

Bake, uncovered, for 45–60 minutes, basting occasionally. Cool. Slice breast off bone.

**Tips:** Best served warm or at room temperature.

Meat will slice easier when cool and is cut against the grain.

An easy way to get honey out of the measuring cup is to coat the cup with oil first and then pour in the honey.

Servings: 6–8
Prep time: 5–10 minutes

# Apricot Turkey Breast

| | |
|---|---|
| 1 | turkey breast, bone in |
| ¼ tsp | garlic powder |
| ¼ tsp | ground ginger |
| | salt and pepper to taste |
| 1 cup | apricot jam |
| ¾ cup | orange juice |
| ¾ cup | dried apricots, chopped |
| ¼ cup | raisins |
| 2 | onions, diced |
| 3 | carrots, peeled and diced |
| 1½ cups | cooking wine |

Preheat oven to 350F.

Place turkey breast in a roasting pan skin side up. Season with garlic, ginger, salt and pepper. Spread jam onto turkey and then pour orange juice over. Place the apricots, raisins, onions and carrots around the turkey. Add wine to the pan. Bake, uncovered, for 1½ hours, basting every 30 minutes. Add more wine if needed. Remove from oven. Let the turkey cool for about 20 minutes before slicing.

Servings: 7–8
Prep time: 20 minutes

# Turkey Meatloaf with Cranberry Glaze

GLAZE

| | |
|---|---|
| ¼ cup | brown sugar |
| ½ cup | jellied cranberry sauce, mashed |

MEATLOAF

| | |
|---|---|
| 2 lbs. | ground turkey |
| ¾ cup | soymilk or apple juice |
| ¾ cup | bread crumbs |
| 3 | eggs, lightly beaten |
| 1½ tsp | salt |
| ⅛ tsp | pepper |
| ¼ cup | red onion, diced |
| ½ cup | chicken broth, just enough to moisten |

**Tip:** May be served warm or at room temperature.

Preheat oven to 350F.

Sprinkle brown sugar onto the bottom of a greased loaf pan. Spread cranberry sauce over sugar. Alternatively, mix cranberry sauce and brown sugar in with ground turkey.

In a large bowl, mix all remaining ingredients until well blended.

Place meat mixture in the loaf pan, laying it out over the cranberry glaze, unless using the alternative method. Bake for 1 hour. Drain off fat. Cool. Turn out the loaf.

Servings: 4–6
Prep time: 10–15 minutes

# meat

# Balsamic Rib-Eye Roast with Roasted Vegetables

*Once you have tried this roast, it will be the one you ask for most often.*

**Tip:** Roast freezes well. Once cooled, cut roast against the grain, then wrap well for freezing.

MARINADE

| | |
|---|---|
| 2½ cups | balsamic vinegar |
| 1¼ cups | dry red wine |
| 2 Tbsp | brown sugar, packed |
| | salt and fresh ground pepper to taste |
| | |
| 3 lb. | rib-eye roast, tied |
| ⅓ cup | olive oil |
| 1½ tsp | coarse salt |
| | fresh ground pepper to taste |
| 2 lbs. | baby potatoes |
| 1 lb. | pearl onions, peeled |
| 4 | carrots, peeled, sliced into rounds |

In a large saucepan, combine balsamic vinegar, wine, brown sugar, salt and pepper. Bring to a boil. Reduce heat. Cover and simmer for approximately 15 minutes. Remove from heat. Set aside to cool.

Place roast in a roasting pan. Pour marinade over roast. Cover. Marinate for 1 hour at room temperature or refrigerate for up to 24 hours.

Preheat oven to 325F.

In a small bowl, combine olive oil, salt and pepper. Set aside.

In large bowl, mix potatoes, onions and carrots with olive oil mixture and toss to coat. Place vegetables on a large greased baking sheet. Put in oven on lowest rack. Bake for 30 minutes, tossing occasionally.

Meanwhile, uncover the roast. Put on middle rack of oven. Bake uncovered, for 1¾ hours. Remove. Let roast stand 10 minutes before slicing.

Servings: 8
Prep time: 50 minutes

# Ginger Ale Brisket

| 3–4 lb. | brisket |
| | salt and pepper to taste |
| 4 cups | ginger ale |
| 2 | large onions, sliced |
| ¾ cup | ketchup |
| ½ cup | apricot jam |
| 3 Tbsp | dry onion soup mix |
| 3 Tbsp | dry mushroom soup mix |

Preheat oven to 400F.

Season meat with salt and pepper.

In a large roasting pan, combine ginger ale, onions, ketchup, jam, onion and mushroom soup mixes. Put meat in pan and turn to coat in sauce. Cover. Put in oven. Bake for approximately 4 hours, or until meat is tender. Turn meat over once or twice during cooking. Slice the meat when cool, place back into gravy.

Reheat to serve.

*Easy! Quick! Tasty!*

Tips: Meat slices easier once it is cool.
Freezes well.

Servings: 8–10
Prep time: 5–10 minutes

# Easy Crock Pot Roast

| ½–1 cup | ketchup |
| 1 (3-lb.) | roast, of choice |
| 2–4 Tbsp | dry onion soup mix |
| 3–5 cups | vegetables of choice, cut into chunks |
| ¼–½ cup | sweet red wine or water |

Rub ketchup into roast until covered. Place roast in the bottom of a greased crock pot. Sprinkle with onion soup mix. Add vegetables. Pour wine into the bottom of the crock pot. Begin to cook roast on low early in the day. Roast will take at least 6–8 hours, depending on the size of the roast.

*This recipe is ideal for when you are out of the house for the whole day.*

Tip: You can put any roast, prepared with any marinade or topping, into a crockpot to slow cook. The roast only needs a little liquid (about ¼–½ cup). Prepare at night and marinate overnight in the refrigerator. Plug crockpot in in the morning; leave it for the whole day. You have a complete meal ready and waiting when you get home.

Servings: 8–10
Prep time: 5 minutes

# Pickled Roast Brisket

| 5 lb. | pickled brisket |
| 2 Tbsp | red wine vinegar |
| ¾ cup | brown sugar |
| ½ cup | ketchup |
| 2 Tbsp | mustard |

Place brisket in a large pot and cover with water. Cover pot and bring to a boil. Drain and refill the pot with water to cover. Bring to a boil again. Reduce heat, cover the pot and simmer for 2–3 hours or until fork tender.

Preheat oven to 375F.

Drain. Cool for ten minutes. Put the brisket in a roasting pan; pour vinegar over the brisket.

In a small bowl, mix brown sugar, ketchup, and mustard. Spread mixture over brisket. Bake, covered, for 25 minutes. Uncover for 5 minutes. Cool; slice against the grain.

Reheats and freezes well.

Serve warm or at room temperature.

*"This is the best corned beef I have ever tasted. I have never had leftovers of this delicious beef."*

Servings: 8–10
Prep time: 10 minutes

# Beef in Beer

| | |
|---|---|
| 1 Tbsp | olive oil |
| 2 lbs. | chuck steak or stewing beef, cut into 2-inch squares |
| 2–3 | onions, peeled, quartered, separated into layers |
| 10 | mushrooms, sliced |
| 2 Tbsp | all purpose flour |
| 1¼ cups | ale or pale-coloured beer |
| 1 Tbsp | tomato paste |
| ½ Tbsp | dried thyme or 1 sprig fresh |
| 1 | bay leaf |
| 1 | clove of garlic, crushed |
| | salt and pepper to taste |

Preheat oven to 275F.

In a large skillet, heat oil until sizzling hot. Sear meat, a few pieces at a time, until it turns brown in colour. Remove meat from skillet onto a plate. Put onions and mushrooms in pan and sauté for approximately 15 minutes until softened. Return meat to skillet along with any juices. Sprinkle with flour. Toss to coat. Lower heat. Continue stirring gently until all juices are soaked up. Gradually stir in ale, tomato paste, thyme, bay leaf, garlic, salt and pepper. Stir thoroughly. When stew begins to simmer, cover with a tight-fitting lid. Transfer to middle shelf of oven. Bake for 2–2½ hours. Cool. Skim fat off when cold. Serve warm.

Servings: 4–6
Prep time: 25–30 minutes

# Best Ever Roast Beef

| | |
|---|---|
| 4–5 lbs. | rib roast |
| 2 Tbsp | margarine, softened |
| 3 Tbsp | Dijon mustard |
| 1 Tbsp | horseradish |
| 2 | cloves of garlic, minced |
| 15–20 | Parisienne potatoes |
| | garlic powder to taste |

Preheat oven to 325F.

Put roast in a roasting pan. Poke holes in roast with a fork or knife.

In a small bowl, combine margarine, Dijon mustard, horseradish and garlic.

Using your fingers or a small knife, rub mixture into roast. Place potatoes around roast. Sprinkle with garlic powder. Bake, uncovered, for about 20–25 minutes per pound. Stir potatoes and baste roast occasionally. Remove roasting pan from oven. Let meat cool thoroughly before slicing.

Servings: 10–12
Prep time: 15 minutes

# BBQ Ribs

| | |
|---|---|
| 4 lbs. | beef ribs |
| 1 cup | onion, sliced |
| 1 cup | ketchup |
| 1 cup | water |
| ¼ cup | vinegar |
| ¼ cup | brown sugar, firmly packed |
| 2 Tbsp | Worcestershire sauce |
| 2 tsp | salt |
| 2 tsp | dry mustard |
| 1 tsp | paprika |

Preheat oven to 350F.

In a heavy frying pan, brown ribs on stovetop or broil in oven for 6 minutes on each side. Set aside.

Combine remaining ingredients. Pour over ribs. Bake, covered, for 1¾ hours, basting occasionally. Uncover, bake an additional 15 minutes.

*Get ready for a delicious mess!*

Tips: Save remaining sauce and freeze to use again as bases for meats, meatballs or anything when you are in a rush.
Freezes well.

Servings: 6–8
Prep time: 15–20 minutes

# Veal Roast in White Wine

Tip: May be served warm or at room temperature.

| 1 | veal roast, any size |
| 2 | cloves of garlic, minced |
| 2 tsp | salt |
| 2 tsp | pepper |
| 2 tsp | oregano |
| 2 tsp | basil |
| ½ cup | dry white wine |

Rinse roast. Pat dry. Combine garlic, salt, pepper, oregano, and basil. Rub over veal. Refrigerate overnight. The following day, bring to room temperature.

Preheat oven to 350F.

Transfer veal to a roasting pan. Pour wine in bottom of pan. Bake, covered, for 2 to 2½ hours or until juice runs clear.

Servings: 8
Prep time: 10 minutes

# Veal Roast with Tomato Sauce

| | |
|---|---|
| 2 | medium tomatoes, chopped |
| 1 | large onion, sliced |
| 1 | large red pepper, chopped |
| 4–5 | cloves of garlic, minced |
| ¼–½ cup | water |
| 2 Tbsp | oil |
| 1 tsp | salt |
| ½ tsp | pepper |
| 1 Tbsp | paprika |
| 5 lb. | veal roll (shoulder) |

Preheat oven to 325F.

Place tomatoes, onion, pepper and garlic on the bottom of a roasting pan. Pour water over the vegetables.

In a small bowl, combine oil with salt, pepper and paprika. Rub mixture over meat, until entirely covered. Pour any excess oil mixture over vegetables. Place roast in pan. Bake, covered, for 2–3 hours, until meat is soft. Cool.

After cooking, push the vegetables through a sieve or food mill, to produce a sauce, not allowing big pieces through. Slice the veal, against the grain, and pour sauce over it to coat.

Tip: Make with beef or turkey roll.

Serve vegetables whole instead of putting through sieve.

Servings: 6–8
Prep time: 20–25 minutes

# Basil Pepper Steak

MARINADE

| | |
|---|---|
| 1 cup | fresh basil leaves, chopped |
| 3 | cloves of garlic, minced |
| ⅓ cup | olive oil |
| 1½ tsp | salt |
| ½ tsp | sugar |
| ½ tsp | pepper |
| 2–3 lbs. | pepper steak, cut into 1-inch strips |
| | lettuce, to garnish |
| | tomatoes, to garnish |

In a small dish, combine basil, garlic, oil, salt, sugar and pepper. Add a small amount of water, as needed, to thin the marinade a little (should be a thick sauce consistency).

Put roast in a shallow glass dish. Rub marinade over meat. Cover. Refrigerate overnight.

Preheat oven to 350F.

In an ovenproof dish, arrange strips of meat in a single layer, and cover with marinade. Bake, uncovered, for 20 minutes.

**Tip:** Serve at room temperature, over a bed of shredded lettuce, with sliced tomatoes around the edge of the plate.

Servings: 6–8
Prep time: 30 minutes, marinate overnight

# Tongue in Tomato Sauce

*"We've been making this for generations."*

| | |
|---|---|
| 1 | tongue |
| 8–10 cups | water |
| 1 Tbsp | vinegar |
| 4–5 | onions, sliced |
| | oil for frying |
| 1–2 Tbsp | brown sugar |
| 2 cups | ketchup |

In a large pot, boil tongue in water mixed with vinegar, for approximately 1½ hours, until a fork comes out easily when stuck into meat. Remove from pot and remove skin while warm. Cool. Slice. Place into a roasting pan.

Preheat oven to 350F.

In a small skillet, sauté onions in oil until golden brown. Remove from heat. Add sugar with ketchup. Taste mixture and adjust seasoning if needed. Pour mixture over tongue. Place in oven. Bake uncovered for 45 minutes.

**Tip:** When preparing ahead of time, freeze before cooking. Defrost prior to cooking.

Add sliced peppers and mushrooms for a heartier dish

Servings: 4–6
Prep time: 15–20 minutes

# Rice and Lamb Chops

| | |
|---|---|
| 4 | large lamb or veal chops or 8 smaller chops |
| 2 tsp | dried rosemary, divided in half |
| 2 | cloves of garlic, minced |
| 1 | onion, sliced |
| 1 cup | long-grain rice, uncooked |
| 1 | red pepper, chopped |
| 1 | green pepper, chopped |
| ⅛ tsp | salt (optional) |
| 2 cups | chicken stock |
| ¼ cup | black olives, sliced (optional) |

Place lamb chops on plate and sprinkle 1 teaspoon rosemary and both cloves of garlic on chops. In a large skillet on medium heat, cook chops, 4 minutes per side, until almost cooked. Remove to plate.

In the same skillet, sauté onions until translucent. Add rice. Mix well. Add peppers, salt, and remaining rosemary. Add chicken stock and bring to a boil. Reduce heat. Cover. Simmer for approximately 20 minutes, or until rice is cooked. Check to make sure there is enough liquid so rice does not burn. Arrange chops on top of rice mixture. Cover. Cook for 5 minutes longer on low, or until heated through. Garnish with olives if desired. Serve.

Servings: 4
Prep time: 25–30 minutes

# Teriyaki Ginger Lamb Chops

MARINADE

| | |
|---|---|
| 3 | cloves of garlic, minced |
| ⅓ cup | teriyaki sauce |
| 2 Tbsp | orange juice |
| 2 Tbsp | orange zest |
| 1 Tbsp | cider vinegar |
| 1 Tbsp | fresh ginger, minced |
| ½ tsp | salt |
| 6 | lamb chops |

In a small bowl, combine all marinade ingredients. Mix well. Place lamb chops in a shallow glass dish. Pour marinade over lamb chops. Cover. Marinate for minimum 4 hours or overnight in the refrigerator.

The following day, heat the barbecue to medium-high heat. Place chops on barbecue. Brush with reserved marinade. Cook for 3–5 minutes per side for medium-rare lamb chops.

Servings: 4–6
Prep time: 10 minutes

# Stromboli

| | |
|---|---|
| 1 (17.3 oz) pkg. | puff pastry, thawed |
| ¼ cup | honey mustard or ketchup |
| 30+ slices | cold cuts, assorted |
| 1 egg wash | 1 egg beaten with 1 Tbsp water |
| | sesame or poppy seeds (optional) |

Preheat oven to 350F.

Roll out puff pastry to size of a cookie sheet, 11 x 17 inches. Be careful not to roll out too thin. Generously spread honey mustard or ketchup on pastry. Layer cold cuts, leaving approximately ½-inch around edges. Starting from the long side (17-inch side), roll up pastry jelly-roll fashion. Place seam side down onto a greased cookie sheet. Seal edges. Brush with egg wash. Sprinkle with sesame or poppy seeds. Slash, with a sharp knife, approximately every 1½ inches, along length. Bake for 30 minutes.

Can be served hot or cold.

*"My grown brothers happen to show up every time I make this deli pinwheel."*

Tip: When using frozen pastry, always defrost overnight in the refrigerator or at room temperature for at least 2 hours.

Puff pastry, whether raw or baked, is best cut using a serrated knife.

Servings: 12–16 slices
Prep time: 10–15 minutes

# Fleishig Pizza

| | |
|---|---|
| 1 lb. | ground beef or chicken or mixture of both |
| 1 cup | fresh mushrooms, sliced |
| ½ | green pepper, sliced |
| ¼ tsp | salt |
| ¼ tsp | pepper |
| 1 (7.5-oz.) can | pizza sauce |
| 1 tsp | Italian herb seasoning |
| 1 lb. | pizza dough |
| | olive oil to rub onto dough |

Do not preheat oven.

In a medium-sized skillet, cook beef or chicken for 5 minutes, stirring constantly and breaking up the chunks with a spoon. Add mushrooms. Stir for 3 minutes until mushrooms are almost tender. Add green pepper, salt and pepper. Stir for an additional minute until mushrooms are tender and chicken is no longer pink. Remove from heat and set aside.

In a small bowl, combine pizza sauce with Italian herb seasoning. Set aside.

Roll out pizza dough onto a greased 12-inch pizza pan. Brush pizza dough with oil. Add ¼ cup of the seasoned pizza sauce to the chicken mixture. Spread remaining sauce over dough. Arrange chicken mixture evenly over pizza sauce.

Place pizza on the bottom rack of a cold oven. Turn oven to 500F and bake 17–20 minutes, depending on oven, until crust is golden brown and topping is bubbly.

Tip: For a more exotic pizza, don't hesitate to add sliced marinated artichokes, roasted peppers and/or sun-dried tomatoes.

Servings: 6–8
Prep time: 25 minutes

# Bourekas with Meat Filling

| | |
|---|---|
| ½ lb. | lean ground beef |
| 1 | egg, separated |
| ¼ cup | dry bread crumbs |
| ¼ cup | tomato sauce |
| 1½ tsp | fresh parsley, chopped |
| 1 tsp | garlic powder |
| | salt and pepper to taste |
| 1 Tbsp | olive oil |
| 2 (17.3-oz.) pkgs. | puff pastry, thawed |
| ¼ cup | honey mustard |
| 1 Tbsp | sesame seeds |

Preheat oven to 350F.

In a small bowl, combine ground beef, egg yolk, bread crumbs, tomato sauce, parsley and spices.

Put olive oil in a frying pan and add beef mixture. Fry on medium setting until cooked, approximately 10–15 minutes.

Roll out puff pastry into a rectangle with a ¼-inch thickness. Cut into 2-inch squares. Spread honey mustard in centre of each square and spoon 1 teaspoon of meat mixture on top. Fold into triangles and press closed. Place on a greased cookie sheet. In a small bowl, gently beat egg white and brush on triangles. Sprinkle sesame seeds on top.

Bake at 350F for approximately 15–20 minutes until brown.

*I got this recipe from an aunt in Israel who can never seem to make enough of these for her children, grandchildren and great grandchildren.*

Tip: "To add a kick, I love to add a few chopped pieces of pepperoni to each one."

Servings: 32 small bourekas
Prep time: 25 minutes

# Stuffed Cannelloni

| | |
|---|---|
| 1½ lbs. | ground veal |
| 2 | eggs |
| 1 | medium onion, minced |
| 1 tsp | oregano |
| ½ tsp | salt |
| | pepper to taste |
| 1 | clove of garlic, minced |
| 2–3 Tbsp | bread crumbs, or as needed to thicken meat |
| 1 (225-g.) box | oven-ready cannelloni |

SAUCE

| | |
|---|---|
| 2½ cups | tomato juice |
| ½ cup | pasta sauce, plain or spiced |
| 2 Tbsp | sugar |
| 1 tsp | oregano |
| ½ tsp | salt |
| | pepper to taste |
| | parsley, chopped, to garnish |

Preheat oven to 350F.

Put ground veal in a large bowl. Add eggs, onion, oregano, salt, pepper and garlic. Mix. Add bread crumbs until meat consistency is not liquid. Stuff cannelloni with meat mixture.

In another bowl, combine sauce ingredients. Spread a thin layer of sauce on the bottom of a 9 x 13-inch baking dish. Arrange stuffed cannelloni in a single layer in dish. Cover with remaining sauce. Bake, covered, for 1 hour. Garnish with fresh parsley.

**Tips:** How to make bread crumbs?

Keep any leftover stale bread in the freezer. When the bag is full, place the bread on a large cookie sheet and toast in the oven at 350F until crispy, approximately 10 minutes. Check periodically. Remove from oven. Cool. Process it in a food processor until fine. Store in a resealable bag and freeze until needed.

To stuff the cannelloni, put the meat mixture in a plastic bag and cut a small hole to squeeze the mixture into the cannelloni.

Servings: 8–10
Prep time: 1 hour

# Veal and Vegetable Meatloaf

**TOPPING**

| | |
|---|---|
| ¼ cup | brown sugar |
| 5 Tbsp | ketchup |
| 1 Tbsp | red wine vinegar |

**FILLING**

| | |
|---|---|
| ¼ cup | oil |
| 1 | small green pepper, chopped |
| 2 | celery stalks, chopped |
| 2 | onions, chopped |
| 2 | cloves of garlic, minced |
| 1 (300-g) pkg. | frozen chopped spinach, thawed |
| 1 cup | mushrooms, sliced, or 1 (10-oz.) can, drained |
| ¼ cup | fresh parsley, chopped |
| 2 lbs. | ground veal |
| 1 cup | bread crumbs |
| 2 | eggs |
| ¼ tsp | pepper |

Preheat oven to 375F.

In a small bowl, combine brown sugar, ketchup and vinegar. Set aside.

In a large skillet, sauté pepper, celery, onions, garlic, spinach, mushrooms, and parsley in oil until soft. Set aside.

In a large bowl, combine veal, bread crumbs, eggs and pepper. Mix well. Add vegetables to meat mixture and form into meatloaf shape. Transfer to a greased loaf pan. Spread topping over surface. Bake uncovered for 1½ hours.

**Tip:** May be served warm or at room temperature.
Slice and serve on a bed of lettuce for an appetizer.

Servings: 8–10
Prep time: 15–20 min

# Festive Sweet Meatballs

MEATBALLS

| 2 lbs. | lean beef or veal, minced |
| 1 | egg, beaten |
| ¼ cup | matza meal or dry bread crumbs, enough to bind |
| 1 tsp | garlic powder |
| 1 tsp | pepper |
| ⅛ tsp | salt |

SAUCE

| 2 | large onions, chopped |
| 1 Tbsp | oil |
| 1 (28-oz.) can | tomato sauce |
| ½–¾ cup | water |
| ½ cup | ketchup |
| ⅓ cup | brown sugar |
| ⅓ cup | white sugar |
| ⅓ cup | apple cider vinegar |

In a large bowl, combine ground meat, egg, matza meal, garlic powder, pepper and salt. Set aside.

In a large pot, sauté onions in oil until translucent. Add tomato sauce, water, ketchup, brown sugar, sugar and vinegar. Bring to a boil. Reduce to simmer.

Form meatballs and drop them into sauce one by one. When all meatballs are made, cover pot. Simmer meatballs for 1 hour.

Tip: Freezes and reheats well. Dip your hands in a bowl of cold water to make rolling meatballs easier.

Servings: 6–8 people
Prep time: 45 minutes

# pastas & side dishes

# Stuffed Shells

| | |
|---|---|
| 1 (250-g) pkg. | jumbo pasta shells |
| 3 | onions, diced |
| | oil for sautéing |
| 1 (300-g) pkg. | frozen spinach, chopped, thawed and drained well |
| 1 (500-g) pkg. | small curd cottage cheese |
| 2 | eggs |
| 2 cups | mozzarella cheese, grated |
| | salt to taste |
| 1 tsp | nutmeg (optional) |
| 1 (25-oz.) jar | prepared marinara sauce |

**Tip: Freezes well.**

Preheat oven to 350F.

In a large pot of boiling water, cook pasta shells until al dente, tender but firm. Drain. Set aside.

Meanwhile, in a large skillet, sauté onions in oil until slightly brown. Remove from heat. Cool. Set aside.

In a medium-sized bowl, combine spinach, onions, cottage cheese, eggs, mozzarella cheese, salt and nutmeg (if using). Stuff shells with mixture. In a lightly oiled baking dish, arrange shells in a single layer, seam side down. Pour marinara sauce over shells. Cover. Bake for 1 hour.

Servings: 8
Prep time: 20 minutes

# Penne with Tomato Cream Sauce

| | |
|---|---|
| 2 Tbsp | olive oil |
| 1 | large onion, chopped |
| 2 | cloves of garlic, chopped |
| 1 (28-oz.) can | tomatoes, chopped, half drained |
| 5 tsp | flour |
| 1½ cups | milk |
| 1–2 tsp | salt |
| | pepper to taste |
| ½ (2½-oz.) can | sun-dried tomatoes in oil, chopped |
| 1–2 Tbsp | oil, from sun-dried tomatoes |
| 1 (2-lb.) pkg. | penne pasta, cooked, rinsed, drained |

In a large skillet, sauté onions and garlic in olive oil until translucent. Add tomatoes. Simmer, covered, for 5 minutes.

In a bowl, make a paste by combining flour with ½ cup of milk. Slowly add the rest of the milk to the bowl, stirring constantly. Once the flour is dissolved in milk, add to tomato mixture and heat on medium, stirring constantly until thickened. Add salt, pepper, ½ can of sun-dried tomatoes and oil to the sauce. Stir. Serve hot over cooked pasta.

*Out of penne? Feel free to substitute any other shaped pasta.*

Tip: You may substitute whipping cream for the milk – flour mixture for a much richer but much higher fat recipe.

Servings: 5–6
Prep time: 15–30 minutes

# Baked Ziti with Mushrooms, Peppers and Parmesan Cheese

| | |
|---|---|
| 3 | large yellow peppers, diced in ¼-inch pieces |
| 1 | large onion, diced |
| 3 | cloves of garlic, minced |
| 3 Tbsp | olive oil, divided 1 Tbsp and 2 Tbsp |
| 1½ cups | heavy cream |
| | salt and pepper to taste |
| 1½ lbs. | mushrooms, thinly sliced |
| 2 | medium red peppers, cut in ¼-inch strips |
| 2 | medium orange peppers, cut in ¼-inch strips |
| 1 lb. | ziti pasta |
| 8 | green onions, green part only, thinly sliced |
| 2 cups | Parmesan cheese, grated, divided 1½ and ½ cup |

Preheat oven to 375F.

In a 4-quart covered saucepan, cook yellow peppers, onion and garlic in 1 tablespoon oil, over medium-low heat. Stir occasionally until peppers become tender, approximately 10 minutes. Gently stir in cream. Remove from heat and transfer, in batches, to a blender to purée. Once complete, transfer to a large bowl and season with salt and pepper. Cool sauce to room temperature.

In deep large skillet, sauté mushrooms and peppers (red and orange) in last 2 tablespoons oil over medium-high heat until peppers become tender and most of the liquid is evaporated, approximately 5 minutes. Season with salt and pepper. Set aside.

Fill a 6–7-quart pot ¾ full with water and a dash of salt. Bring to a boil. Stir in ziti. Cook until just tender, approximately 10 minutes. Reserve 1 cup of water. Rinse and drain pasta.

Add ziti, mushroom mixture, green onions, 1½ cups Parmesan and reserved cooking water, to the sauce. Adjust seasonings. Transfer mixture into 3-quart shallow baking dish and sprinkle with remaining ½ cup Parmesan. Bake in middle of oven until pasta begins to brown, approximately 15 minutes. Good warm or at room temperature.

Servings: 4–6
Prep time: 45 minutes

# Tomato and Artichoke Pasta

| 250-g | pasta of choice |
|---|---|
| 3–4 | medium tomatoes, diced |
| 1 (19-oz.) can | artichoke hearts, cut up |
| ½ cup | fresh parsley, chopped |
| 2 Tbsp | fresh lemon juice |
| 4 tsp | lemon zest, grated |
| 1 Tbsp | olive oil |
| 1 tsp | salt |
| | freshly ground pepper to taste |

Cook pasta according to package directions. Drain, rinse in cold water and set aside.

In a serving bowl, combine tomatoes, artichoke, parsley, lemon juice and rind, oil, salt and pepper. Marinate for an hour. Add pasta to bowl just before serving. Mix well.

PARVE

*Yummy!*

Servings: 4–6
Prep time: 20 minutes, marinate for 1 hour

# Szechwan Noodles: Hot -Tossed Noodles with Peanut Sauce

| 4–6 | green onions, sliced diagonally |
|---|---|
| 1 bunch | broccoli, cut up |
| 3 Tbsp | canola oil, divided 1 Tbsp and 2 Tbsp |
| 6 Tbsp | peanut butter (crunchy variety is best) |
| 1 Tbsp | sesame oil |
| ¼ cup | soy sauce |
| ¼ cup | vegetable stock or water |
| 1½ lb. | fresh or frozen Chinese or Japanese noodles, cooked |
| 1 cup | toasted almonds or pecans, to garnish |

In a skillet, sauté green onions and broccoli in 1 tablespoon of canola oil. Stir in peanut butter, oils, soy sauce and stock. Remove from heat.

Place noodles on a serving platter. Add vegetables. Toss. May be served warm, refrigerated or at room temperature. Garnish with nuts before serving.

PARVE

Servings: 6–8
Prep time: 15–20 minutes

# Peanutty Linguini

SAUCE

| | |
|---|---|
| 6 | cloves of garlic, minced |
| ½ cup | soy sauce |
| ¼ cup | fresh cilantro |
| 3 Tbsp | sugar |
| 3 Tbsp | vinegar |
| 1 Tbsp | fresh ginger, grated |
| 1 Tbsp | peanut oil |
| 1 Tbsp | dark sesame oil |
| ¼ tsp | chili powder |

NOODLES

| | |
|---|---|
| 1 (15-oz.) pkg. | linguini noodles, cooked, rinsed, drained |
| 6 | green onions, minced |
| ¼ cup | chopped peanuts, garnish |
| | cilantro sprigs, garnish |

**Tip:** Add a light splash of oil to the pasta after draining to loosen it up.

Place all sauce ingredients in a blender or food processor. Process until smooth. Set aside.

In a large serving bowl, combine pasta and green onions. Pour sauce over pasta. Toss to coat. Garnish with peanuts and sprigs of cilantro.

Servings: 6–8
Prep time: 15–20 minutes

# Tangy Oriental Noodles

| 1 lb. | thick Shanghai Chinese noodles (usually found frozen), defrosted |
| 3½ Tbsp | sesame oil |
| 3½ Tbsp | soy sauce |
| 1½ Tbsp | balsamic vinegar |
| 2 Tbsp | sugar |
| 2 tsp | kosher salt |
| ¼ cup | green onions, chopped |
| 1 Tbsp | sesame seeds |
| 1 tsp | chili flakes (optional) |

Bring an 8-quart pot of water to boil. Meanwhile, fluff noodles with hands to detangle. Put noodles in water and swish with chopsticks to separate strands. Cook until al dente. Drain immediately in colander. Place under cold running water. Return noodles to pot or large bowl.

In a small bowl, combine oil, soy sauce, balsamic vinegar, sugar and salt. Pour over noodles. Toss. Adjust seasonings to taste.

Cover. Store overnight in refrigerator. Before serving add onions, sesame seeds and chili flakes. Serve at room temperature.

PARVE

*A beautiful dish with a blend of tangy and sweet flavours.*

Tip: Kosher salt is coarser than regular table salt.
Prepare the night before. Flavour peaks on second day.
Keeps 4–5 days.

Servings: 6–8
Prep time: 25 minutes

# Tomato Herbed Fettuccine

| | |
|---|---|
| ¾ of a (12-oz.) pkg. | plain fettuccine, cooked, rinsed, drained |
| ¾ of a (12-oz.) pkg. | coloured fettuccine, cooked, rinsed, drained |
| 2–3 | large tomatoes, diced |
| 2 Tbsp | fresh basil, chopped |
| 1 tsp | salt |
| ¼ tsp | pepper |
| 2 | cloves of garlic, minced |
| ¼ cup | green onions, chopped |
| ⅓ cup | olive oil |

In a large serving bowl, combine pasta. Set aside.

In a small bowl, combine tomatoes, basil, salt and pepper. Set aside.

In a large skillet, sauté garlic and green onions in oil for 1 minute. Do not brown the ingredients. Add tomato mixture. Cook on medium heat for 2–3 minutes, to heat through. Pour over pasta. Toss and serve.

# Basil Pesto Fusilli

PESTO SAUCE

| | |
|---|---|
| 2 | cloves of garlic, peeled |
| 2 cups | fresh basil leaves, packed |
| ½ cup | chicken stock (parve) |
| ¼ cup | olive oil |
| 3 Tbsp | pine nuts |
| 2 tsp | lemon juice |
| ¼ tsp | salt |
| 1 (450-g) box | fusilli pasta |

Combine pesto sauce ingredients in a food processor until finely minced. Pulse until blended.

Cook pasta according to package directions. Drain. Add pesto, tossing to coat.

# Three Pepper Pasta Salad

PARVE

*For those who enjoy sweet pasta.*

DRESSING

| | |
|---|---|
| 8–10 | fresh basil leaves, chopped |
| ¼ cup | oil |
| 3 Tbsp | balsamic vinegar |
| ½ tsp | salt |
| ½ tsp | black pepper |
| 3 Tbsp | brown sugar |
| ½ tsp | paprika |

SALAD

| | |
|---|---|
| 1 (450-g) pkg. | Scooby do pasta, cooked and drained |
| ¼ cup | dried cranberries |
| ¼ cup | pine nuts |
| ¼ | red pepper, cut in strips |
| ¼ | yellow pepper, cut in strips |
| ¼ | green pepper, cut in strips |

In a small jar or cruet, combine basil leaves, oil, balsamic vinegar, salt, pepper, brown sugar and paprika. Cover. Shake well. Set aside.

In a large serving bowl, combine pasta with dressing. Toss to coat. Add cranberries, pine nuts, and peppers. Mix well.

Servings: 10
Prep time: 20 minutes

# Grilled Vegetable Penne

DRESSING

| | |
|---|---|
| 3 | cloves of garlic, minced |
| ½ cup | vinegar |
| ½ cup | olive oil |
| 2 tsp | oregano |
| ½ tsp | salt |
| ½ tsp | pepper |
| | |
| 3 | Portobello mushrooms, sliced |
| 2 | zucchini, sliced lengthwise with peel |
| 1 | large red pepper, sliced lengthwise, 1 inch wide |
| 1 | large yellow pepper, sliced lengthwise, 1 inch wide |
| 1 | large orange pepper, sliced lengthwise, 1 inch wide |
| 1 | eggplant, sliced |
| 2 Tbsp | oil |
| 3 Tbsp | balsamic vinegar |
| ⅛ tsp | salt |
| 1 (900-g.) pkg. | penne pasta, cooked, rinsed, drained |
| ½ cup | feta cheese |

In a large jar or cruet, combine garlic, vinegar, olive oil, oregano, salt and pepper. Cover. Shake well. Set aside.

Preheat oven to broil.

Place vegetables on a parchment-lined cookie sheet. Pour oil, balsamic vinegar and salt over vegetables. Broil the vegetables in the oven or grill them on a barbecue, until slightly blackened. Remove from oven or barbecue. Set aside.

Put penne in a wide serving dish. Lay the vegetables over the penne. Crumble Feta cheese over the top. Thirty minutes before serving, pour dressing over penne mixture. Toss and serve.

Servings: 10–12
Prep time: 20–25 minutes

# Pasta and Meat Sauce

| | |
|---|---|
| 1 (900-g) bag | spaghetti, cooked and drained |
| 1 | large onion, chopped |
| 3 | medium carrots, peeled and sliced |
| 3 | stalks of celery, chopped |
| 3 Tbsp | olive oil or as needed |
| 2 lbs. | ground beef |
| 1 (28-oz.) can | whole tomatoes, chopped, plus liquid |
| | basil to taste |
| | oregano to taste |
| ⅛ tsp | pepper |
| 2 tsp | sugar (optional) |
| 2–4 Tbsp | HP sauce®, to taste |

In a large skillet, sauté onion, carrots, and celery in oil. Add beef, constantly stirring to avoid beef clumping. Brown on all sides. Add tomatoes, herbs, pepper and sugar. Reduce heat. Simmer, uncovered for 10 minutes. Add HP sauce®. Remove from heat. Pour beef mixture over spaghetti. Toss and serve.

Tip: Serve with fresh green salad.

Servings: 6
Prep time: 20 minutes

# Savory Pecan Rice

PARVE

| | |
|---|---|
| 2 cups | wild rice, uncooked |
| ½ cup | onion, chopped |
| 2 cups | mushrooms, chopped |
| 1 cup | celery, diced |
| ½ cup | margarine |
| 1 tsp | salt |
| ½ tsp | pepper |
| ½ tsp | marjoram |
| ⅛ tsp | sage |
| ⅛ tsp | thyme |
| ⅔ cup | pecans, finely chopped |
| | water, to moisten |

Preheat oven to 350F.

Prepare rice according to package directions.

In a large skillet, sauté onion, mushrooms and celery in margarine. Stir in salt, pepper, marjoram, sage and thyme. Remove from heat.

Stir in rice, pecans and water. Put in a greased 9 x 13-inch casserole dish. Bake, covered, for 30 minutes. Remove cover. Bake for an additional 30 minutes.

Tip: Replace wild rice with 1 cup raw wild rice and 1 cup raw regular white rice. Cook white rice in 2 cups water and simmer for 20 minutes and cook wild rice in 2 cups boiling water and simmer for 1 hour.

Servings: 8
Prep time: 30 minutes

# Spicy Rice and Bean Casserole

| | |
|---|---|
| 1 Tbsp | oil |
| 2 | cloves of garlic, minced |
| 1 | onion, chopped |
| 1 cup | long-grain brown rice, uncooked |
| 1 tsp | cumin |
| 2 cups | chicken stock |
| 1 cup | mild chunky salsa |
| 1 (14-oz.) can | red kidney beans, rinsed and drained |
| 1½ cups | corn nibblets |
| ½ tsp | salt |
| ¼ tsp | pepper |
| 1 (28-oz.) can | stewed tomatoes, diced |

Preheat oven to 350F.

In a large skillet, sauté garlic and onion in oil until softened. Stir in rice and cumin, continuing to stir for 1 minute. Add stock, salsa, beans, corn, salt and pepper. Transfer to a 9 x 13-inch casserole dish. Bake, covered, for 45 minutes or until rice is tender and a little liquid remains. Remove from oven. Pour tomatoes over rice. Cover. Return to oven for an additional 10–15 minutes.

Servings: 6–8
Prep time: 15–20 minutes

# Wild & White Rice Pilaf with Portobello Mushrooms & Green Onions

PARVE

| | |
|---|---|
| 1½ cups | white rice, uncooked |
| ½ cup | wild rice, uncooked |
| 2 Tbsp | margarine |
| 2 Tbsp | oil |
| 2 cups | Portobello mushrooms (approximately 3), chopped in large pieces |
| 2 | cloves of garlic, crushed |
| 3 | green onions or chives, chopped |
| 1 Tbsp | dried rosemary |
| 2 tsp | chicken soup powder |
| | salt and pepper to taste |
| 2 Tbsp | shelled pumpkin seeds, salted or raw |

Prepare rice as directed on package and transfer to a large serving bowl. Stir in margarine until absorbed. Set aside.

Heat oil in non-stick skillet over medium heat. Add mushrooms and garlic. Cook, stirring often, for approximately 5 minutes or until tender. Add green onions, rosemary and soup powder. Cook for another minute. Combine with rice. Add salt and pepper to taste. Stir in pumpkin seeds before serving. Can be served hot or cold.

Tip: Replace pumpkin seeds with toasted almonds or pine nuts.

Servings: 8
Prep time: 30 minutes

# Wild Rice Surprise

| ½ cup | dried cranberries |
|---|---|
| 1 cup | white rice, cooked |
| 1 cup | wild rice, cooked |
| 6 | green onions, chopped |
| 1 | celery stalk, chopped |
| 1 | yellow pepper, chopped |
| 1 | red pepper, chopped |
| 2 | cloves of garlic, minced |
| 1 Tbsp | olive oil |
| ¼ cup | pine nuts or almonds, toasted |

In a small bowl cover the cranberries with hot water and soak for 15 minutes.
Set aside.

Put white rice in a serving bowl. Add drained cranberries, onions, celery,
peppers, garlic and oil. Mix well. Add wild rice.

Sprinkle nuts over before serving. Can be served warm or cold.

Servings: 6–8
Prep time: ½ hour

Tip: Orzo is a quick cooking
pasta that looks like large
grains of rice.

# Herbed Vegetable Orzo

| 1 cup | orzo, uncooked |
|---|---|
| ½ cup | fresh basil, chopped |
| ½ cup | fresh thyme, chopped |
| ¼–⅓ cup | olive oil |
| 2 cups | fresh mushrooms, sliced |
| 2 | cloves of garlic, minced |
| ⅓ cup | sun-dried tomatoes, soaked in boiled water to cover for 10 minutes, drained, chopped |
| | salt to taste |

Cook orzo according to package directions. Drain. Rinse. Set aside.

In a large skillet, heat herbs in oil on low for 3–4 minutes to release the flavours,
being careful not to brown. Add mushrooms and garlic. Sauté an additional
5 minutes, adding more oil if needed. Add orzo and tomatoes. Add salt to taste.
Stir thoroughly. Serve warm.

Servings: 6–8
Prep time: 15 minutes

# Risotto Primavera

| | |
|---|---|
| 4 cups | chicken or vegetable stock |
| 1 Tbsp | margarine |
| 1 | onion, chopped |
| 1 | carrot, peeled and chopped |
| 2 | cloves of garlic, minced |
| ¼ tsp | pepper |
| 2 cups | arborio rice, uncooked |
| ½ cup | white wine or vegetable stock |
| 1 | red pepper, chopped |
| 1 | yellow pepper, chopped |
| 2 Tbsp | fresh parsley, chopped, (optional) |

In small pot, bring chicken stock to a boil. Reduce heat to low. Set aside.

In a large pot, sauté onion, carrot, garlic and pepper in margarine until vegetables are softened. Stir in arborio rice until well coated. While stirring the rice mixture, add ½ cup of warm stock, stirring constantly until all liquid is absorbed. Add wine, stirring until all the wine is absorbed. Add red and yellow peppers. Continue adding ½ cup stock at a time, stirring after each addition until completely absorbed. Rice should be tender and creamy once all the liquid has been added, approximately 20 minutes. Be sure to keep heat on low to avoid the rice sticking. Stir in parsley if desired.

Tips: The high-starch kernels of this Italian-grown grain are shorter and fatter than any other short-grain rice. Arborio is traditionally used for risotto because its increased starch lends this classic dish its requisite creamy texture.

The trick to ensuring a successful risotto dish is to constantly be stirring the rice.

Servings: 6–8
Prep time: 35–45 minutes

# Quinoa Pilaf

| | |
|---|---|
| 2 Tbsp | vegetable oil |
| 2 Tbsp | slivered almonds |
| 2 Tbsp | cashew pieces |
| 2 Tbsp | pine nuts |
| 1 | onion, chopped |
| ½ tsp | cumin |
| 4 | cloves of garlic, minced |
| 2-inch piece | fresh ginger, peeled, grated or chopped |
| 1 cup | quinoa |
| 2 cups | water |
| ½ cup | raisins or currants |
| | salt to taste |
| 1 Tbsp | sunflower seeds, for garnishing |

In a deep saucepan, sauté almonds, cashews and pine nuts in oil until they begin to brown. Transfer to a bowl.

In the same saucepan, sauté onion, cumin, garlic and ginger until onion is soft. Add quinoa and nut mixture. Stir. Add water. Bring to a boil. Reduce heat. Simmer, covered, until water has evaporated. Remove from heat. Let stand for 10 minutes. Add raisins and mix well. Add salt to taste. Garnish with sunflower seeds.

**Tips:** Quinoa is a white grain, the size of mustard seed. The cooked grain will have a sweet flavour and soft texture.

Quinoa is an excellent source of iron, magnesium, phosphorus, potassium, zinc, copper, thiamin and riboflavin.

Easy cooking: 1 part quinoa to 2 parts water

Servings: 4–6
Prep time: 30 minutes

# Pecan Pumpkin Loaf

| | |
|---|---|
| 3 cups | flour |
| 2 cups | sugar |
| 2 tsp | baking powder |
| 2 tsp | baking soda |
| ½ tsp | cinnamon |
| ½ tsp | salt |
| ½ tsp | cloves |
| 1 cup | oil |
| 1 (16-oz.) can | pumpkin purée |
| 1 cup | pecans, chopped |

Preheat oven to 350F.

Grease 5 mini loaf pans (5¾ x 3¼ inches).

In a large mixing bowl, using an electric or hand-held mixer, mix flour, sugar, baking powder, baking soda, cinnamon, salt and cloves. Add oil and pumpkin purée. Mix until smooth. Stir in pecans.

Pour batter into greased loaf pans. Bake for 50–60 minutes.

PARVE

*This recipe is delicious and tastes like a cake. It is a great side dish for those allergic to eggs.*

**Tips:** This recipe may be served as a side dish or a dessert.
You can substitute or add chocolate chips.
Can also be served as a muffin and prepared in muffin tins.

Servings: 15–20
Prep time: 15–20 minutes

# Carrot Muffins

| | |
|---|---|
| 2 | eggs |
| 1 (8-oz.) jar | baby food carrots |
| 1 cup | all purpose flour |
| ¾ cup | sugar |
| ½ cup | applesauce |
| 1 Tbsp | vanilla sugar |
| 1 tsp | vanilla |
| ½ tsp | baking soda |
| ½ tsp | baking powder |
| ½ tsp | salt |

Preheat oven to 350F.

In a large mixing bowl, combine all ingredients. Mix until just combined. Pour into greased muffin tins. Bake for 25 minutes.

PARVE

*Kids will love this!*

Servings: 2 dozen mini muffins or 1 dozen regular
Prep time: 10–15 minutes

# More Than Apple Kugel

| | |
|---|---|
| 4 | apples, peeled, cored and sliced |
| 1 | carrot, peeled, diced or shredded |
| 1 | handful dried cranberries or raisins |
| 1 cup | all purpose flour |
| 1 cup | sugar |
| 2 tsp | baking powder |
| ¾ cup | oil |
| 1 tsp | lemon juice |
| 1 tsp | vanilla |
| 2 | eggs, beaten |
| | cinnamon to taste |

Preheat oven to 350F.

In a medium-sized bowl, combine apples, carrots and cranberries. Set aside.

In another bowl, mix together flour, sugar, baking powder, oil, lemon juice, vanilla and eggs. Mix well. Add fruit to batter. Mix well. Place in a greased 8-inch round glass dish. Sprinkle cinnamon on top. Bake for 45–50 minutes until golden on top.

Servings: 12
Prep time: 10–15 minutes

# Apple Kugel

| | |
|---|---|
| 2 | eggs, beaten |
| 1 cup | sugar |
| ¾ cup | oil |
| 1 tsp | vanilla |
| 1¼ cups | all purpose flour |
| 1 tsp | baking powder |
| 5 | large apples, peeled and chopped in small pieces |
| 1 tsp | cinnamon |

Preheat oven to 350F.

Blend eggs, sugar, oil and vanilla in a large bowl. Add flour and baking powder. Mix well. Add apples and mix until just combined. Pour into an ungreased 9-inch pie plate. Sprinkle cinnamon on top. Bake for 1 hour or until light brown.

PARVE

*"This is the best apple kugel I have ever tasted."*

Tip: This recipe can also be prepared in greased muffin tins. Once the batter is prepared, drop spoonfuls of it into muffin tins. Bake for 20 minutes until golden brown.

Servings: 8
Prep time: 10 minutes

# Squash Kugel

| | |
|---|---|
| 1 (3–4 lb.) | butternut squash, peeled, seeded and cut in half lengthwise |
| 1 cup | all purpose flour |
| ½ tsp | baking powder |
| 6 Tbsp | margarine |
| 1 cup | sugar |
| 4 | eggs |
| ¼–½ cup | non-dairy milk |
| ½ tsp | vanilla |
| | cinnamon to taste |

Preheat oven to 350F.

Place squash cut side down on a greased baking sheet and bake for 45–60 minutes (until soft). Remove from sheet, place in a small bowl and mash. Set aside.

Meanwhile, grease a bundt pan or 9 x 13-inch pan.

Combine flour and baking powder. Set aside. With an electric or hand held-mixer, cream margarine and sugar. Blend in eggs, milk and vanilla.Add flour mixture.  Add mashed squash and cinnamon until just combined. Pour into prepared pan and bake for 45 minutes to 1 hour or until golden.

Servings: 8–10
Prep time: 60 minutes

# Zucchini Kugel

| 6 | medium-sized zucchini, peeled, grated and drained (yields 6 cups) |
| 3 | onions, grated (yields 2 cups) |
| 3 | eggs, beaten |
| 1½ cups | all purpose flour |
| 1 tsp | baking powder |
| ¾ cup | water |
| ¾ cup | oil |
| 1 Tbsp | chicken soup powder |
| 1 tsp | salt |
| | pepper to taste |

Preheat oven to 350F.

In a large mixing bowl, combine all ingredients. Pour into an ungreased 9 x 13-inch pan. Bake, uncovered, for 1 hour.

# Sweet Apricot Noodle Kugel

| 1 (12-oz.) pkg. | medium egg noodles, cooked, drained |
| 3 | eggs |
| 1 cup | non-dairy creamer |
| 1 (2.8-oz.) pkg. | vanilla pudding mix |
| ½–1 cup | apricot jam |
| 2 (.43-oz.) pkgs. | vanilla sugar |
| ¼ cup | oil |

Preheat oven to 350F.

In a large bowl, combine all ingredients. Mix well. Pour into a greased 9 x 13-inch baking dish. Bake, uncovered, for 50–60 minutes or until golden.

PARVE

Tip: Zucchini retains a lot of water. To avoid having a kugel that is very watery, squeeze the grated zucchini with your hands to get rid of excess moisture before mixing it with the rest of the ingredients.

Servings: 10-12
Prep time: 15 minutes

PARVE

*This is for the person who likes a sweet taste without any fruit pieces.*

Tip: Substitute soymilk for non-dairy creamer, a healthier option.

Servings: 10–12
Prep time: 15 –20 minutes

# Yerushalmi Kugel

| 1 cup | sugar |
| ½ cup | oil |
| 5 cups | boiling water |
| 1 tsp | salt |
| 1 tsp | black pepper |
| 1 (12-oz.) pkg. | thin egg noodles |
| 3 | eggs, lightly beaten |

**Tip:** This recipe comes out great baked in the same sauce pan it is prepared in. Once it cools slightly, run a flexible spatula around the edges and turn over onto a serving plate.

Preheat oven to 350F.

In a large saucepan, melt sugar with oil on medium heat until honey-coloured, stirring constantly. Remove from heat. Cool 5 minutes. Slowly add 1 cup of water to the caramel mixture. Add remaining 4 cups of water. Return saucepan to heat. Boil caramel mixture until all the sugar is dissolved. Add salt, pepper and egg noodles. Continue to boil for another 5 minutes. Remove from heat. Cool for 10 minutes. Slowly add eggs to noodle mixture. Stir to combine. Transfer mixture to a greased ovenproof 9 x 13-inch baking dish. Place in oven. Bake, uncovered, for 40 minutes.

Turn out onto plate to serve.

Servings: 8–10
Prep time: 15–20 minutes

# Eggplant Casserole

| | |
|---|---|
| 1 | large eggplant, peeled, quartered |
| ½ tsp | salt |
| ¼ cup | margarine |
| 3 Tbsp | flour |
| 1 (28-oz.) can | stewed tomatoes, undrained |
| 1 | onion, grated |
| 1 Tbsp | brown sugar |
| | cornflake crumbs, to garnish |

Preheat oven to 350F.

Soak eggplant in a dish, covered with salt water, for 30 minutes to 1 hour.

Drain. Cut into 1-inch pieces. Boil in water until tender but not too soft. Drain well.

In a 6-quart pot, combine salt, margarine, flour, stewed tomatoes, onion and brown sugar. Cook until thick. Add eggplant. Mix well.

Transfer to an 8 x 8-inch baking dish or similar-sized oval dish. Sprinkle top with cornflake crumbs.

Bake, uncovered, for 30–40 minutes.

Serve hot and enjoy.

*You won't believe how delicious this casserole is. The stewed tomatoes really enhance the flavours in the dish.*

Servings: 6–8
Prep time: 30 minutes

# Roasted Vegetable Strudel

| | |
|---|---|
| 1 lb. | fresh asparagus, cleaned, left whole |
| 2 | red peppers, halved, cleaned |
| 1 | yellow pepper, halved, cleaned |
| 2 | zucchinis, cut lengthwise in thick pieces |
| 2 | large Portobello mushrooms, sliced |
| 1 | red onion, thickly sliced |
| 4 | cloves of garlic, peeled |
| ½ cup | feta cheese, cubed |
| ½ cup | fresh basil, chopped |
| | salt and pepper to taste |
| 2 Tbsp | balsamic vinegar |
| 12–24 | phyllo sheets (6 per strudel) |
| | melted butter |
| | sesame seeds to sprinkle on top |

Preheat oven to 450F.

Place asparagus, peppers, zucchinis, mushrooms, red onion and garlic on a large greased baking sheet. Put in oven for 20 minutes. Remove from oven and chop.

Add feta, basil, salt, pepper and vinegar.

Lay out 1 phyllo sheet. Brush with melted butter. Put another sheet on top of the first, brushing it with melted butter. Continue this process with 4–6 sheets of phyllo, depending on the thickness that you want the strudel to be. Spread some roasted vegetables across the bottom of the phyllo sheets. Start rolling up sheets over vegetables, jellyroll style. Fold over ends and continue rolling. Brush with butter on top. Sprinkle with sesame seeds. Score with 4 diagonal cuts along top of strudel. Bake for 15 minutes.

Freezes well.

**Tips:** This recipe will make 2–4 strudels.

Grilled vegetables are divine on their own or even with pasta.

Servings: 2–4 strudels
Prep time: 30–45 minutes

# vegetables

# Grilled Asparagus with Orange Wasabi Dressing

*These asparagus are absolutely mouthwatering.*

DRESSING

| | |
|---|---|
| 2 Tbsp | soy sauce |
| 2 Tbsp | orange juice |
| 1 tsp | sugar |
| 1 tsp | wasabi powder |
| ½ tsp | ground ginger |

SALAD

| | |
|---|---|
| 2 Tbsp | sesame oil |
| 30 | asparagus spears, trimmed |
| ¼ tsp | freshly ground black pepper |
| 1½ cups | shredded napa cabbage (optional) |

In a small bowl, combine dressing ingredients. Set aside.

Pour oil into a shallow baking dish and add asparagus. Sprinkle with pepper.

Roll asparagus in oil to coat.

Broil asparagus 4–6 minutes or until tender crisp, being careful not to burn it.

Pour dressing over asparagus. If serving asparagus on the napa cabbage,

pour dressing over both.

**Tips:** To revitalize fresh asparagus that is wilted, sprinkle with cool water, wrap in a towel and refrigerate for 1½ hours.

To choose the best asparagus, keep the following in mind. Use straight firm green asparagus, thin stalks for salads and thick for side dishes. The tips should be tightly closed with a purple tinge to the tips. To store, remove rubber band, wrap in a towel, place in a Ziploc bag and refrigerate for up to 2 days. (1 lb asparagus – 3 cups chopped)

Servings: 6–8
Prep titme: 15–20 minutes

# Asparagus with Toasted Pine Nuts

DRESSING

| | |
|---|---|
| 1 | clove of garlic, minced |
| ¼ cup | olive oil |
| 1 Tbsp | lemon juice |
| ½ tsp | oregano |
| ½ tsp | basil |
| ½ tsp | salt |
| 1 lb. | asparagus, trimmed |
| 3 Tbsp | pine nuts, toasted, chopped (optional) |

In a small bowl, combine dressing ingredients. Set aside.

Place asparagus in a pot of boiling water. Steam for 5 minutes. Remove from heat. Rinse immediately with cold water. Lay flat on a kitchen towel.

Place asparagus in a serving dish. Drizzle with dressing. Sprinkle with pine nuts.

# Sesame Green Beans

| | |
|---|---|
| 2 lbs. | fresh green beans, ends trimmed |
| 1 Tbsp | sesame seeds |
| 2 Tbsp | soy sauce |
| 1 Tbsp | fresh ginger, minced, or ¾ tsp ground ginger |
| 2 tsp | sesame oil |

Boil or steam beans until tender crisp, approximately 1 minute. Rinse under cold water. Drain. Place in serving bowl. Set aside.

In a small non-stick skillet, toast sesame seeds, until golden brown, shaking the skillet frequently. Gently stirring, add soy sauce, ginger and oil. Remove from heat. Pour over beans.

PARVE

*"I always keep this dressing on hand in the refrigerator to use on steamed broccoli or green beans as well. Make sure to use toasted pine nuts–the toasting brings out the wonderful nutty flavour."*

Tip: You'll never boil asparagus again. Roast in a single layer at a high temperature (400F) with a little olive oil, salt and lemon juice, (optional), for approximately. 15 minutes. Turn once.

Servings: 6–8
Prep time: 20–25 minutes

PARVE

*"This recipe has become a staple in my family."*

Servings: 6
Prep time: 10–15 minutes

# Cauliflower Pesto with Parsley

| | |
|---|---|
| 1 | cauliflower, broken into flowerets |
| 1 cup | fresh parsley, chopped |
| ¼ cup | bread crumbs, soft and fresh |
| ¼ cup | olive oil |
| 1 Tbsp | lemon juice |
| ½ tsp | lemon zest, grated |
| ¼ tsp | dried thyme |
| ⅛ tsp | dried oregano, to taste |
| ⅛ tsp | salt |
| ⅛ tsp | pepper |

Preheat oven to 350F. Grease a 9-inch pie plate.

In a pot of boiling water, cook cauliflower for 5 minutes until tender. Drain. Transfer to a bowl. Set aside.

Combine parsley, bread crumbs, oil, lemon juice and zest and thyme in food processor. Process until smooth. Add to cauliflower. Toss to coat. Season with oregano, salt and pepper to taste. Place into ovenproof dish. Bake for 25–30 minutes.

Servings: 6–8
Prep time: 20–25 minutes

# Fasoulia – Green Beans Sephardic Style

| | |
|---|---|
| 1 tsp | olive oil |
| 1–2 | large onions, sliced |
| ½ lb. | fresh mushrooms, sliced |
| 1 (8-oz.) can | tomato sauce |
| 2 (8-oz.) cans | tomatoes, chopped |
| | salt and pepper to taste |
| ¼ cup | parve chicken broth |
| 2–3 lbs. | fresh green beans, cooked |
| ½ | lemon, juiced |

Preheat oven to 350F.

In a large skillet, sauté onion in oil until translucent. Add mushrooms and sauté until tender and water in mushrooms is absorbed. Add tomato sauce and tomatoes. Cook for an additional 3–5 minutes. Add salt, pepper and chicken broth. Combine well.

Place green beans in ovenproof dish and pour sauce over beans. Bake, covered, for 30–45 minutes. Remove from oven and drizzle lemon juice. Mix well. Serve hot.

Tip: Reheats well.
Use frozen green beans to save time.

Servings: 8–10
Prep time: 15 minutes

# Glazed Carrots and Parsnips

PARVE

| | |
|---|---|
| 1¼ cups | chicken broth (1 tsp chicken broth powder/ 1¼ cups water) |
| ¼ cup | margarine |
| 3 Tbsp | sugar |
| 1 tsp | salt |
| 2 lbs. | carrots, peeled and julienne |
| 2 lbs. | parsnips, peeled and julienne |
| 3 Tbsp | fresh parsley, finely chopped |

In a large pot, combine broth, margarine, sugar and salt. Bring to a boil. Add carrots and cook for 2 minutes. Add parsnips and cook for an additional 5 minutes.

Remove carrots and parsnips from broth and place in a serving dish. Continue to boil broth until liquid reduces to approximately ⅓ of a cup and slightly thickens. Pour broth over vegetables.

Sprinkle parsley over vegetables just before serving.

*This recipe is great for Rosh Hashanah!*

Servings: 8
Prep time: 15–20 minutes

# Zucchini and Tomato Sauté

| | |
|---|---|
| 2 | onions, medium, sliced |
| 1 | clove of garlic, crushed |
| 4 Tbsp | olive oil |
| 4 | zucchini, medium, sliced in rounds |
| 4 | tomatoes, peeled and diced, or 1 (28-oz.) can of whole tomatoes, chopped, plus liquid |
| ½ tsp | salt |
| ⅛ tsp | pepper |
| | basil to taste |
| | oregano to taste |

In a large skillet, sauté onions and garlic in oil until golden brown. Add zucchini and sauté until softened. Add tomatoes and spices and herbs. (May need to add small amount of boiling water if using whole tomatoes.) Stir well. Cover. Simmer for 20 minutes.

**Tips:** Recipe doubles and triples easily.

Freezes well.

To peel tomatoes easily, put tomatoes in a bowl of boiling water for a few seconds. Do not leave longer or they begin to cook.

Servings: 6
Prep time: 20 minutes

# Italian Stuffed Tomatoes

| 12 | plum tomatoes |
| 1 cup | fresh parsley, chopped |
| 8 | cloves of garlic, minced |
| ¾ cup | olive oil |
| | salt and pepper to taste |

Preheat oven to 350F.

Cut tomatoes in half lengthwise and scoop out seeds and flesh to make 24 tomato cups. Reserve flesh and seeds.

In a small bowl, combine parsley, garlic, scooped-out flesh and seeds, oil, salt and pepper. You can use a food processor to mix. Fill tomato halves with the mixture.

Place tomatoes on parchment-lined baking sheet or pan. Bake for 45–60 minutes. Sprinkle with additional olive oil several times during baking. Remove from oven. Serve at room temperature.

Servings: 10–12
Prep time: 20–30 minutes

*Yams – a great source of vitamins*

Servings: 4 to 6
Prep time: 15–20 min.

# Candied Yams

| | |
|---|---|
| 4 | medium-sized yams |
| ¼ cup | margarine |
| ⅓ cup | brown sugar |
| ¼ cup | coffee liqueur |

In a medium-sized pot, bring water to boil, then add yams. Cook until tender but firm, approximately 20–25 minutes. Cool. Peel and slice them in half, length-wise. Set aside.

In a skillet, melt margarine with sugar. Add coffee liqueur and stir for 1 minute. Add yams to mixture and toss to coat. Cover skillet and simmer on low heat for approximately 15 minutes. Turn yams once before serving.

# Oranges and Yams

| | |
|---|---|
| 3 | large yams, boiled, peeled, sliced into thick rounds |
| 2 | small seedless oranges, unpeeled, sliced with ring intact |
| 1 cup | orange juice |
| ⅔ cup | brown sugar or honey |
| 1 Tbsp | potato starch |
| 1 Tbsp | margarine |

Preheat oven to 325F.

Place yams slices in a single layer in a greased casserole dish. Set a slice of orange on top of each yam.

In a saucepan over low heat, combine orange juice, sugar, and potato starch. Cook, stirring until thick and clear. Remove from heat. Add margarine. Stir until melted. Pour mixture over yams. Bake covered, for 25 minutes. Uncover. Continue baking for additional 20 minutes.

Servings: 6 – 8
Prep time: 20 minutes

# Lemon Herb Potatoes

PARVE

| | |
|---|---|
| ⅓ cup | oil |
| ¼ cup | lemon juice |
| 3 Tbsp | Dijon mustard |
| 8 | potatoes, peeled and diced |
| 1 tsp | garlic powder |
| | salt and pepper to taste |
| ⅛ tsp | oregano |
| ⅛ tsp | basil |
| ⅛ tsp | tarragon |
| ⅛ tsp | dill |

Preheat oven to 350F.

In a small bowl, combine oil, lemon juice and mustard. Reserve.

Put potatoes in a casserole dish. Season with garlic powder, salt, pepper, oregano, basil, tarragon and dill. Pour sauce over potatoes. Coat well. Cover. Bake for 1 hour, or until potatoes are soft. Stir once or twice.

*"I make these often because they are fuss free and delicious."*

Servings: 8
Prep time: 15–20 minutes

Servings: 4
Prep time: 20 minutes

PARVE

**Tips:** You can mix baby white, red and purple potatoes or sweet potatoes and white potatoes for a beautiful presentation.

Chop or cut leaves of fresh herbs finely. The more cut surface is exposed, the more flavour is released.

Rubbing dry herbs between your fingers will expose more surface area and release more flavour.

Servings: 6
Prep time: 5–10 minutes

# Waffle Potatoes

| | |
|---|---|
| 4 | large potatoes, halved |
| 1 Tbsp | olive oil |
| 2 | cloves of garlic, minced |
| 1 tsp | salt |
| | fresh ground pepper to taste |

Preheat oven to 400F.

Cut potatoes in half lengthwise. Make 4 diagonal cuts across potato face about ½ inch in depth. Cut again at right angle to the first cuts. Potato face will resemble a waffle.

In a non-stick baking pan, combine the olive oil, garlic, salt and pepper. Coat cut side of potatoes in oil mixture and then place cut side down in the same pan. Bake for 35 minutes, until golden.

# Herbed Roasted Baby Potatoes

| | |
|---|---|
| 2 Tbsp | olive oil |
| 2 | cloves of garlic, minced |
| 1 tsp | salt |
| 1 Tbsp | fresh rosemary, chopped, or 1 tsp dried |
| 1 Tbsp | fresh thyme, chopped, or 1 tsp dried |
| 2 lbs. | baby white or red potatoes, cleaned, halved, not peeled |
| | pepper to taste |

Preheat oven to 425F.

In a medium-sized bowl, combine oil, garlic, salt, rosemary and thyme. Add potatoes and toss to coat. Place potatoes in a single layer on a parchment-lined baking pan. Bake for 35–45 minutes, until brown and crispy.

# Summer Barbecued Vegetables

PARVE

### VINAIGRETTE

| | |
|---|---|
| ¾ cup | extra virgin olive oil |
| ⅓ cup | balsamic vinegar |
| 3 Tbsp | fresh coriander, chopped |
| 10–12 | thin asparagus, trimmed and cut |
| 8 | cloves of garlic, peeled |
| 8–10 | large mushrooms, sliced |
| 8–10 | shiitake mushrooms, sliced |
| 1 | small zucchini, sliced |
| 1 | small eggplant, sliced |
| 1 | red pepper, sliced |
| 1 | green pepper, sliced |
| 1 | yellow pepper, sliced |
| 1 | red onion, sliced |

In a small jar or cruet, combine olive oil, balsamic vinegar and coriander. Cover. Shake well. Set aside.

Place vegetables in a large bowl. Toss with dressing. Transfer the vegetables to a grill basket. Grill on the barbecue over medium-high heat, turning periodically for 15–20 minutes or until tender and lightly charred.

**Tip:** Red onion rings develop a wonderful smoky-sweet flavour from grilling.

Servings: 6
Prep time: 20–30 minutes

# Savory Roasted Winter Vegetables

| | |
|---|---|
| 2 | turnips, peeled |
| 2 | parsnips, peeled |
| 2 | sweet potatoes, medium, peeled |
| 4 | potatoes, washed, unpeeled |
| 1 (284-g) bag | pearl onions, peeled |
| 1 | clove of garlic, peeled |
| 2 Tbsp | olive oil |
| 1 Tbsp | coarse salt, or to taste |
| | pepper to taste |

Preheat oven to 425F.

Slice turnips, parsnips and potatoes into a variety of cuts – wedge, round, sticks. Try to keep thickness similar. In a large bowl combine all vegetables and garlic. Drizzle with olive oil and sprinkle with salt and pepper. Place vegetables and garlic on a large baking sheet with sides. Roast for 1 hour until golden and tender. Turn occasionally.

**Tip:** You can substitute red potatoes for yellow potatoes.

Coarse salt is also called kosher salt. It contributes less salt to a dish than table salt due to its bulk.

Servings: 6–8
Prep time: 20–25 minutes

# Sesame Tofu with Green Beans

PARVE

| | |
|---|---|
| ¼ cup | light olive oil |
| 1½ tsp | sesame oil |
| ⅓ cup | soy sauce |
| 2 (8-oz.) pkgs. | firm tofu, washed, pressed, cut into bite-size cubes |
| 1–2 Tbsp | light olive oil |
| ½ tsp | sesame oil |
| ½-inch chunk | ginger, peeled, thinly sliced |
| 4 cups | green string beans, trimmed, uncut |
| | soy sauce, to taste |
| | toasted sesame seeds, to garnish |

Preheat oven to 400F.

In a bowl, combine ¼ cup olive oil, 1½ teaspoons sesame oil, soy sauce and tofu. Toss lightly. Place mixture on a baking sheet and bake uncovered, for 10 minutes. Remove from oven. Turn tofu. Bake for additional 10 minutes. The longer you bake the tofu, the firmer and crispier it will become. Remove the tofu. Place in a serving dish.

Heat 1–2 tablespoons olive oil and ½ teaspoon sesame oil in a large skillet. Add ginger and sauté until it becomes dark brown. Add beans. Sauté on high heat until the beans are slightly blackened. Add soy sauce to taste. Check the beans for the level of crispiness you prefer. Place the beans on top of the tofu so that the tofu is showing at the edges. Garnish with sesame seeds.

*"This recipe is so tasty that I nibbled the whole thing and didn't have anything left for the testing committee to try!"*

Tip: This recipe may also be prepared ahead of time and re-heated in a low (250F) oven, but then cover it with foil so that it doesn't dry out.

Servings: 6
Prep time: 25–30 minutes

# Teriyaki Tofu Stir-Fry

| | |
|---|---|
| ½ cup | teriyaki sauce |
| 1 tsp | brown sugar |
| 1⅓ cups | firm tofu, cubed |
| 1 tsp | cornstarch |
| 1 Tbsp | water |
| 2 tsp | olive oil |
| ½ | onion, sliced |
| ½ | green pepper, seeded, julienned |
| ½ | red pepper, seeded, julienned |
| 1 tsp | fresh ginger, grated |
| 1 | clove of garlic, minced |
| 2 cups | broccoli florets cut into 1-inch pieces |
| 3 cups | hot cooked rice |
| 2 Tbsp | parsley, fresh, chopped |

In a medium-sized bowl, stir teriyaki and brown sugar together until sugar dissolves. Add tofu and stir until evenly coated. Cover and refrigerate at least 10 minutes or up to 4 hours. In a small bowl, stir cornstarch with water until smooth. Set both aside.

In a large non-stick frying pan, heat oil on medium heat. Add onion, peppers, ginger and garlic. Stir-fry for 3 minutes. Add broccoli and continue to stir-fry for an additional 2 minutes until tender crisp. Add tofu. Stir cornstarch mixture and add to pan. Cook, stirring often until sauce is thickened and broccoli is tender, 3–4 minutes.

Serve over rice. Garnish with parsley.

**Tip:** Tofu can become soggy if it is left longer than the required amount of time in the fridge to marinate.

**Servings:** 4 servings
**Prep time:** 20 minutes

# desserts

# Caramelized Apple-Cranberry Strudel

| ½ cup | fresh cranberries |
| 1 Tbsp | cornstarch |
| 2 Tbsp | margarine |
| 4 | medium baking apples, peeled, chopped |
| ½ cup | sugar |
| ½ cup | dried cranberries |
| 1 tsp | ground ginger |
| ½ tsp | cinnamon |
| 6 sheets | phyllo dough |
| ¼ cup | margarine, melted |
| ½ Tbsp | coarse or vanilla sugar, to garnish |
| | icing (confectioner's) sugar, to garnish |

Preheat oven to 400F.

Toss fresh cranberries with cornstarch. Set aside.

In a medium saucepan, melt margarine and add fresh cranberries, apples and sugar. Gently stir and continue cooking for about 5 minutes or until cranberries begin to split. Stir in dried cranberries, ginger and cinnamon. Cool to room temperature.

Lay out one sheet of phyllo dough and brush with melted margarine. Add remaining sheets of phyllo, brushing with margarine between each layer. Spoon apple mixture along long edge, leaving 2-inch border along bottom and on each side. Fold over the excess border on each short side and then roll long side up. Press together.

Place strudel with seam side down on a parchment-lined baking sheet. Brush margarine on top. Sprinkle with sugar. Using sharp knife, poke five vent holes in strudel. Bake for 20 minutes until golden. Sprinkle with icing sugar before serving.

Serve sliced warm or at room temperature.

Freezes well.

**Tips:** Use phyllo dough when it has just been defrosted. Cover open, unused dough with a damp cloth so it does not dry up and become difficult to work with.

Check the phyllo's expiration date. Try to buy it fairly fresh.

Defrost the package in the fridge the day before you plan to use it to make sure it thaws.

Servings: 8
Prep time: 30 minutes

# Blueberry Flan

CRUST

| | |
|---|---|
| 1½ cups | all purpose flour |
| ⅛ tsp | salt |
| 3 Tbsp | sugar |
| ¾ cup | margarine, cold |
| 1½ Tbsp | vinegar |

FILLING

| | |
|---|---|
| 4½ cups | blueberries or raspberries |
| ¾ cup | sugar |
| 3 Tbsp | all purpose flour |
| ⅛ tsp | cinnamon |
| | icing (confectioner's) sugar, garnish |

Preheat oven to 400F.

**CRUST:** Grease and flour an 11-inch fluted tart pan with removable bottom. Combine flour, salt, and sugar in food processor. Add margarine and pulse 6–8 seconds. Add vinegar and pulse for 2 more seconds. Do not allow mixture to become doughy. With your fingers, press dough into a thin crust in bottom and up sides of pan.

**FILLING:** Mix together all ingredients except 1 cup berries. Pour mixture into crust. Bake for 1 hour.

Remove from oven and sprinkle with remaining berries. Let cool. Once cooled, remove rim of flan pan. Dust with icing sugar before serving.

Tip: To make this into a bumble berry flan, use 4½ cups of a combination of blueberries, raspberries, blackberries, strawberries and cranberries.

Servings: 8
Prep time: 15 minutes

# Harvest Apple Spice Cake

Tips: Always bake with eggs that are at room temperature. It makes the batter fluffier.

Freezing a cake before frosting will help frosting spread more easily.

Apple guide: For cakes and sauces: Cortland, Golden Delicious, Idared, Jonalgold, Mutsu-Crispin, Northern Spy and Spartan.

For sauces and spreads: Empire, Gravenstein, McIntosh, Royal Gala, Granny Smith

For pies and baked apples: Golden Delicious, Northern Spy

CAKE

| | |
|---|---|
| 1 cup | oil |
| 1¼ cups | sugar |
| ½ cup | brown sugar, packed |
| 4 | eggs |
| 1 tsp | vanilla |
| ¼ cup | applesauce |
| 3 cups | all purpose flour |
| 2½ tsp | cinnamon |
| ¾ tsp | allspice |
| 1 tsp | baking soda |
| 1½ tsp | baking powder |
| ½ tsp | salt |
| 3–4 cups | apples, peeled, thinly sliced |

ICING

| | |
|---|---|
| ¼ cup | brown sugar, packed |
| 2½ Tbsp | parve whipping cream |
| 2 Tbsp | margarine |
| ⅔ cups | confectioner's sugar |
| | |
| 2 Tbsp | pecans, chopped |

Preheat oven to 350F.

In a large mixing bowl, using an electric or hand-held mixer, beat oil, sugars, eggs and vanilla. Add applesauce and stir until just combined. In a separate bowl, combine flour, cinnamon, allspice, baking soda, baking powder and salt. Add dry ingredients to liquid ingredients. Stir until just combined. Add apples. Gently stir until combined. Pour into a greased and floured 10-inch tube pan. Bake for 1¼–1½ hours. Test with a toothpick to see when it is ready. Cool and turn out onto serving dish.

In a saucepan, combine sugar, cream and margarine. Heat until sugar dissolves and mixture comes to a boil. Remove from heat. Cool. Add icing sugar until it is drizzling consistency. Drizzle icing over cake. Decorate with chopped pecans.

Servings: 10–12
Prep time: 20 minutes

# Raspberry Pound Cake

PARVE

| 1 cup | margarine, softened |
| 1⅔ cups | sugar |
| 5 | eggs |
| 2 cups | all purpose flour |
| ½ tsp | salt |
| 1 tsp | vanilla |
| 1 cup | raspberry jam |

Preheat oven to 325F.

In a large bowl, cream margarine, sugar and eggs. Stir in flour, salt and vanilla. Mix well.

Pour half the batter into a greased and floured Bundt pan. Carefully spoon jam in a thin strip in the centre of the batter. Pour remainder of the batter on top.

Bake for 1¼ to 1½ hours, or until toothpick comes out clean when inserted.

Allow cake to cool before removal from pan.

**Tip:** Cake can also be baked in a 9 x 5-inch loaf pan, using the same directions.

Serve with a scoop of vanilla ice cream and fresh raspberries.

Servings: 10–12
Prep time: 20 minutes

# Amaretto Pound Cake

CAKE

| | |
|---|---|
| 2 cups | all purpose flour |
| 2 cups | sugar |
| 1 (2.8-oz.) pkg. | instant vanilla pudding mix |
| 2 tsp | baking powder |
| 4 | eggs |
| ¾ cup | orange juice |
| ⅔ cup | oil |
| ¼ cup | vodka |
| ¼ cup | almond liqueur |

ALMOND GLAZE

| | |
|---|---|
| 1 cup | icing (confectioner's) sugar |
| 1 tsp | almond extract or 1 tsp almond liqueur |
| 1–2 Tbsp | water |
| | |
| 2 Tbsp | toasted sliced almonds |

Preheat oven to 350F.

In a large mixing bowl, combine flour, sugar, pudding mix and baking powder. Using an electric or hand-held mixer, slowly add eggs, orange juice, oil, vodka and almond liqueur. Mix well. Pour mixture into a greased Bundt pan. Bake for 1 hour. Remove from oven. Cool.

In a small bowl, combine icing sugar and almond extract. Add water until drizzle consistency. Glaze cake. Sprinkle almonds on top before glaze hardens.

Servings: 12
Prep time: 10 minutes

# Banana Cake

| | |
|---|---|
| ½ cup | margarine |
| 1½ cups | sugar |
| 2 | eggs, slightly beaten |
| 2 cups | all purpose flour |
| ½ tsp | baking powder |
| ¾ tsp | baking soda |
| ½ tsp | salt |
| ¼ cup | orange juice or apple juice or water or soy milk |
| 1 tsp | vanilla |
| 3–4 | ripe bananas, mashed |

Preheat oven to 350F.

In a large mixing bowl, using an electric or hand-held mixer, cream margarine and sugar until light and fluffy. Beat in eggs. Set aside.

In a small bowl, combine flour, baking powder, baking soda and salt. Set aside.

In another bowl, combine juices, water or soy milk, vanilla and bananas. Add dry mixture alternately with banana mixture to margarine mixture. Mix well.

Pour into greased Bundt pan. Bake for 25–30 minutes, until batter is firm to the touch and springs back when touched.

**Tips:** Ripe yellow freckled and fragrant bananas are ideal for baking banana loaves.

Add 1 cup chocolate chips before baking for Banana Chocolate Chip Cake.

Servings: 8–10
Prep time: 15 minutes

# Chocolate Chip Coffee Cake

TOPPING

| | |
|---|---|
| ½ cup | brown sugar |
| ¼ cup | cinnamon |

CAKE

| | |
|---|---|
| 2 cups | all purpose flour |
| 1 tsp | baking powder |
| ⅛ tsp | baking soda |
| ⅛ tsp | salt |
| 1 cup | sugar |
| 1 cup | sour cream |
| ½ cup less 1 Tbsp | margarine |
| 2 | eggs |
| 1 tsp | vanilla |
| ½ cup | chocolate chips |

Preheat oven to 350F.

In a small bowl, combine brown sugar and cinnamon. Set aside.

In a medium-sized mixing bowl, combine flour, baking powder, baking soda and salt. Set aside. In a large mixing bowl, using an electric or hand-held mixer, blend sugar, sour cream, margarine, eggs and vanilla. Add flour mixture to wet mixture. Mix well. Fold in chocolate chips. Pour into a greased and floured 10-inch spring-form pan. Spread the topping over cake, using only as much as you like. Bake for 45–60 minutes. Toothpick should come out clean.

Tip: If you do not have brown sugar in the house, combine 1 cup of white granulated sugar with 3–4 tablespoons molasses. Pulse in a processor to blend. For a darker brown sugar, simply add more molasses.

Servings: 8–10
Prep time: 15 minutes

# Honey Cake

| 1¼ cups | sugar |
| ¾ cup | oil |
| 3 | eggs |
| 1 cup | alfalfa honey, warm |
| 1 cup | water, warm |
| 3 cups | all purpose flour |
| 2 tsp | baking powder |
| ½ tsp | baking soda |
| ½ tsp | cinnamon |
| ½ tsp | nutmeg |
| | icing (confectioner's) sugar, garnish (optional) |

Preheat oven to 325F.

In a large mixing bowl, using an electric or hand-held mixer, combine sugar, oil, eggs, honey and water. In a separate bowl, mix flour, baking powder, baking soda, cinnamon and nutmeg. Add dry mixture to liquid ingredients. Mix well. Batter will be quite thin. Transfer batter into a greased 10-inch tube pan, bake for 1 hour, or or if using a 9 x 13-inch pan, bake for 45–50 minutes. Cover loosely with foil if it starts becoming too brown.

**Tip:** Tastes better the next day as the honey has a chance to settle and get absorbed.

Sprinkle with icing sugar before serving.

Servings: 8
Prep time: 10–20 minutes

# Captivating Coconut Cake

BATTER

| | |
|---|---|
| 1 cup | sugar |
| 2 | eggs |
| 1 cup | all purpose flour |
| 1 tsp | baking powder |
| 1 tsp | salt |
| ½ cup | milk |
| 2 Tbsp | butter, melted |
| 1 tsp | vanilla |

TOPPING

| | |
|---|---|
| ⅓ cup | brown sugar |
| 3 Tbsp | butter |
| 2 Tbsp | milk |
| ½ cup | flaked coconut |

Preheat oven to 350F.

In a large bowl, using an electric or hand-held mixer, blend sugar and eggs. Add flour, baking powder, salt, milk, melted butter and vanilla. Mix well. Pour into a greased 8 x 8-inch pan. Bake for ½ hour.

When cake is almost done, combine brown sugar, butter and milk in a saucepan. Bring to a boil. Simmer for 2 minutes, stirring often. Remove cake from oven. Pour topping mixture over cake. Sprinkle with coconut. Return to oven. Bake for an additional 5 minutes, or until coconut is browned.

Servings: 6–8
Prep time: 30 minutes

# Simply Sensational Chocolate Cake

### CAKE

| | |
|---|---|
| 2 cups | sugar |
| 1¾ cups | all purpose flour |
| ¾ cup | cocoa powder |
| 1½ tsp | baking soda |
| 1½ tsp | baking powder |
| 1 tsp | salt |
| 2 | eggs |
| 1 cup | soy milk (or ½ cup water and ½ cup soy milk) |
| 2 tsp | vanilla |
| ½ cup | oil |
| 1 cup | boiling water |

### GLAZE

| | |
|---|---|
| 2 cups | icing sugar |
| 2 Tbsp | corn syrup |
| 3–4 Tbsp | parve milk |
| 1 oz. | semi-sweet chocolate, melted |

Preheat oven to 350F.

In a large mixing bowl, combine sugar, flour, cocoa powder, baking soda, baking powder and salt. Mix by hand. Add eggs, milk, vanilla and oil. Mix. Add boiling water and continue mixing. Batter will be loose. Pour into a greased and floured Bundt pan. Bake for 30–35 minutes until toothpick comes out clean. Cool.

In another bowl, stir sugar, syrup and milk until smooth. Turn cake onto a baking sheet. Pour glaze over cake to cover completely. Drizzle melted chocolate over cake. Transfer cake to a serving platter.

Tip: When a recipe says to grease and flour pan, you can use icing (confectioner's) sugar instead of flour when it comes to cakes. If the cake is chocolate, use cocoa powder.

Servings: 10–12
Prep time: 10 minutes

# Chocolate Mocha Cake

*This icing is out of this world. You can adapt it to any chocolate cake recipe.*

CAKE

| | |
|---|---|
| ⅓ cup | instant coffee powder |
| 1⅓ cups | boiling water |
| 1⅔ cups | sugar |
| 3 | eggs |
| 1 tsp | vanilla |
| 1 cup | mayonnaise |
| 3 squares | unsweetened chocolate, melted and cooled |
| 2½ cups | all purpose flour |
| 1½ tsp | baking soda |

ICING

| | |
|---|---|
| 4 squares | unsweetened chocolate |
| ½ cup | parve milk |
| 2 Tbsp | instant coffee powder |
| 1 cup | margarine, softened |
| 3 cups | icing (confectioner's) sugar |
| 1 | egg |
| ¼ cup | chocolate-covered coffee beans, for garnishing |

Preheat oven to 350F.

Grease 2 9-inch cake pans and line them with parchment paper.

Dissolve coffee in boiling water. Set aside.

In a large mixing bowl, using an electric or hand-held mixer, beat sugar, eggs and vanilla until light and fluffy. Blend in mayonnaise and melted chocolate. Combine flour and baking soda and add to egg mixture alternately with coffee mixture on low speed. Divide batter between the prepared 9-inch cake pans. Bake for 35 minutes or until cake tester comes out clean. Cool. Slice each cake round into 2 layers.

ICING: In a medium-sized bowl, melt chocolate, parve milk and coffee powder in microwave (2 minutes on medium power). Blend until smooth. Cool. In a mixing bowl, cream margarine and sugar until light and fluffy. Add egg and beat at high speed for 1 minute. Add chocolate mixture to margarine mixture and blend well. Ice first layer and place another layer of cake on top. Repeat process and finish with icing on top. Garnish with coffee beans. Refrigerate.

Greasing the pan: Grease pan with cooking spray, and cut parchment paper to fit bottom of pan. Spray cooking spray on top. It is recommended to have the parchment a bit smaller than the bottom of the pan. The purpose of the parchment paper is to make the bottom (which will be the top of the cake) smooth.

Tip: Using mayonnaise as the fat in this recipe keeps the cake very moist. If you use light mayonnaise, it will also lessen the calories.

Servings: 8–10
Prep time: 15 minutes

# Cardamom Cake

| | |
|---|---|
| 1 cup | margarine, softened |
| 3 cups | sugar |
| 6 | eggs |
| 3 cups | cake and pastry flour |
| 4½ tsp | baking powder |
| 1½ tsp | salt |
| 1½ tsp | cardamom |
| 1 cup | parve whipping cream |
| 2 Tbsp | vanilla |
| | icing (confectioner's) sugar, to garnish |

Preheat oven to 350F.

In a large mixing bowl, using an electric or hand-held mixer, beat margarine and sugar together until light and fluffy. Add eggs. Beat well. Set aside.

In a separate bowl, combine dry ingredients. Set aside.

In a cup, combine whipping cream and vanilla. Set aside.

Alternately beat in dry ingredients with wet ingredients, adding them to the batter, beginning and ending with dry ingredients. Pour batter into a greased 10-inch tube or Bundt pan. Bake for 1 hour, or until inserted toothpick comes out clean. Garnish with icing sugar before serving.

*This makes a large rich-tasting cake!*

**Tip:** Refrigerating this cake enhances its flavour.
Cardamom has a strong lemon flavour that perks up pilafs, cakes, fruits and spiced wine.

Servings: 10–12
Prep time: 15 minutes

# Peanut Butter Mousse Cake

PARVE

*You will "wow" them with this dessert.*

CRUST

| | |
|---|---|
| 2 cups | chocolate sandwich cookie crumbs or chocolate wafer crumbs |
| ½ cup | peanuts, chopped |
| ¼ cup | sugar |
| 2 Tbsp | margarine, melted |

MOUSSE

| | |
|---|---|
| 1¾ cups | parve whipping cream |
| 2 cups | creamy peanut butter |
| 2 (8-oz.) tubs | tofutti cream cheese, softened |
| 2 cups | icing (confectioner's) sugar |
| 2 Tbsp | vanilla |

TOPPING

| | |
|---|---|
| ¼ cup | sugar |
| ¼ cup | parve whipping cream |
| 1 cup | semi-sweet chocolate chips |
| ½ cup | peanuts, chopped, to garnish |

Preheat oven to 350F.

**CRUST:** In a large bowl, combine cookie crumbs, peanuts, ¼ cup sugar and melted margarine. Press into a 10-inch springform pan. Bake for 15 minutes. Cool. Set aside.

**MOUSSE:** Using an electric or hand-held mixer, beat whipping cream until stiff. Set aside.

In another mixing bowl, beat together peanut butter and tofutti cream cheese until smooth. Stir in icing sugar and vanilla, mixing well. Gently fold in beaten whipping cream, a quarter at a time. Pour into baked crust. Refrigerate until set, approximately 2 hours.

**TOPPING:** In a medium-sized saucepan, combine sugar and whipping cream. Stir over medium heat until sugar dissolves and mixture comes to a boil. Remove from heat. Add chocolate chips. Stir until melted and smooth. Remove cake from refrigerator. Spread topping evenly over filling. Garnish with peanuts. Refrigerate until cold. Serve chilled.

Tip: Freezes well.

Servings: 16
Prep time: 20 minutes, plus
2 hours to set cake

# Peanut Butter Marble Cake

CAKE

| | |
|---|---|
| 2¾ cups | all purpose flour |
| 2 tsp | baking powder |
| 1 tsp | baking soda |
| ½ tsp | salt |
| 1 cup | sugar |
| ½ cup | brown sugar, packed |
| ¾ cup | shortening |
| ¾ cup | creamy peanut butter |
| 3 | large eggs |
| 1½ tsp | vanilla |
| 1 cup | soy milk |
| ¾ cup | chocolate syrup |

GLAZE

| | |
|---|---|
| 1 cup | icing (confectioner's) sugar |
| ¼ cup | chocolate syrup |
| 1 tsp | vanilla |
| approx. 1 tsp | water |

Preheat oven to 350F.

In a large bowl, combine flour, baking powder, baking soda and salt. Set aside.

In a second large bowl, using an electric or hand-held mixer, combine the sugars, shortening and peanut butter. Beat until creamy. Beat in eggs, 1 egg at a time. Add vanilla. Add the dry ingredients to the second bowl, alternating with the soy milk. Beat at low speed until mixed. Reserve 2 cups of batter. Add chocolate syrup to the rest mixing well. Pour reserved batter in a greased 10-inch Bundt pan. Add chocolate batter on top. Bake for 70–80 minutes or until toothpick inserted in centre comes out clean. Cool.

Meanwhile, prepare glaze. In a small bowl, combine glaze ingredients until they reach drizzle consistency. Drizzle over cooled cake.

Servings: 10–12
Prep time: 20 minutes

# Mum's Apple Pie

PARVE

*This recipe is a little different because the crust is like a cookie crust.*

FILLING

| | |
|---|---|
| 6 | cooking apples, peeled, cored and thinly sliced |
| 2 Tbsp | sugar |
| 2 Tbsp | cornstarch |
| 1 tsp | vanilla sugar |
| 1 tsp | cinnamon |
| | handful of raisins (optional) |

CRUST

| | |
|---|---|
| 2½ cups | all purpose flour |
| ¾ cup | sugar |
| 1 tsp | baking powder |
| 1 | egg |
| 1 cup | margarine, melted |

TOPPING

| | |
|---|---|
| 2 Tbsp | sugar |
| ½ tsp | cinnamon |

Preheat oven to 350F.

FILLING: In a large bowl, combine apples, sugar, cornstarch, vanilla sugar, cinnamon and raisins, if using. Set aside.

CRUST DOUGH: In another large bowl, mix together flour, sugar, baking powder and egg. Add melted margarine and blend well.

Divide crust dough in two and set one portion aside. Roll out one portion between two sheets of waxed paper and place in a 9-inch pie plate. Put filling in pie shell.

Roll out second portion of crust dough between two sheets of waxed paper and set them over filling to cover pie completely.

Cut excess dough away from dish rim and tuck edges in and under.

Combine topping ingredients and sprinkle over pie. Prick dough with fork so that steam can escape.

Bake for 45–50 minutes, or until crust is golden brown.

Servings: 6–8
Prep time: 25 minutes

# Heavenly Chocolate Pecan Pie

CRUST

| | |
|---|---|
| 2 cups | all purpose flour |
| ½ tsp | salt |
| ⅔ cup + 2 Tbsp | shortening – do not make substitutions |
| 5–6 Tbsp | cold water |

FILLING

| | |
|---|---|
| 1 cup | semi-sweet chocolate chips |
| ⅔ cup | corn syrup |
| ⅓ cup | sugar |
| 3 | eggs |
| 1½ cups | pecan halves or as needed |

**Tip:** Top with whipping cream or icing.

In a food processor, mix flour and salt until blended. Add shortening and process until mixture resembles slightly moist cornmeal. Add water, 1 tablespoon at a time, until you get large clumps in the dough. Dough shouldn't be too sticky. Form dough into a ball and lightly wrap it in plastic wrap. Refrigerate for ½ hour.

Meanwhile, melt chocolate chips and corn syrup together, either in a double boiler or microwave. Set aside.

In a food processor, beat sugar and eggs. Add chocolate mixture to egg mixture and process until blended. Set aside.

Preheat oven to 400F.

Roll out dough and place in a greased 9-inch pie pan. Pour chocolate mixture into piecrust and top with pecan halves, starting in the centre and working your way to the outside in concentric circles. Bake for 10 minutes. Reduce heat to 350F for an additional 20 minutes. Cool. To garnish, drizzle melted chocolate over pecan halves.

Servings: 8–10
Prep time: 25 minutes + refrigeration of 1½ hours

# Bavarian Apple Torte

*"My friends have been waiting months for this recipe!"*

CRUST

| | |
|---|---|
| ½ cup | margarine, softened |
| ⅓ cup | sugar |
| ½ tsp | vanilla |
| 1 cup | all purpose flour |

BATTER

| | |
|---|---|
| 1 (8-oz.) pkg. | cream cheese, softened |
| ¼ cup | sugar |
| 1 | egg |
| ½ tsp | vanilla |

APPLE

| | |
|---|---|
| ⅓ cup | sugar |
| ½ tsp | cinnamon |
| 4 cups | apple, peeled, cored and sliced |
| ½ cup | slivered almonds |

Tip: Freezes well.

Preheat oven to 450F.

**CRUST:** In a large mixing bowl, using an electric or hand-held mixer, cream margarine and sugar. Add vanilla. Blend in flour. Mix well. Spread on bottom of 9-inch spring-form pan.

**BATTER:** In another large bowl, blend cream cheese and sugar. Add egg and vanilla. Mix well. Pour mixture onto crust.

**APPLE:** In a third mixing bowl, combine sugar and cinnamon. Add apples. Spoon apple-sugar mixture over cream cheese layer. Bake for 10 minutes. Reduce heat to 400F and bake for an additional 25 minutes. Cool. Garnish with almonds right before serving so that they do not get soggy.

Servings: 8–10
Prep time: 25 minutes

# Royal Apple Cake

CRUST

| | |
|---|---|
| 2 cups | all purpose flour |
| ½ cup | margarine, softened |
| 2 | egg yolks |
| ¼ cup | sugar |
| 1½ tsp | baking powder |
| 2 Tbsp | brandy |
| | |
| 5–6 | apples, peeled, cored, diced |

FILLING

| | |
|---|---|
| ½ cup | orange juice |
| 1 | egg |
| 2 Tbsp | sugar |
| 1–2 Tbsp | lemon juice |
| 1 Tbsp | cornstarch |

TOPPING

| | |
|---|---|
| 1½ cups | all purpose flour |
| ½ cup | margarine |
| ½ cup | sugar |
| | icing (confectioner's) sugar, to decorate |

Preheat oven to 350F.

In a large mixing bowl, using an electric or hand-held mixer, combine crust ingredients. Press evenly into a greased 9 x 13-inch pan. Arrange apples on dough.

In a small bowl, combine the filling ingredients. Blend well. Pour over apples.

In another small bowl, mix topping ingredients until a crumbly consistency results. Sprinkle evenly over filling. Bake for 1 hour. Remove and let cool. Sprinkle with icing sugar before serving.

Servings: 10–12
Prep time: 15–20 minutes

# Peach Cobbler

| | |
|---|---|
| 6 | large peaches, skinned, pitted and sliced |
| ¼ cup | brown sugar |
| 2 tsp | cornstarch |
| 1 tsp | fresh lemon juice |
| 1 tsp | vanilla |
| ¼ tsp | cinnamon |

TOPPING

| | |
|---|---|
| 1 cup | all purpose flour |
| 1 cup | sugar |
| 1 tsp | baking powder |
| ¼ tsp | salt |
| 6 Tbsp | cold margarine, cut into pieces |
| ¼ cup | boiling water |

Preheat oven to 425F.

In a 2-quart baking dish, combine peaches with brown sugar, cornstarch, lemon juice, vanilla and cinnamon. Mix well. Bake for 10 minutes.

Meanwhile, in a large bowl, mix together flour, sugar, baking powder and salt. Mix in margarine by hand or using a pastry blender, until mixture is crumbly. Stir in water until just combined.

Remove peaches from oven and drop spoonfuls of topping over them. Bake until topping is golden, about 18–20 minutes. Topping will spread as it bakes and will be custard-like when done. Serve warm or at room temperature.

Tip: To skin peaches: place peaches in a bowl and cover with boiling water. After a minute or so, peaches will peel easily.

Store peaches at room temperature and use within a couple of days.

Servings: 6–8
Prep time: 15–20 minutes

# Strawberry, Blueberry & Rhubarb Crumble

### CRUMBLE TOPPING

| | |
|---|---|
| 2 cups | all purpose flour |
| 2 cups | rolled oats |
| 1 cup | dark brown sugar |
| 1 cup | unsalted margarine, softened |
| 1½ tsp | ground cinnamon |

### FRUIT FILLING

| | |
|---|---|
| 2 cups | fresh blueberries |
| 2 cups | fresh sliced strawberries |
| 2 cups | fresh sliced rhubarb |
| 1 cup | granulated sugar |
| ¼ cup | corn starch |
| 1 Tbsp | fresh lemon juice |

Preheat oven to 375F.

Mix crumble topping ingredients by hand until ingredients are incorporated and crumbly. Set aside.

Toss together fruit filling and put in a 10-inch pie dish. Cover with aluminum foil and bake in 375F oven for 45 minutes or until fruit begins to bubble at edges. Remove from oven and remove aluminum foil. Sprinkle crumble mixture evenly over fruit. Return to oven and bake for an additional 15 minutes or until golden brown.

Servings: 6–8
Prep time: 15 minutes

# Israeli Tiramisu

| | |
|---|---|
| ⅓ cup | warm water |
| 2 Tbsp | coffee |
| ¼ cup | liqueur, any kind |
| 2 Tbsp | sugar |
| 2½ cups | parve whipping cream, divided |
| 2 (8-oz.) pkg. | cream cheese or tofu cream cheese, softened |
| 1 (2.8-oz.) pkg. | vanilla pudding mix |
| ½ cup | icing (confectioner's) sugar |
| 2 (5.25-oz.) pkgs. | chocolate-flavour biscuits |
| | chocolate shavings, to garnish |

FUDGE

| | |
|---|---|
| ¼ cup | sugar |
| ¼ cup | water |
| ¼ cup | margarine, softened |
| 2 Tbsp | cocoa powder |

*To make this a true Israeli delicacy, use products that have been made in Israel.*

In a small bowl, mix water, coffee, liqueur and sugar. Set aside.

In a large mixing bowl, whip whipping cream. Set aside ½ cup. In the large bowl, beat whipped cream with cream cheese, vanilla pudding mix and icing sugar for approximately 5–8 minutes. Dip half the biscuits in the liqueur mixture, then line a glass trifle bowl with them. Pour half of the whipped cream mixture on top. Repeat process. Top with reserved whipped cream. Garnish with chocolate shavings.

In a small saucepan, on low heat, combine sugar, water, margarine and cocoa powder. Stir constantly until everything melts. Pour on top of tiramisu. Cover. Refrigerate for 1 hour before serving.

**Tips:** Chocolate curls make an impressive dessert garnish and are easy to make. Use a vegetable peeler to slice strips from a block of chocolate. Make sure bowl and beaters are cold for better volume.

---

*For a different version of this recipe, assemble tiramisu in greased 10-inch spring-form pan.*

| | |
|---|---|
| ½ cup | extra strong instant coffee |
| 2 Tbsp | brandy/orange liqueur or orange juice |
| 24 | dry lady fingers |

Combine coffee and brandy. Dip lady fingers in coffee mixture and line bottom and sides of the pan. Prepare layers as directed in recipe above.

Servings: 10
Prep time: 20 minutes + refrigerate for 1 hour

# Chocolate Babka

### CAKE

| | |
|---|---|
| 1 tsp | sugar |
| ½ cup | warm water |
| 2 Tbsp | active dry yeast |
| ⅓ cup | sugar |
| 4½–5 cups | all purpose flour |
| 3 Tbsp | butter or margarine, softened |
| ½ tsp | salt |
| ½ tsp | vanilla extract |
| 3 | eggs |
| ⅔ cup | warm milk or soy milk |
| 3 Tbsp | butter or margarine, melted |

### COCOA FILLING

| | |
|---|---|
| ⅔ cup | sugar |
| ⅓ cup | unsweetened cocoa, sifted |
| 1 cup | walnuts or pecans, chopped |
| 1 tsp | water |

### STREUSEL TOPPING

| | |
|---|---|
| 2 Tbsp | butter or margarine, softened |
| ¼ tsp | cinnamon |
| ⅓ cup | icing (confectioner's) sugar |
| ¼ cup | all purpose flour |

**Tip:** To make sure your yeast is really active, stir 1 tablespoon of active dry yeast with 3 tablespoons of lukewarm water and a pinch of sugar. In 5 minutes it should begin to bubble.

In a medium-sized bowl, dissolve 1 teaspoon sugar in warm water. Sprinkle yeast over and stir. Let stand 8–10 minutes, then stir.

Combine sugar, flour, butter, salt and vanilla in a food processor. Pulse until just combined. Add yeast mixture and process 20 seconds. Separate one of the eggs, reserving the white for glaze. While processing, add egg yolk, 2 eggs and warm milk. Once the dough has formed a ball, continue to process for another minute.

Turn out dough onto a lightly floured board. Knead dough for 1–2 minutes. Turn out dough into a greased bowl, turning to coat dough. Cover with plastic wrap and a towel. Let dough rise in a warm place until doubled in bulk (45 minutes to 1 hour).

Punch dough down. Cover with inverted bowl and let rest for 10 minutes.

Divide dough into two equal parts. Roll each half out on a floured surface to a 10 x 20-inch rectangle. Brush half of the melted butter over each rectangle of dough, leaving about ½-inch margin on all edges.

Cocoa filling: In a small bowl, mix sugar and cocoa until well combined and no lumps remain. Sprinkle half of the cocoa filling evenly over the surface of each rectangle and then sprinkle each rectangle with half of the nuts.

Starting with a 20-inch side, roll each rectangle of dough tightly, jellyroll fashion. Pinch edge to seal. Place on a greased baking sheet. Cover with a tea towel and let rise until almost doubled in bulk (35–45 minutes).

Preheat oven to 350F.

In a small dish, beat reserved egg white with 1 teaspoon water; brush egg white mixture over loaves.

Streusel topping: In a medium-sized bowl, beat butter with cinnamon until fluffy. Gradually add icing sugar and flour until mixture becomes crumbly and uniformly combined.

Sprinkle each loaf with half of the streusel topping.

Bake on middle rack for 30–35 minutes until cakes are well-browned. Remove loaves from baking sheets and let cool on wire racks.

Servings: 2 cakes
Prep time: 1 hour plus

# Oh Henry Cheesecake

CRUST

| | |
|---|---|
| 1 cup | peanuts, honey roasted, finely chopped |
| ⅔ cup | sugar |
| ⅔ cup | graham cracker crumbs |
| 5 Tbsp | margarine, melted |

FILLING

| | |
|---|---|
| 1 (2.8-oz.) pkg. | vanilla pudding mix |
| 2 cups | whipping cream |
| 2 (8-oz.) pkgs. | cream cheese, softened |
| ⅔ cup | sugar |
| 3 | eggs |
| 1 tsp | vanilla |
| 1 tsp | liqueur (any kind) |
| 1 cup | boiling water |

TOPPING

| | |
|---|---|
| 1 (320-g) bag | mini Oh Henry bites, chopped (use only as much as you want) |
| | caramel sundae sauce |

Preheat oven to 350F.

**CRUST:** In a large bowl, mix together all crust ingredients. Press the crust firmly on bottom of a greased 10-inch round spring-form pan.

**FILLING:** In a small bowl, whip vanilla pudding and whipping cream together. Set aside. In a large bowl, mix cream cheese, sugar, eggs, vanilla and liqueur. Fold pudding-cream mixture into the cheese mixture. Pour into pan over crust.

Cover the outside bottom and sides of the spring-form pan with 2 layers of aluminum foil. Place in a larger pan with a cup of boiling water poured in bottom or fill with water to 1 inch of sides. Bake for 1½ hours or just until set. Cool.

**TOPPING:** When cake is cool, sprinkle Oh Henry bars on top of cake. Drizzle with caramel sauce. Refrigerate.

**Tips:** Freezes well.
Remove from freezer 20 minutes before serving and let thaw.

Servings: 15
Prep time: 1 hour

# Parve Cheese Cake

CRUST

| | |
|---|---|
| 1½ cups | graham cracker crumbs |
| ¼ cup | sugar |
| 2 Tbsp | margarine, melted |

FILLING

| | |
|---|---|
| 3 (8-oz.) pkgs. | tofu cream cheese, softened |
| 3 | eggs |
| 1 cup | sugar |
| 1 Tbsp | liqueur, your choice |

TOPPING

| | |
|---|---|
| 1 (14-oz.) can | cherry pie filling |

Preheat oven to 350F.

In a large mixing bowl, combine graham cracker crumbs, sugar and melted margarine. Mix well. Press firmly into the bottom of a 10-inch round spring-form pan. Set aside.

In another bowl, using an electric or hand-held mixer, combine cream cheese, eggs, sugar and liqueur. Mix well. Pour into crust. Bake for 40 minutes. Once cooled, spread cherry pie filling on top.

Tip: In place of cherry pie topping, drizzle chocolate syrup on top in a circular pattern.

Servings: 6–8
Prep time: 10 minutes

# Orange Tang Ice Cream

*Brings back memories of a Creamsicle. This recipe requires some time but the efforts are well worth it.*

| 2 cups | parve whitener |
| ½ cup | water |
| ¾ cup | Tang crystals®* |
| 1 cup | non-dairy whipping cream* |
| 1 tsp | vanilla sugar |
| 3 | egg whites |
| ¼ cup | sugar |

You will need three bowls.

In bowl 1: Using an electric or hand-held mixer, beat whitener with water and Tang®. Pour half the liquid into freezer-safe extra-large plastic container or glass dish. Freeze (approximately 2 hours). Set reserved liquid aside.

In bowl 2: Using an electric or hand-held mixer, beat whipping cream with vanilla sugar until soft peaks form. Set aside.

In bowl 3: Using an electric or hand-held mixer, beat egg whites with sugar to stiff peaks. Gently fold into contents of bowl 2.

Place the above mixtures on top of orange layer. Freeze. Once completely frozen (approximately 2 hours), add reserved liquid from bowl 1. Freeze.

*Quantities may be adjusted if you like more orange or more whipping cream content.

Servings: 10–12
Prep time: 1 hour + freezing time

# Coffee Ice Cream Deluxe

PARVE

*This makes a very large ice cream cake with a delicious fudgy icing. It is great to prepare and freeze until you need it.*

CRUST

| | |
|---|---|
| 2 cups | chocolate sandwich cookies, crushed, or chocolate wafer crumbs |
| ½ cup | sugar |
| 2 Tbsp | margarine, melted |
| 8 | egg yolks |
| ¾ tsp | instant coffee |
| 1½ cups | non-dairy whipping cream |
| ¾ cup | icing (confectioner's) sugar |
| 1 tsp | vanilla |
| 8 | egg whites |
| ⅔ cup | chocolate chips |
| ¼ cup | sugar |
| ¼ cup | margarine |
| 2 | eggs |

Preheat oven to 350F.

You will need three bowls.

Mix crust ingredients in food processor. Press into the bottom of a 10-inch spring form pan. Bake for 15 minutes. Cool.

Bowl 1: Mix egg yolks and coffee dissolved in a drop of water.

Bowl 2: Whip up non-dairy whipping cream. Add icing sugar and vanilla. Mix again.

Bowl 3: Beat egg whites to stiff peaks, then fold all ingredients from all bowls together.

Spread coffee mixture into cooled crust and freeze until set.

Melt chocolate chips, sugar and margarine together. Cool.

Add 2 eggs (one at a time) to cooled chocolate mixture and pour as top layer and freeze again.

Servings: 10–12
Prep time: 15–20 minutes, plus freezing and setting

# Halva Ice Cream

| | |
|---|---|
| 4 | eggs, separated |
| 1 cup | sugar, divided into thirds |
| 2 cups | non dairy whipping cream |
| 1 tsp | vanilla |
| 7–9 oz. | halva, grated |

You will need 3 bowls.

Bowl 1: Using an electric or hand-held mixer, beat the egg whites until very stiff, adding ⅓ cup of sugar, 1 tablespoon of sugar at a time, for approximately 3–5 minutes.

Bowl 2: Using an electric or hand-held mixer, beat the whipping cream, ⅓ cup sugar and vanilla, until very firm, for approximately 4–6 minutes.

Bowl 3: Using an electric or hand-held mixer, beat the egg yolks and remaining sugar for approximately 2 minutes.

Fold whipped cream into the egg whites. Fold egg yolks into the mixture. Fold in the grated halva. Transfer contents into a freezer-safe container. Freeze.

**Variations:** Halva can be replaced or added to with almost anything, e.g.: chocolate chips, fruit purée, nuts, marshmallows.

**Tip:** Freeze ice cream in mini cupcake holders to pass around at a party.

Servings: 8–10
Prep time: 15–30 minutes

# Rice Crisp Ice Cream

DAIRY OR PARVE

| | |
|---|---|
| 1 quart | parve or dairy ice cream, vanilla, vanilla fudge or chocolate chip |
| 1 cup | rice crisp cereal |
| 1 cup | creamy peanut butter, warm |
| 1 cup | maple syrup, warm |

Put ice cream in a large bowl and let melt until it is soft enough to mix with other ingredients. Add rice cereal and peanut butter and mix together. Add maple syrup. Mix.

Transfer mixture to a sealable, freezer-safe container or 10-inch spring form pan. Freeze for several hours or overnight.

Servings: 10–12
Prep time: 10 minutes

# Caramel Pudding

DAIRY

| | |
|---|---|
| 3 (300-mL) cans | condensed milk |
| 1 (450-g) box | graham crackers |
| 1 (16-oz.) box | whipping cream, whipped chocolate sauce (optional) |

*Decadent!*

Place unopened cans of condensed milk in large pot. Fill pot to the top with water. Cover and bring to a boil. Reduce to low and cook for 3 hours. Check depth of water throughout the cooking as the cans must always be covered with a few inches of water. At this point the condensed milk becomes caramel. Leave cans to cool.

Meanwhile, layer graham crackers on the bottom of a rectangular 9 x 13-inch dish. Add a layer of caramel. Add a layer of cream. Repeat. To garnish, drizzle with chocolate sauce or crumble crackers on top. Chill.

Tip: For a nice party alternative, spoon caramel pudding into parfait glasses. Chill and top with whipped cream right before serving.

Servings: 8–10
Prep time: 15 minutes

# Pavlova

| | |
|---|---|
| 6 | egg whites |
| ⅛ tsp | salt |
| 1½ cups | sugar |
| 1½ tsp | vinegar |
| 1½ tsp | vanilla |
| 1 Tbsp | cornstarch |
| 1 (8-oz.) box | parve whipping cream |
| | fresh fruit – see below |
| | mint leaves to garnish |

Preheat oven to 400F. Spray an aluminum pizza pan with non-stick cooking spray. Set aside.

In a large mixing bowl, using an electric or hand-held mixer beat egg whites with salt for 5–6 minutes until stiff, slowly adding sugar, a tablespoon at a time. Continue beating until very stiff. Add vinegar and vanilla. Beat again. Gently fold in cornstarch. Place spoonfuls of mixture on pan and spread evenly, building up sides.

Reduce oven to 250F. Bake for 1½ hours. Cool.

In a small bowl, beat non-dairy whipping cream until stiff. Spread over Pavlova.

### TOPPING A

| | |
|---|---|
| 2 cups | mixed blueberries and raspberries, fresh or frozen |
| ½ cup | sugar |
| 2 Tbsp | orange liqueur or Sabra |

In a small saucepan, combine berries, sugar and liqueur. On medium heat bring to a boil. Simmer for 15–20 minutes, uncovered. Drain liquid. Cool. Spread on top of Pavlova.

### TOPPING B

| | |
|---|---|
| 5–6 | peaches, peeled, cut into wedges |
| 1 cup | fresh blackberries |
| 2–3 Tbsp | sugar |
| 1 Tbsp | orange liqueur |

In a small saucepan, combine peaches, blackberries, sugar and liqueur. Bring to a boil, then simmer for 5 minutes. Drain. Cool. Spread on top of Pavlova.

**Tips:** If you use a large, flat ovenproof ceramic dish, the presentation will be beautiful.

A wet knife will cut through meringue without tearing it.

You can always top with fresh fruit instead.

Garnish with mint leaves.

Servings: 10
Prep time: 20 minutes

# Spicy Sugared Nuts

| 1 | egg white |
| 2 cups | unsalted mixed nuts, e.g., cashews, almonds, pecans |
| ¼ cup | sugar |
| ½ tsp | cinnamon |
| ½ tsp | cayenne pepper |
| ¼ tsp | salt |

Preheat oven to 325F.

In a large bowl beat egg white until foamy. Stir in nuts until well coated. Set aside.

In a small bowl, combine sugar, cinnamon, pepper and salt. Add this blend to nuts and toss until coated.

Spread on greased cookie sheet. Place in oven for 20–25 minutes, stirring often, until golden. Remove and let cool.

Store in airtight container for up to 2 weeks.

**Tips:** Can be used in Mango Salad page 47.

To refresh stale nuts, put them in the oven at 250F for 5–10 minutes.

Servings: 2 cups
Prep time: 5–10 minutes

---

Tip: A great last minute dessert.

For added calories top with a spoon of ice-cream!

# Fried Bananas

---

| 2 | ripe bananas, peeled |
| 3 Tbsp | sugar |
| 1 tsp | cinnamon |
| 2–3 Tbsp | margarine |

Cut bananas in half and then slice each in half lengthwise.

In a small bowl, combine sugar and cinnamon. Mix well. Dip banana pieces in mixture.

In a skillet, melt the margarine. Place banana slices in skillet and fry for 2–3 minutes watching closely so as not to burn bananas.

Servings: 4
Prep time: 5 minutes

# cookies & squares

*A very elegant cookie!*

# Cinnamon Maple Swirls

DOUGH

| | |
|---|---|
| 2 cups | all purpose flour |
| ¼ cup | sugar |
| 1 cup | shortening or margarine |
| ¼ cup | pure maple syrup |
| 1–2 Tbsp | ice water |

FILLING

| | |
|---|---|
| ¼ cup | sugar |
| 4 tsp | cinnamon |
| ¼ cup | maple syrup to brush on top of cookies |

Mix flour, sugar, shortening and maple syrup in a food processor. Add ice water, 1 tablespoon at a time, until dough is firm but not sticky. Remove from bowl and separate dough into 2 equal balls. Wrap each ball in plastic wrap. Refrigerate for 2 hours.

In a small dish, combine sugar and cinnamon. Set aside.

Remove dough from refrigerator. Roll out each ball into a 10 x 12-inch rectangle, approximately ¼-inch thick. Sprinkle with cinnamon sugar. Roll dough up-jelly roll fashion, starting from the long side and forming cylinders. Roll each cylinder in plastic wrap. Refrigerate for 1 hour.

Preheat oven to 325F.

Remove dough from refrigerator. Cut dough into ¼-inch slices. Dip the knife into flour between each cut. Lay slices flat on an ungreased baking sheet 1 inch apart. Gently press down cookies. Brush tops lightly with maple syrup. Bake for 16–17 minutes.

Servings: 3 dozen cookies
Prep time: 25–30 minutes

# Crackle Ginger Cookies

PARVE

| | |
|---|---|
| ½ cup | margarine, softened |
| ½ cup | sugar |
| ½ cup | molasses |
| 1 | egg |
| 1 tsp | vanilla |
| 2 cups | all purpose flour |
| 1 Tbsp | ginger |
| 2 tsp | cinnamon |
| 1 tsp | baking soda |
| ½ tsp | salt |
| ¼ cup | sugar for rolling |

Preheat oven to 350F.

In a large mixing bowl, beat margarine and sugar together until creamy. Add molasses, egg and vanilla. In a separate bowl, combine flour, ginger, cinnamon, baking soda and salt. Gradually add dry ingredients to creamed mixture until thoroughly combined.

Shape dough into 1-inch balls and roll in sugar. Place balls 2 inches apart on a greased cookie sheet. Bake for 13–15 minutes. Cool on wire racks.

*If you love ginger, then you will love this cookie!*

Tip: Cookies freeze well.

Servings: 4 dozen
Prep time: 15–20 minutes

# Craisins Oatmeal Cookies

| | |
|---|---|
| ¾ cup | margarine, softened |
| 1 cup | brown sugar, packed |
| ⅓ cup | sugar |
| 1 | egg |
| 2 Tbsp | water |
| 2 tsp | vanilla |
| ¾ cup | all purpose flour |
| ¾ tsp | baking soda |
| 1 tsp | cinnamon |
| 3 cups | oatmeal |
| 1 cup | dried cranberries |
| ½ cup | chocolate chips (optional) |
| ½ cup | pecans, chopped (optional) |

**Tip:** Parchment paper makes cleanup a breeze.

Preheat oven to 350F.

In a large mixing bowl, beat margarine, sugars, egg, water and vanilla until light and creamy.

In a small bowl, combine flour, baking soda and cinnamon. Add to creamed mixture, beating on low speed until blended. Stir in oatmeal and cranberries, by hand. Add chocolate chips and pecans if desired. Drop dough in heaping spoonfuls onto greased baking sheets. Press flat for crisp cookies; leave rounded for chewy cookies. Bake for 12–15 minutes, until edges are golden brown.

Servings: 4 dozen
Prep time: 15–20 minutes

# Great & Healthy Chocolate Chip Cookies

| | |
|---|---|
| 1¾ cups | all purpose flour |
| 1 tsp | baking soda |
| ½ tsp | salt |
| 1¼ cups | brown sugar, firmly packed |
| ½ cup | sugar |
| ½ cup | margarine, softened |
| ½ cup | unsweetened applesauce |
| 2 | large egg whites |
| 1 Tbsp | vanilla |
| 2½ cups | quick-cook or old-fashioned oats |
| 2 cups | semi-sweet chocolate chips |

Preheat oven to 375F.

In a small bowl, combine flour, baking soda and salt. Set aside.

In a large mixing bowl, using an electric or hand-held mixer, beat brown sugar, sugar, margarine and applesauce together. Beat in egg whites and vanilla. Gradually beat in flour mixture. Stir in oats and chocolate chips. Cover and refrigerate for ½ hour or more, until dough hardens somewhat.

Drop dough by rounded tablespoons onto greased baking sheet. Flatten cookies. For chewy cookies, bake for 8–10 minutes. For crispy cookies, bake for 12–13 minutes. Remove from oven. Let stand for 2 minutes. Transfer to wire racks to cool completely.

Servings: **4 dozen**
Prep time: **10 minutes**

# Choco-Mania Cookies

| | |
|---|---|
| 2¼ cups | all purpose flour |
| ⅔ cup | cocoa, sifted |
| 1 tsp | baking soda |
| ⅛ tsp | salt |
| 1 cup | margarine, softened |
| ¾ cup | sugar |
| ⅔ cup | brown sugar, packed |
| 1½ tsp | vanilla |
| 2 | eggs |
| 1¼ cups | white chocolate chips |
| 1¼ cups | chocolate chips |

Preheat oven to 350F.

In a small bowl, combine flour, cocoa, baking soda and salt. Set aside.

In a large mixing bowl, using an electric or hand-held mixer, beat margarine, sugars and vanilla until creamy. Mix in eggs. Gradually add flour mixture, beating at low speed until just combined. Stir in 1 cup of each type of chocolate chips.

Drop dough by tablespoons onto cookie sheets lined with parchment paper. Sprinkle a few chocolate chips onto the top of each cookie. Bake for 15 minutes.

### Types of Chocolate

| Type | Description |
|---|---|
| Unsweetened Chocolate, Semi-Sweet Chocolate and Sweet (dark) Chocolate | Used for baking and cooking |
| Milk Chocolate | Sweet chocolate with milk added. Not for cooking unless recipe asks for it specifically |
| Cocoa Powder | Form of pure chocolate with almost all the cocoa butter removed |
| White chocolate | Not really chocolate, used for cooking and candy making |
| Chocolate flavoured | Has flavour of chocolate but not enough to meet government standards to be labelled chocolate |
| Artificial chocolate | Mostly chemical, not chocolate |

Servings: 4 dozen
Prep time: 15–20 minutes

# White Chocolate Delight

| | |
|---|---|
| 1 cup | margarine, softened |
| 1 cup | sugar |
| ½ cup | brown sugar, packed |
| 2 tsp | vanilla |
| 2 | eggs |
| 2¼ cups | all purpose flour |
| 1 tsp | baking soda |
| ¼ tsp | salt |
| 1 cup | white chocolate chips (parve) |

Preheat oven to 325F.

In a large bowl, beat margarine, sugars, vanilla and eggs until fluffy. Add flour, baking soda and salt. Mix well. Add chocolate chips. Mix until doughy in texture. Form dough into golf-size balls and place onto ungreased cookie sheet. Bake 7 minutes or until bottom edges of cookies are golden brown. Cool. Store in airtight container.

May be made dairy and colourful by substituting m&m's® instead of white chocolate chips.

Freezes well.

PARVE

*"This delicious cookie has dough that is soft and easy to work with. It has become a favourite dough that I adapt to any kind of cookie."*

**Tip:** Dark brown sugar and light brown sugars are virtually interchangeable in recipes, but dark contains more molasses, which will give a deeper, spicier flavour.

Servings: 30 cookies
Prep time: 15 minutes

# Chocolate Mocha-Nut Cookies

| 1 cup | margarine, melted |
| ½ cup | cocoa |
| 3 | eggs |
| ¾ cup | sugar |
| ½ cup | brown sugar |
| 1 Tbsp | vanilla |
| 2 Tbsp | coffee liqueur |
| 2½ cups | flour |
| 1½ tsp | baking powder |
| ¼ tsp | salt |
| 6 oz. | white chocolate, chopped |
| 6 oz. | semi-sweet chocolate, chopped |
| 1 cup | pecans, chopped |

In a small bowl, whisk cocoa into margarine until smooth.

In a separate bowl, beat eggs and sugars for 4–5 minutes. Add margarine mixture. Add vanilla, liqueur, flour, baking powder and salt. Stir in chocolates and pecans. Refrigerate for 1 hour.

Remove dough from refrigerator. Preheat oven to 325F. Cut dough into 4 equal pieces. Shape each piece into a log 1½ x 8 inches. Place on cookie sheet lined with parchment paper.

Bake 25–30 minutes until tops crack and toothpick comes out clean. Place logs on cutting board. Cool for 15 minutes. Cut into 1-inch slices.

**To store chocolate:** Wrap in brown paper or aluminum foil and put in a cool dry place (65–70 degrees). Chocolate stored at the right temperature will retain freshness for over a year.

Servings: 2 dozen
Prep time: 30 minutes

# Chocolate Biscotti

| ½ cup | margarine, softened |
| ¾ cup | sugar |
| 2 | eggs |
| 2 Tbsp | Sabra, Kahlua or double-strength coffee |
| 2 cups+2 Tbsp | all purpose flour |
| ⅓ cup | cocoa, sifted |
| 1½ tsp | baking powder |
| ¼ tsp | salt |
| ⅔ cup | toasted almonds, coarsely chopped |
| ⅔ cup | chocolate chips |

Preheat oven to 325F.

In a large bowl, using an electric mixer or hand-blender, cream margarine and sugar until light and fluffy. Mix in eggs and liqueur. In a separate bowl, combine flour, cocoa, baking powder and salt. Add to margarine mixture. Add almonds and chocolate chips. Blend well.

Divide dough into equal parts. On a baking sheet lined with parchment paper, shape dough into 2 logs. Lightly score the log, not cutting all the way through. Bake for 30 minutes, or until lightly browned. Transfer to a cutting board. Let cool for 5 minutes. Slice into ½-inch thick slices. Place on baking sheet, cut side up, ½ inch apart and return to oven for 10–15 minutes. Cool and store in an airtight container.

**Tip:** For low-cal version, substitute 5 Tbsp olive oil and 3 Tbsp water for the ½ cup margarine.

For chewier biscotti, decrease second baking by 5 minutes.

Servings: 2½ dozen
Prep time: 15–20 minutes

# Nut-Free Chocolate Chip Biscotti

*A great nut free adition to your child's lunchbox.*

| | |
|---|---|
| 4 | large eggs |
| 1 cup | oil |
| 1¼ cups | sugar |
| ¼ cup | applesauce |
| 1 tsp | vanilla |
| 3½ cups | all purpose flour |
| 1 tsp | baking powder |
| 1 tsp | cinnamon |
| 1 cup | quick-cooking oats |
| 2 Tbsp | wheat germ |
| 1 cup | chocolate chips |

TOPPING

| | |
|---|---|
| ½ cup | sugar |
| 2 tsp | cinnamon |

**Tip:** Let cookies cool completely before storing. Store at room temperature in a tin or plastic container with a tight-fitting lid. If layering or stacking cookies, put sheets of waxed paper or parchment between layers.

Preheat oven to 350F.

In a large bowl, beat eggs, oil, sugar, applesauce and vanilla with an electric mixer. In separate bowl, combine flour, baking powder and cinnamon. Gradually add to egg mixture until just combined. Stir in oats, wheat germ and chocolate chips. Divide dough in half and shape dough into 2 logs about 1 inch high and 4 inches wide. Place logs on 2 greased cookie sheets. Bake for 30 minutes.

Slice each log into approximately 18 pieces (depending on desired thickness of biscotti) then place each piece on its side. Lower temperature to 250F. Return cookie sheets to oven and bake until golden brown, approximately 20 minutes. Remove biscotti, turn over and bake for another 20 minutes. Remove and let cool for approximately 15 minutes.

In a small bowl or resealable bag, combine sugar and cinnamon. While biscotti are still warm, dip each slice into cinnamon sugar mixture to coat. Lay slices down on a rack to continue cooling.

Servings: 3 dozen
Prep time: 25–30 minutes

# Mandel with Cranberries and Cherries

| | |
|---|---|
| ½ cup | margarine, softened |
| 2 cups | sugar |
| 4 | eggs |
| 1½ tsp | lemon zest, grated |
| ½ tsp | vanilla extract |
| ¼ tsp | almond extract |
| 5 cups | all purpose flour |
| 2 tsp | baking soda |
| 1 tsp | baking powder |
| ½ tsp | salt |
| 1 cup | dried cranberries |
| 1 cup | dried tart cherries |
| ¼ cup | almonds, coarsely chopped |

Preheat oven to 325F.

In a large mixing bowl, using an electric or hand-held mixer, beat margarine and sugar until creamy. Add eggs, 1 at a time, beating after each one. Add lemon zest, vanilla and almond extract, mixing well.

In a separate bowl, combine flour, baking soda, baking powder and salt. Add to creamy mixture, beating just until dry ingredients are moistened.

Turn dough out onto a lightly floured surface. Lightly flour hands, and knead in cranberries, cherries, and almonds (or you can add in the mixer).

Divide dough in half. Shape each portion into a 14 x 2-inch log on a lightly-greased baking sheet. Flatten logs slightly. You can also make smaller logs.

Bake for 30–35 minutes or until golden brown. Cool on a baking sheet for 5 minutes. Transfer to a wire rack to cool completely.

Cut each log diagonally into ½-inch thick slices with a serrated knife, using a gentle sawing motion. Place slices on ungreased baking sheets cut side up. Return to oven. Bake for an additional 10 minutes. Turn cookies over. Bake 10 additional minutes. Remove to wire racks to cool.

**Tip:** Substitute raisins, dates or chopped dried apricots for the cherries or cranberries.

Servings: 30–36 cookies
Prep time: 45 minutes

# Raving Rogelach

DOUGH

| | |
|---|---|
| 1-oz. | fresh cake yeast or 4½ tsp dry (2 (8-g) packages) |
| 1 tsp | sugar |
| ¼ cup | warm water |
| 3 cups | all purpose flour |
| 1 cup | margarine, softened |
| ⅓ cup | sugar |
| 2 | eggs |
| 1 tsp | vanilla |
| ¼ cup | margarine, softened |
| 1 | egg, beaten |

FILLING 1

| | |
|---|---|
| ⅔ cup | sugar |
| ⅓ cup | cocoa |
| 2 tsp | vanilla |

FILLING 2

| | |
|---|---|
| ¾ cup | sugar |
| ¼ cup | cinnamon |

FILLING 3

| | |
|---|---|
| ¼ cup | apricot jam or enough to cover dough |
| ½ cup | nuts, finely chopped |
| ½ cup | sugar |

Tip: May be sprinkled with icing (confectioner's) sugar when cooled.

In a large bowl, dissolve yeast in sugar and water. Let stand for 10 minutes. When yeast begins to bubble, add flour, 1 cup margarine, sugar, eggs and vanilla. Mix well. Place dough into a greased bowl. Cover. Let rise until dough doubles in size – about 1 hour. Alternatively, cover and refrigerate overnight.

Prepare desired filling by mixing ingredients in a small bowl. Set aside.

Preheat oven to 350F.

Divide dough into thirds. Roll each third into a 10-inch round circle. Brush with softened margarine. Spread filling over dough. Cut into 10–12 wedge shapes, starting from the centre of the dough. Roll each wedge starting at wide end. Place onto a greased cookie sheet. Brush with beaten egg.

Bake for 20 minutes.

Servings: 2 dozen rogelach
Prep time: 25 minutes

# Hamentashen/Cookie Dough

| 2 cups | all purpose flour |
| 2 tsp | baking powder |
| ½ tsp | salt |
| ½ cup | margarine, softened |
| 1 cup | sugar |
| 1 | egg |
| 1 tsp | vanilla |
| 2 Tbsp | orange juice or water |

In a medium-sized mixing bowl, mix flour, baking powder and salt. Set aside.

In a large mixing bowl, with an electric or hand-held mixer, cream margarine and sugar together, until light and fluffy. Add egg, vanilla and juice. Add dry ingredients. Mix well. Cover and refrigerate for 2 hours.

Remove dough from refrigerator. Roll dough out to ¼-inch thickness on a lightly floured surface.

Preheat oven to 375F.

**FOR HAMENTASHEN:** Using a cup, cut out circles. Add a tiny drop of jam. Shape into triangles.

**FOR COOKIE:** Using a cookie cutter, cut shapes out of the dough. Add topping if desired-sprinkles or dip half the cookie in melted chocolate after baking.

Place on lightly greased cookie sheet. Bake for 15 minutes or until edges start browning.

PARVE

*A versatile recipe you will use over and over again.*

Tip: Freezes well.
In order to prevent rolled-out dough from sticking to counters and rolling pin, place the dough between sheets of waxed paper.

Servings: 24–36 hamentashen / cookies
Prep time: 10 minutes

# Sugar Cookie Cut-Outs

PARVE

| ¾ cup | margarine |
| 1¼ cups | sugar |
| 2 | eggs |
| 2 tsp | vanilla |
| 3 cups | all purpose flour, may need to add additional ½ cup |
| 1 tsp | baking powder |
| ¾ tsp | salt |

### CHOCOLATE GANACHE

| ½ cup | non-dairy whipping cream |
| 4 oz. | semi-sweet chocolate, chopped |

In a large mixing bowl, using an electric or hand-held mixer, cream margarine, sugar, eggs and vanilla. Add flour, baking powder and salt. If dough is too soft or sticky, add more flour. Cover bowl. Refrigerate dough for 1 hour.

Preheat oven to 375F.

Remove dough from fridge. Roll dough out on a lightly floured surface into ¼-inch thickness. Cut into shapes. Transfer cookies onto a parchment-lined baking sheet. Bake for 8–10 minutes until edges are golden.

**CHOCOLATE GANACHE:** In a small saucepan over medium heat, bring cream to simmer. Add chocolate. Stir until chocolate melts. Remove from heat. Refrigerate until filling sets a little, is spreadable and no longer runny, approximately ½ hour.

Turn one cookie upside down, so flat part is facing you. Add a drop of ganache and press another cookie right side up on ganache. Place sandwich cookies back on baking sheet. Drizzle tops with remaining chocolate; you may have to mix with a little water so that chocolate is drizzle consistency.

Servings: 2 dozen cookies
Prep time: 10 minutes, 1 hour refrigerate

# Magic Mushroom Meringues

This recipe is worth the
effort put forth to prepare
it. Sure to delight children
of all ages who have a
sweet tooth.

| | |
|---|---|
| 7 | large egg whites |
| ½ tsp | cream of tartar |
| ½ tsp | salt |
| 2 cups | sugar |
| 2 tsp | pure vanilla extract |
| ¾ cup | chocolate chips |
| ½ cup | margarine |
| | cocoa for decoration |

**Tip:** To give it a more "mushroom look" use a toothpick to create lines running from underneath the centre of the cap to the edges before inserting the stem into the cap.

In a large mixing bowl, beat egg whites at low speed. When foamy (6–7 minutes), add cream of tartar and salt. Gradually add 1 cup of sugar, a tablespoon at a time, increasing the speed. Add vanilla extract. Continue adding the remaining sugar, at high speed, until the whites look glossy and are stiff.

Preheat oven to 200F.

Line two baking sheets with parchment paper, securing the corners with a little meringue mixture. With a piping bag or a decorating syringe, pipe round caps onto the first baking sheet. On the second sheet, pipe the stems in small, flat strips of egg whites. The size is not important, since mushrooms come in all shapes and sizes.

Bake on middle rack at 200F for 1 hour. Turn oven off and continue baking the stems for 20–25 minutes and the caps for approximately 40 minutes. Occasionally they dry faster. Check the caps for readiness when you remove the stems. They should lift easily from the parchment paper. If they are under-baked, they will go mushy. If they are over-baked, they will have the texture of Styrofoam. Timing is everything so the baking may require a little practice.

In a small saucepan, heat chocolate chips and margarine until melted. Dust the top of caps with cocoa, using a small sifter. Then, cover the underside of the caps with chocolate mixture letting it drip onto the mushroom from a small spoon. Poke a small hole into the centre of each mushroom cap using a paring knife. Dip the stem into the soft chocolate and insert into hole in centre of cap. Set them upside down in a muffin tin until they harden. The inside will have the consistency of a marshmallow.

Serving: approximately 28
Prep time: 30 minutes

# Palmiers

| | |
|---|---|
| 1½ cups | all purpose flour |
| ½ cup | frozen margarine, cut into chunks |
| ½ cup | parve whipping cream, mixed with 1 teaspoon lemon juice |
| ½ cup | sugar – may need to add more |

Put flour in the bowl of a food processor. Add margarine. Process until the mixture resembles coarse crumbs. Add whipping cream. Process until dough forms a ball. Remove it from bowl. Place onto a lightly floured surface and flatten into a rectangle. Transfer onto a cookie sheet. Cover and refrigerate for several hours.

Heavily sugar a pastry cloth. Keep the dough well sugared, front and back, so it won't be sticky. Roll it into a large rectangle. Determine the centre of the dough and mark it lightly with a vertical line. Then fold each side three times towards the centre, so that there is a ½-inch space between the finished rolls. Lift one roll and place on the other. Wrap it well. Refrigerate for an hour or so.

Preheat the oven to 400F. Grease two cookie sheets.

Slice the rolls, making sure that they are not overly thin – about ¼ inch. Place onto cookie sheets. Bake for 12 minutes on 1 side or until light brown. Remove from oven. Turn cookies over. Return to oven. Bake for additional 6–8 minutes. Remove cookies from sheets. Cool on racks.

**Tip:** Use parchment paper (not waxed paper) for everything: on cookie sheets, in casseroles, under kugels. To wrap salmon before baking – everything comes out easier with no sticking and no mess.

Servings: 2½ dozen
Prep time: 5 minutes.
Refrigerate dough for several hours

# Chocolate Raspberry Brownies

| | |
|---|---|
| 1 cup | margarine |
| 1 cup | semi-sweet chocolate chips |
| 2 cups | sugar |
| 4 | large eggs |
| 2 tsp | vanilla extract |
| 1¼ cup | all purpose flour |
| 1 tsp | baking powder |
| ½ tsp | salt |
| ½ cup | seedless raspberry jam |
| ¼ cup | margarine |
| ½ cup | semi-sweet chocolate chips |

Preheat oven to 350F.

In a small saucepan or microwave-safe dish, melt 1 cup margarine and 1 cup chocolate chips.

In a separate bowl, combine sugar, eggs and vanilla. Add chocolate mixture. Add flour, baking powder and salt and mix well. Spread 2 cups of the batter into a greased 9 x 13-inch pan. Freeze till firm, approximately 10 minutes. Spread jam over frozen brownie layer. Spoon remaining batter over jam. Let stand at room temperature, for 20 minutes, to thaw bottom layer. Bake for 35 minutes. Remove from oven. Cool.

Melt ¼ cup margarine and ½ cup chocolate chips together. Pour over brownies. Let it set. While still a little soft, cut brownies into squares and let them set completely.

**Tip:** Decorate with a fresh raspberry on each brownie.

Servings: 36 squares
Prep time: 45 minutes

# Secret Mint Squares

PARVE

*No longer a secret.*

CAKE

| 2 squares | unsweetened chocolate |
| ½ cup | margarine, softened |
| 2 | eggs |
| 1 cup | sugar |
| ¼ tsp | peppermint extract |
| ½ cup | all purpose flour |
| pinch | salt |
| ½ cup | chopped walnuts or almonds (optional) |

FILLING

| 2 Tbsp | margarine, softened |
| 1 cup | icing (confectioner's) sugar, sifted |
| 1 Tbsp | parve whipping cream |
| ¾ tsp | peppermint extract |
| ¼ tsp | green food colouring (optional) |

GLAZE

| 1 Tbsp | margarine, softened |
| 1 square | unsweetened chocolate |

Preheat oven to 350F.

**CAKE:** Melt chocolate and margarine in a double boiler. Remove from heat and cool. Cream together eggs, sugar, cooled chocolate mixture and peppermint extract. Add flour, salt and nuts. Mix well. Pour into a greased 9-inch square pan and bake for 20–35 minutes. Cool in pan.

**FILLING:** Blend all ingredients. Mixture should be thick not runny. Spread over cooled cake. Refrigerate.

**GLAZE:** Melt margarine and chocolate in a double boiler. Mix well. Pour hot glaze over icing to cover. Refrigerate.

Cut into bars when cool.

**Tips:** You can use dairy products in this recipe as well by substituting butter for margarine and using dairy chocolate.

Three tablespoons unsweetened cocoa plus 1 tablespoon shortening equals 1 ounce (1 square) unsweetened baking chocolate.

Servings: 16 squares
Prep time: 20–25 minutes

# Brown Bottom Cupcakes

*The proportions in the recipe work best with mini muffin tins.*

| 1½ cups | all purpose flour |
| 1 cup | sugar |
| ¼ cup | cocoa |
| ½ tsp | salt |
| 1 tsp | baking soda |
| 1 cup | water |
| ⅓ cup | oil |
| 1 Tbsp | vinegar |
| 1 tsp | vanilla |

### CHEESE TOPPING

| 1 (8-oz.) pkg. | cream cheese, softened |
| 1 | egg |
| ⅓ cup | sugar |
| ⅛ tsp | salt |
| 1 cup | chocolate chips (preferably mini) |

**Tip:** Freezes well.

Preheat oven to 350F. Line mini muffin tins with paper cups. Set aside.

In a large mixing bowl, combine flour, sugar, cocoa, salt and baking soda. Mix well. Add water, oil, vinegar and vanilla. Mix well. Fill each muffin cup half full with chocolate mixture. Set aside.

In another bowl, combine cheese, egg, sugar and salt. Beat well. Add chocolate chips. Place a teaspoon of this mixture on top of each cupcake. Bake for 20 minutes, until cheese topping just barely browns.

**Servings:** 48 mini cupcakes
**Prep time:** 25–30 minutes

# Peanut Buddy Bars

| | |
|---|---|
| 1 cup | creamy light peanut butter |
| ½ cup | margarine, softened |
| 1¼ cups | sugar |
| 3 | eggs |
| 1 tsp | vanilla |
| 1 cup | all purpose flour |
| ¼ tsp | salt |
| 2 cups | chocolate chips, divided in half |

Preheat oven to 350F.

In a large mixing bowl, using an electric or hand-held mixer, combine peanut butter and margarine. Mix until smooth. Add sugar, eggs, and vanilla, mixing well after each addition, until creamy. Add flour and salt. Fold in 1 cup of chocolate chips. Pour into a greased 9 x 13-inch baking pan. Bake for 25–30 minutes. Remove from oven. Sprinkle with remaining chocolate chips. Let stand for 5 minutes. Spread the "melted chocolate chips" on top. Cool. Cut into bars.

Servings: 24 squares
Prep time: 10 minutes

# Rice Krisp Circles

| | |
|---|---|
| 1 cup | sugar |
| ¾ cup | corn syrup |
| ¼ cup | marshmallow fluff |
| 1 cup | creamy peanut butter |
| 6 cups | rice crisp cereal |
| 1¼ cups | chocolate chips |

In a small saucepan over medium heat, bring sugar, corn syrup and fluff to a boil.

Remove from heat. Stir in peanut butter. Mix in cereal. Set aside.

In a microwavable bowl, melt chocolate chips for 1–1½ minutes on high. Stir chocolate chips into cereal mixture. Press mixture into mini muffin tins. Refrigerate to set. To remove from tin, gently loosen with a knife or teaspoon.

Servings: 48 mini muffin-sized portions
Prep time: 15–30 minutes

*This recipe is so quick and easy but the end result looks and tastes like you spent the whole day preparing it.*

**Tips:** To make marbled bark, replace half the chocolate with white chocolate.

Freezes well.

To make this recipe even quicker, melt chocolate in the microwave, remove and stir in chopped cookies.

Servings: 8–10
Prep time: 15 minutes

**Tips:** Freezes well.

If brown sugar becomes hard, place a slice of apple in with the brown sugar and microwave briefly until it softens.

# Cookie Crunch Bark

| 8 | squares semi-sweet chocolate, chopped |
| | OR |
| 2 cups | semi-sweet chocolate chips |
| 1 cup | chocolate sandwich cookies, chopped |

Line a baking sheet that has sides with parchment paper.

In a small double boiler, carefully heat chocolate until two-thirds melted.

Remove from heat and continue stirring until completely melted and smooth.

Stir in chopped cookies. Pour mixture onto baking sheet. Gently smooth the surface with a spoon.

Refrigerate until firm, about one hour. Break bark into pieces.

Store in an airtight container in refrigerator.

# Praline Brittle

| 12 | cinnamon graham crackers, 5 x 2½-inch each |
| 1 cup | margarine |
| 1 cup | brown sugar, firmly packed |
| 1 cup | pecans, chopped |

Preheat oven to 350F.

Spray baking sheet with non-stick cooking spray. Cover with 1 layer of crackers.

In a saucepan, melt margarine and brown sugar until mixture boils. Remove from heat. Add pecans. Pour mixture over crackers. Bake for 10 minutes. Cool for ½ hour. Break up into bars.

Servings: 10–12
Prep time: 10–15 minutes

# passover

# Other recipes that can be used for Passover

| Recipe | Category | D/M/P* | Page | Modifications |
|---|---|---|---|---|
| Three-Coloured Fish Loaf | Appetizer | P | 7 | None |
| Stuffed Zucchini | Appetizer | P | 11 | None |
| Marinated Eggplant Salad | Appetizer | P | 15 | None |
| Algerian Roasted Peppers & Tomatoes | Appetizer | P | 19 | No chili powder |
| Lemon Parsnip Soup | Soup | P | 31 | None |
| Squash & Fennel (Anise) Soup | Soup | P | 32 | None |
| Zucchini Potato Soup | Soup | P | 36 | None |
| Roasted Tomato Bisque | Soup | P | 40 | None |
| Asparagus Soup | Soup | P | 41 | None |
| Chilled Strawberry Soup | Soup | P | 43 | None |
| Cranberry Sauce | Soup | P | 44 | None |
| Grilled Tuna Nicoise | Salad | P | 70 | No green beans |
| Chicken Salad with Avocado Dressing | Salad | M | 74 | No corn |
| Honey-Lemon Dressing | Salad | P | 80 | None |
| Broccoli-Cheese Stuffed Potatoes | Brunch | D | 98 | None |
| Steamed Halibut with Simmering Vegetables and Feta Cheese | Fish | D | 116 | None |
| Sole Fillets Meridian | Fish | D | 117 | None |
| Moroccan Coriander Fish | Fish | P | 118 | None |
| Tilapia | Fish | P | 118 | None |
| Portobello Chicken | Poultry | M | 123 | None |
| Sliced Chicken with Lemon-Basil Vinaigrette | Poultry | M | 124 | None |
| Chicken with Lemon and Artichoke | Poultry | M | 125 | None |
| Sweet Chicken Cutlets | Poultry | M | 127 | None |
| Rosemary Grilled Chicken | Poultry | M | 133 | None |
| Apricot Turkey Breast | Poultry | M | 147 | None |
| Balsamic Rib-Eye Roast with Roasted Vegetables | Meat | M | 150 | None |
| Ginger Ale Brisket | Meat | M | 151 | None |
| Easy Crock Pot Roast | Meat | M | 151 | None |
| Veal Roast in White Wine | Meat | M | 156 | None |
| Veal Roast with Tomato Sauce | Meat | M | 157 | None |
| Basil Pepper Steak | Meat | M | 159 | None |
| Tongue in Tomato Sauce | Meat | M | 160 | None |
| Veal and Vegetable Meatloaf | Meat | M | 167 | Substitute matza meal for bread crumbs |
| Festive Sweet Meatballs | Meat | M | 168 | Substitute matza meal (no bread crumbs) |
| Glazed Carrots and Parsnips | Vegetable | P | 201 | None |
| Zucchini and Tomato Sauté | Vegetable | P | 202 | None |
| Italian Stuffed Tomatoes | Vegetable | P | 203 | None |
| Oranges and Yams | Vegetable | P | 204 | None |
| Waffle Potatoes | Vegetable | P | 206 | None |
| Herbed Roasted Baby Potatoes | Vegetable | P | 206 | None |

*D = dairy   M = meat   P = parve

# Gefilte Fish with Salsa Topping

| | |
|---|---|
| 2 | eggs |
| 2 | large onions |
| 3 Tbsp | sugar |
| 2 tsp | salt |
| ¼ tsp | pepper |
| 1½ lb. | chopped fish |
| 1 (8-oz.) jar | mild salsa, chunky |
| 2 tsp | oil |
| ½ | red pepper, cut into ½-inch strips |
| ½ | green pepper, cut into ½-inch strips |
| ½ | yellow pepper, cut into ½-inch strips |
| 1 | red onion, cut into strips |

Preheat oven to 350F.

In a food processor, process eggs and onions until smooth. Add sugar, salt, pepper and chopped fish. Process until smooth.

Divide mixture into 2 equal loaves.

Place each loaf into a greased loaf pan. Pour salsa over each loaf. Bake covered for 45 minutes. Uncover. Bake for an additional 15 to 30 minutes until loaf feels firm.

Meanwhile, in a small skillet, sauté peppers and onion in oil until tender. Pour over fish. Cover and refrigerate.

Tip: To serve, cut into slices and top with some vegetables.

Servings: 10–12
Prep time: 10 minutes

# Potato Cheese Casserole

| | |
|---|---|
| 2 | large onions, chopped |
| 2 | cloves of garlic, minced |
| 2 Tbsp | butter |
| 4 | large baking potatoes, grated |
| 1½ cups | Cheddar cheese, grated |
| ½ tsp | salt |
| ¼ tsp | pepper |
| 2 cups | milk |
| 2 Tbsp | fresh parsley, chopped |

Preheat oven to 400F.

In a large skillet, sauté onions and garlic in butter until tender. Add potatoes, cheese, salt, pepper, milk and parsley. Mix. Transfer to a greased 9 x 9-inch baking dish. Bake, uncovered, for 1¼ hours. Let stand for 10 minutes before serving.

Servings: 6–8
Prep time: 20 minutes

**Tip:** This recipe also fits nicely into 8-inch pie plate.

# Quistada

| | |
|---|---|
| | oil to grease pan |
| 3 (300-g) boxes | frozen chopped spinach, thawed, drained |
| 3 sheets | matza, soaked, squeezed |
| 1 heaping cup | cottage cheese |
| ½ lb. | feta cheese, crumbled |
| | salt to taste |
| 8 | eggs, well beaten |
| ½ cup | Parmesan cheese |
| 1 Tbsp | butter (approximately) |

Preheat oven to 350F.

Heat oiled 9 x 13-inch pan.

In a large mixing bowl, combine, spinach, matza, cottage cheese, feta cheese and salt. Add eggs mix well. Pour into oiled pan. Sprinkle with Parmesan cheese. Dot with butter. Bake, uncovered, for 30–40 minutes until golden brown.

Servings: 10–12
Prep time: 20–25 minutes

# Spinach Mushroom Soufflé

PARVE

| | |
|---|---|
| 6 cups | water |
| 1 (16-oz.) pkg. | frozen chopped spinach |
| 1 | large onion, chopped |
| 1 Tbsp | oil |
| 2 cups | fresh mushrooms, sliced |
| 1 cup | mayonnaise |
| 3 | eggs, slightly beaten |
| 1 cup | non-dairy creamer |
| 3 Tbsp | potato starch |
| | salt and pepper to taste |

Preheat oven to 350F.

In a large pot, combine water and spinach. Boil for 10 minutes. Drain well. Set aside.

In a skillet, sauté onion in oil until lightly browned. Add mushrooms and sauté for an additional 10 minutes.

In a bowl, combine onion-mushroom mixture, spinach, mayonnaise, eggs, creamer, potato starch, salt and pepper. Pour into a greased, round, 9-inch deep casserole dish. Bake, uncovered, for 1 hour.

**Tip:** Add 1 cup of grated mozzarella to the mixture and sprinkle additional mozzarella on top.

Servings: 8–10
Prep time: 20 minutes

# Zucchini Frittata

| | |
|---|---|
| 1½ lbs. | zucchini, peeled, grated, drained |
| 1 | onion, chopped |
| 3 Tbsp | oil |
| 5 | matzas |
| 5 | eggs, beaten |
| 1¼ cups | Cheddar cheese, grated |
| 1 cup | cottage cheese |
| 1 tsp | salt |
| 8 | cherry tomatoes, halved |
| ¼ | small red onion, finely chopped |

Preheat oven to 350F.

In a small skillet, sauté zucchini and onion in oil for 5 minutes. Pour off excess water onto matzas. Briefly soak matzas and squeeze dry. Break matzas into small pieces and place in a medium-sized bowl. Add onion-zucchini mixture along with eggs, cheeses and salt. Mix together. Add tomatoes and onion and toss gently. Transfer mixture to a greased 9 x 13-inch pan. Bake, uncovered, for 50 minutes.

**Tips:** Can be frozen.
Reheats well.
To determine whether an egg is fresh, put it in water. It will sink if it's fresh.

Servings: 8
Prep time: 15 minutes

# Pesach Schnitzel

| | |
|---|---|
| 2 | eggs, lightly beaten |
| 1 (1.5-oz.) pkg. | mashed potato flakes |
| 2 tsp | garlic powder |
| 2 tsp | onion powder |
| 1 tsp | dried parsley |
| | salt and pepper to taste |
| 6 | chicken breasts, boneless, skinless and pounded flat (¼ inch thickness) |
| ¼ cup | oil |

Preheat oven to 350F.

Break eggs into a shallow bowl and beat them lightly. Set aside.

Combine potato flakes with spices in a shallow bowl. Dip chicken into beaten eggs, then into potato mix.

In a large skillet, heat oil over medium heat. Quickly brown chicken on both sides, 1 to 2 minutes per side. Place browned chicken on a baking sheet. Bake, uncovered, for 15–20 minutes or until just done.

**Tip:** Works well with turkey scaloppini.

Servings: 4–6
Prep time: 20 minutes

# Glazed Chicken with Vegetables

| | |
|---|---|
| 2 cups | apricot jam |
| ¾ cup | ketchup |
| 2 Tbsp | brown sugar (optional) |
| 8 | chicken thighs, skinless, boneless or with 1 bone removed, washed, and dried |
| 2 Tbsp | olive oil |
| 1 | large onion, cut into ½-inch strips |
| 1 | green pepper, cut into ½-inch strips |
| 1 | red pepper, cut into ½-inch strips |
| ½ lb. | fresh mushrooms, sliced |

Preheat oven to 350F.

In a small bowl, combine apricot jam, ketchup and brown sugar. Set aside.

Place chicken in a shallow baking dish. Pour mixture over chicken. Bake, uncovered, for 40 minutes.

Meanwhile, in a small skillet, sauté onion, green and red peppers and mushrooms in oil until tender. Pour over chicken and bake for additional 15 minutes.

Servings: 6–8
Prep time: 20 minutes

# Chicken Cacciatore

| | |
|---|---|
| 1 (3–4 lb.) | chicken, skinned, cut into eighths |
| 3 Tbsp | oil |
| 1 cup | mushrooms, sliced |
| ½ cup | onion, chopped |
| 1 | clove of garlic, minced |
| 1 cup | ketchup |
| 1 cup | water |
| 2 Tbsp | dry red wine |
| 1 Tbsp | parsley, chopped |
| | salt to taste |

In a large skillet, heat half of the oil and brown chicken on both sides, approximately 3–5 minutes. Remove from pan onto paper towels to drain.

Add fresh oil to the skillet and heat. Sauté mushrooms, onion and garlic until browned. Gently stir in ketchup, water, wine and parsley. Add salt to taste. Add chicken. Mix. Simmer, uncovered, for 30–40 minutes until sauce is thickened and chicken is tender.

Servings: 6–8
Prep time: 15 minutes

# Meat Lasagna

| | |
|---|---|
| 5 | potatoes, peeled |
| | water, to cover |
| 2 Tbsp | margarine |
| ½ tsp | salt |
| ½ tsp | pepper |
| 2 Tbsp | olive oil |
| 2 | medium eggplants, unpeeled, cut into 1-inch slices |
| 1 | large onion, chopped |
| 2 Tbsp | olive oil |
| 2 lbs. | ground beef |
| 1 Tbsp | dry onion soup mix |
| 1 cup | tomato sauce |
| 1 tsp | thyme |
| 1 tsp | oregano |
| 1 | clove of garlic, minced |

Boil potatoes in a medium-sized pot with water to cover. Once they are soft, remove from heat. Drain pot of water. Mash potatoes. Add margarine, salt and pepper. Mix well. Set aside. Spread potatoes on bottom of a greased 9 x 13-inch pan.

Preheat oven to broil setting.

On a baking sheet, sprinkle olive oil over eggplant slices. Broil in oven, until soft and lightly brown. Remove from oven. Set aside. Reduce setting to 350F.

In a large skillet, sauté onion in olive oil until golden. Add ground beef, onion soup mix, tomato sauce, thyme, oregano and garlic. Cook, stirring often, until beef is brown. Drain. Cool. Spread meat mixture alternately with eggplant onto potatoes, ending with eggplant on top. Bake, covered, for 30 minutes.

Servings: 8–10
Prep time: 30–40 minutes

# Vegetable Kugel

| | |
|---|---|
| 3 | large zucchini, peeled, grated, to equal approximately 5 cups |
| 2 | carrots, peeled and grated |
| 1 | potato, grated |
| 2 | celery stalks, grated |
| 2 | onions, grated |
| 3 cups | matza farfel |
| 4 | eggs, beaten |
| ½ cup | margarine, melted |
| 3 Tbsp | dry onion soup mix |
| 1 tsp | oil, to grease pan |

Preheat oven to 350F.

In a large bowl, combine zucchini, carrots, potato, celery and onions. Add farfel and eggs. Mix well. Add margarine and onion soup. Mix well. Pour into a greased 9 x 13-inch ovenproof dish.

Bake for 60–90 minutes or until browned.

Servings: 8–10
Prep time: 15–20 minutes

# Zucchini Kugel

| | |
|---|---|
| ½ | onion, finely chopped |
| ½ | red pepper, finely chopped |
| 1 tsp | oil |
| 6 | eggs |
| 1½ tsp | salt |
| ½ tsp | pepper |
| | garlic powder to taste |
| 6 | zucchini, unpeeled, grated, drained |
| 1 cup | matza meal |
| 1 Tbsp | oil |
| | paprika, to garnish |

Preheat oven to 350F.

In a small skillet, sauté onion and red pepper in oil until tender, not brown. Remove from heat. Set aside.

In a large bowl, beat eggs with salt, pepper and garlic powder. Add zucchini, onion, red pepper and matza meal, mixing well after each addition.

Pour oil in a 9-inch square pan and place in oven until hot, about 5 minutes. Remove baking pan from oven and pour oil into zucchini mixture, leaving a little grease in the bottom of pan. Pour zucchini mixture into baking pan. Garnish with paprika on top. Bake, uncovered, for 45 minutes or until browned.

Servings: 8–10
Prep time: 20 minutes

# Passover Apple Kugel

**Tip:** Freezes well.

| | |
|---|---|
| 2 cups | matza meal |
| 1 cup | potato starch |
| 3 tsp | baking powder |
| 3 cups | sugar |
| 1½ cups | oil |
| 12 | eggs |
| 3 tsp | vanilla |
| 10 | cooking apples, peeled, cored and thinly sliced |
| | cinnamon to taste |

Preheat oven to 350F.

Grease 2 8 x 8-inch pans and 1 9 x 13-inch pan.

Combine matza meal, potato starch and baking powder in a medium-sized bowl. Set aside.

In a large bowl, blend sugar, oil, eggs and vanilla. Add matza meal mixture. Mix well.

Fold in apples until just combined.

Pour into prepared baking pans and sprinkle with cinnamon. Bake uncovered for ½ hour, cover and continue baking for ½ hour more.

Servings: 20–24
Prep time: 15–20 minutes

# Parve Pesach Kishka

| | |
|---|---|
| 2 cups | matza meal |
| 2 | carrots, peeled, diced |
| 2 | stalks of celery, diced |
| 1 | large onion, diced |
| 1 | egg, beaten |
| ½ cup | oil or melted margarine |
| 1 Tbsp | sugar |
| 1 tsp | salt |
| ½ tsp | pepper |
| ⅛ tsp | garlic powder |

Preheat oven to 375F.

Put matza meal in a large bowl. Set aside.

Put in a food processor bowl carrots, celery, onion, egg, oil, sugar, salt, pepper and garlic powder. Pulse until finely chopped. Pour over matza meal. Mix well. Divide into 2 equal pieces. Form each piece into a roll and place them on separate greased pieces of foil. Wrap and seal. Place on baking sheet. Bake for 45–60 minutes. Serve hot.

Tip: Freezes well.

Servings: 10–12
Prep time: 15 minutes

# Pesach Cheese Cake

| | |
|---|---|
| 20 | lady fingers |
| 2 Tbsp | margarine |
| 2 (8-oz.) pkgs. | cream cheese, softened |
| 1 cup | sugar |
| 3 | large eggs |
| 2 cups | sour cream |
| 1 Tbsp | vanilla |
| 1½ cups | chocolate chips |

Preheat oven to 350F.

In a food processor bowl, combine lady fingers and margarine. Pulse until mixture is fine in texture. Press evenly into bottom of a 9 x 13-inch or 10-inch spring-form pan.

In a medium-sized bowl, using an electric or hand-held mixer, beat cream cheese until smooth. Add sugar, eggs, sour cream and vanilla, blending well. Stir in 1 cup of chocolate chips.

Pour filling into crust and sprinkle remaining chocolate chips on top. Bake for 30–40 minutes. Turn off oven and leave cheesecake for 1 hour to set. Serve chilled.

Servings: 8–10
Prep time: 10–20 minutes

# Lemon Meringue

| | |
|---|---|
| 5 | egg yolks |
| 1¼ cups | sugar |
| 2 cups | parve whipping cream |
| ¾ cup | lemon juice |
| 1 | lemon zest, optional |
| 2 | egg whites |
| ¼ cup | sugar |

In a small bowl, using an electric or hand-held mixer, beat yolks until thick and creamy. Add sugar. Continue beating until light yellow.

In another bowl, whip cream. Add lemon juice and zest. Fold whipped cream mixture into yolk mixture. Pour into a 9–10-inch spring-form pan. Cover. Freeze at least 5 hours.

Preheat broil element.

In large bowl, beat egg whites with sugar until stiff peaks form. Remove cake from freezer and spread egg white mixture over the top of the lemon mousse. Place on top rack of oven. Broil for 1 minute. Watch very closely since it burns quite fast. Cover. Return to freezer. Serve frozen.

*Put the caterers out of business with this delightful dessert.*

Servings: 6–8
Prep time: 15 minutes

# Frozen Lemon Meringue Cake

### JELLY ROLL

| | |
|---|---|
| 5 | eggs, separated |
| ½ cup | sugar, divided into ¼ cup and ¼ cup |
| ¼ cup | potato starch |
| ⅓ cup | jam, of your choice |

### LEMON MOUSSE

| | |
|---|---|
| 6 | eggs, separated, reserve 3 whites for meringue |
| ½ cup | lemon juice |
| ½ | lemon, zest, grated |
| 1½ cups | sugar, divided into 1¼ cups plus ¼ cup |

### MERINGUE

| | |
|---|---|
| 3 | egg whites (from above) |
| 1 Tbsp | sugar |

Preheat oven to 400F.

**JELLY ROLL:** In a small bowl, beat egg yolks and ¼ cup sugar. Set aside.

In a separate bowl, using an electric or hand-held mixer, beat whites with ¼ cup sugar until stiff peaks form. Add 1 cup of egg whites to yolk mixture. Mix gently. Pour yolk mixture into whites. Sift in potato starch. Gently fold together.

Spread onto a parchment paper-lined baking sheet (leave some parchment overhanging on 2 ends of pan so you can get cake out easily). Bake for 12 minutes. Remove cake from pan and lay it flat on a clean dishtowel. Roll up cake from the short side in towel. Cool.

**LEMON MOUSSE:** Combine egg yolks, lemon juice, zest and 1¼ cups sugar in a double boiler, or microwave. Cook until thickened. Put in refrigerator to cool. It will thicken more when cooled.

In a large mixing bowl, beat 3 whites and ¼ cup sugar until stiff peaks form. Fold into lemon mixture.

Unroll jelly-roll cake. Spread it with jam and roll up again from the short side. Cut into ½-inch slices and line a spring-form pan, bottom and sides with the slices. Fill with lemon mousse and freeze for at least 5 hours.

**Tip:** Try lining the spring form pan with sliced sponge cake instead of jelly-roll slices.

Servings: 8–10
Prep time: 1 hour before + 5 hours to freeze mousse

**MERINGUE:** Preheat broil element.

In a separate mixing bowl, beat remaining 3 egg whites with sugar until stiff peaks form. Spread over lemon mousse. Place in top rack of oven for about 5 minutes until golden browned. Watch very closely since it browns quite fast. Remove from oven. Refreeze.

Remove from freezer 15 minutes before serving to allow to thaw.

## Strawberry Mousse

PARVE

| | |
|---|---|
| 1 quart | strawberries, puréed |
| 3 | egg whites |
| 1 cup | sugar |
| 1 Tbsp+ 1 tsp | lemon juice |
| ⅛ tsp | salt |

In a large mixing bowl, with an electric or hand-held mixer, beat all the ingredients together at high speed, for at least 15 minutes. Cover and freeze.

Remove from freezer ½ hour before serving.

Scoop into serving bowls.

Tips: To make this creamier rather than icy, add ¼ cup whipping cream.

Serve with fresh berries and crisp wafer cookies.

Kids will love this if you freeze it in individual muffin cups or you can insert a Popsicle stick when the mousse is half frozen.

Servings: 12
Prep time: 15 minutes

# Passover Chocolate Rolls

CAKE

| 10 | eggs, separated |
| ⅔ cup | sugar |
| ⅔ cup | sugar |
| 1 cup | potato starch |
| ⅓ cup | oil |
| ½ | lemon, juiced |
| 1 Tbsp | vanilla sugar |
| 1 tsp | baking powder |

ICING

| 7 Tbsp | margarine, melted |
| ¾ cup | cocoa, sifted |
| ⅓ cup | whipped topping |
| ¼ cup | water |
| 1 tsp | vanilla extract |
| 3–4 cups | icing (confectioner's) sugar |

Preheat oven to 350F.

**CAKE:** In a large mixing bowl, using an electric or hand-held mixer, beat egg whites until stiff. Slowly stir in ⅔ cup of sugar. Set aside.

In another bowl, combine egg yolks with ⅔ cup sugar, potato starch, oil, lemon, vanilla sugar and baking powder. Fold egg whites into egg yolk mixture. Pour batter into 2 10 x 15-inch parchment-lined and sprayed jelly-roll pans. Bake, one pan at a time, for 14–15 minutes.

**ICING:** Meanwhile, in a large mixing bowl, combine margarine with cocoa. Blend in whipped topping, water, vanilla and icing sugar. Add more or less icing sugar until desired thickness is achieved. Set aside.

Dampen a dishcloth or tea towel with water, cover with parchment paper and sprinkle icing sugar over it. Turn baked cake over onto new parchment paper and peel parchment paper off the cake. Spread thin layer of icing over cake while warm. Roll up cake beginning at the short side. Put paper and tea towel over rolled-up cake. Leave for 15 minutes to cool and keep shape. When cooled, remove from tea towel and paper. Repeat process with second roll.
Ice the outside of the cake.

Servings: makes 2 rolls, 10–12 slices per roll
Prep time: 30 minutes

# Super Moist Chocolate Nut Cake
# for Passover (not Gebroktz)

| 12 | eggs, separated |
| 1½ cups | sugar, divided 1 cup and ½ cup |
| 2 cups | ground walnuts or filberts |
| 3 Tbsp | potato starch |
| 2 tsp | vanilla sugar |
| 7 oz. | bittersweet chocolate, melted and cooled slightly |

Preheat oven to 350F.

In a large mixing bowl, using an electric or hand-held mixer, beat egg yolks. Add 1 cup sugar. Beat until light in colour.

In a separate bowl beat egg whites. Gradually add remaining ½ cup of sugar. Beat until stiff. Blend together egg yolks, walnuts or filberts, potato starch, vanilla sugar and chocolate. Fold egg whites into egg yolk mixture. Pour batter into a greased 9 x 13-inch pan. Bake for 45 minutes. Test for readiness by inserting a toothpick into middle of cake.

*"This is a great gluten-free cake that you can use all year round."*

Tips: Serve with raspberry sauce or squirts of chocolate sauce with icing (confectioner's) sugar on top.

Egg whites are easiest to beat when they are at room temperature. Leave them out for about ½ hour before use.

Servings: 10–12
Prep time: 20 minutes

# Sour Cream Pesach Cake

**Tip:** For Pesach baking, when adding dry ingredients to wet, combine with very few strokes. matzo or cake meal will turn lumpy and heavy when over-mixed.

| | |
|---|---|
| 1 cup | sour cream |
| 1 tsp | baking soda |
| ½ cup | margarine, softened |
| 1 cup | sugar |
| 2 | eggs |
| 1 tsp | vanilla |
| 1 cup | cake meal |
| ¼ cup | potato starch |
| 1 tsp | baking powder |
| ½ cup | brown sugar (can be replaced with white sugar) |
| 1 tsp | cinnamon |
| | ground nuts, (optional) |

Preheat oven to 350F.

Grease a large loaf pan approximately 11½ x 4¼ x 2¼ inches, or use 2 smaller pans. The longer cake is more elegant.

In a large bowl combine sour cream and baking soda. Reserve. In a mixer, cream margarine and sugar well. Add eggs and vanilla, beating until the margarine is well blended.

In a separate bowl, combine cake meal, potato starch and baking powder. Mix well. (Use a food processor to eliminate lumps.)

Add sour cream mixture to batter. Then, using a light hand – most important step – barely blend dry ingredients into the batter.

Pour half the batter into loaf pan. In a small bowl, combine sugar, cinnamon and ground nuts. Place half of this mixture in the middle of the cake. Pour remaining batter on top and sprinkle with rest of the sugar-nut mixture. Bake for 45–50 minutes. The top cake will crack, lending to its "homey" appearance.

You can substitute Bundt pan for loaf pans.

Serves: 8–10
Prep time: 20 minutes

# Marshmallow Brownies

| | |
|---|---|
| 1¾ cups | chocolate chips |
| ½ cup | margarine |
| 2 | eggs |
| ¾ cup | sugar |
| 1 tsp | vanilla |
| 1 tsp | instant coffee (dissolved in a drop of water) |
| ½ cup | cake meal |
| 1 Tbsp | potato starch |
| ⅛ tsp | salt |
| 1 cup | mini marshmallows |
| ½ cup | chopped nuts |
| | icing (confectioner's) sugar to garnish |

Preheat oven to 350F.

Melt chocolate and margarine in a double boiler. Cool. Set aside.

In a large mixing bowl, beat eggs, sugar, vanilla and coffee. Set aside.

In a small bowl, combine cake meal, potato starch and salt. Add dry mixture to egg mixture and mix well. Add cooled chocolate mixture and mix. Fold in marshmallows and nuts until just combined. Pour into a greased 8 x 8-inch pan.

Bake for 35–40 minutes – do not over bake. When cool, sprinkle with icing sugar and cut into squares.

*"These brownies are so unbelievable. When I made these brownies as a gift for a friend of mine, they were so good, that the family finished all of them before Passover even began."*

Servings: **16 squares**
Prep time: **10 minutes**

# The Best Brownies Ever

*"This recipe is an old family recipe and still a favourite every year. It is so delicious; you will not believe it is kosher for Passover."*

| | |
|---|---|
| 2 cups | chocolate chips |
| 1 cup | margarine |
| 8 | eggs |
| 2⅔ cups | sugar |
| ½ tsp | salt |
| 2 cups | matza cake meal |

Preheat oven to 350F.

Melt chocolate chips and margarine in a double boiler. Set aside to cool. In a large mixing bowl, beat together eggs, sugar and salt. Add chocolate mixture and mix well. Add cake meal and mix well. Pour into a greased 9 x 13-inch pan. Bake for 30 minutes.

**Servings:** 16 squares
**Prep time:** 10 minutes

# Passover Chocolate Chip Cookies

| | |
|---|---|
| 3 | eggs |
| ½ cup | margarine, softened |
| ½ cup | brown sugar |
| ½ cup | sugar |
| 1 Tbsp | vanilla sugar or 1 tsp vanilla extract |
| 1 cup | cake meal |
| ½ cup | potato starch |
| ¼ tsp | salt |
| 1½ cups | chocolate chips |

Preheat oven to 350F.

In a large mixing bowl, using an electric or hand-held mixer, beat eggs, margarine and sugars and vanilla. Set aside.

In a separate bowl, combine cake meal, potato starch and salt. Add dry ingredients to egg mixture. Add chocolate chips. Mix until chocolate chips are evenly distributed in dough. Drop dough by spoonful onto a greased cookie sheet. Bake for 10–15 minutes or until lightly browned.

**Tip:** Add cocoa to the dough and a little extra sugar to make it into chocolate cookies. They freeze well too.

**Servings:** 2 dozen cookies
**Prep time:** 10–15 minutes

# Caramel Pecan Squares

| | |
|---|---|
| 4 | plain matzas |
| 1 cup | margarine |
| 1 cup | brown sugar, packed |
| 1 cup | chopped pecans |
| ¾ cup | semi-sweet chocolate pieces |
| 1 cup | slivered almonds |

Preheat oven to 350F.

Line bottom of well-greased or parchment-lined baking sheet (15 x 10 inches) that has sides with matzas, breaking as necessary, to fit pan.

In medium saucepan over medium-high heat, combine margarine, brown sugar and pecans. Bring to boil, stirring with wooden spoon. Reduce heat to medium and boil 2 minutes, stirring constantly. Pour over matzas.

Bake for 7 to 8 minutes. Remove from oven and sprinkle with chocolate. Return to oven and bake an additional 2 minutes to melt chocolate. Remove and spread chocolate. Sprinkle with almonds, pressing into chocolate. Cut while still warm, or when cool, break into pieces. Chill in refrigerator until set.

Servings: 10–12
Prep time: 15 minutes

# Pesach Mandelbread

| ¼ cup | sugar |
| 1 tsp | cinnamon |
| 3 | eggs |
| ½ cup | sugar |
| ½ cup | oil |
| 1 tsp | vanilla |
| 1 cup | cake meal |
| ½ cup | almonds, finely crushed |
| 2 Tbsp | potato starch |
| ½ cup | chocolate chips |

Preheat oven to 350F.

In a small dish, combine ¼ cup sugar and cinnamon. Set aside.

In a large mixing bowl, beat eggs, ½ cup sugar, oil and vanilla. Slowly add cake meal, almonds and potato starch. Mix well. Stir in chocolate chips. Divide dough into 3 equal portions. Shape each portion into a log. Place each log on a lightly greased baking sheet. Bake for 12–15 minutes.

Remove from oven, and cut into slices. Place on baking sheet cut side up and sprinkle with cinnamon-sugar mixture. Return to oven. Bake for additional 10 minutes on each side or until golden.

Tip: Freezes well.

Servings: 3 dozen
Prep time: 15–20 minutes

# Conversion charts

## Standard Measures

### Liquid or Dry Measurements

3 tsp = 1 Tbsp
2 Tbsp = ⅛ cup
4 Tbsp = ¼ cup
5 Tbsp plus 1 tsp = ⅓ cup
16 Tbsp = 1 cup

### Liquid Measurements

1 oz. = 2 Tbsp
2 oz. = ¼ cup
8 oz. = 1 cup
2 cups = 1 pint
2 pints = 1 quart
4 quarts = 1 gallon

### Other Equivalents

1 Tbsp fresh herbs = 1 tsp dried herbs
1 Tbsp fresh spices = 1 tsp powdered spices
Dash cayenne or red pepper = few drops of hot pepper sauce

## Metric Equivalent Measures

### Equivalent Liquid Measurements

¼ tsp = 1.5 mL
½ tsp = 3 mL
1 tsp = 5 mL
1 Tbsp = 15 mL
⅓ cup = 80 mL
½ cup = 125 mL
¾ cup = 200 mL
1 cup = 250 mL
1000 mL = 1 L
1 quart = 1.25 L
1 gallon = 5 L

### Equivalent Dry Measurements

¼ lb. = 125 g
½ lb. = 250 g
1 lb. = 500g = 16 oz.
2 lbs. = 1 kg
3 lbs. = 1.5 kg
4 lbs. = 2 kg
5 lbs.= 2.5 kg

### Weights

1 oz. = 28.5 g
8 oz. = 225 g
16 oz. = 454 g
2.2 lbs. = 1 kg

### Equivalent Oven Temperatures

200 F = 96 C
250 F = 120 C
300 F = 150 C
350 F = 175 C
400 F = 205 C
450 F = 230 C
500 F = 260 C

### Baking Pan Conversions

1 quart casserole = 1 litre casserole
8" square x 2" deep = 20 cm x 5 cm
7" x 11" x 2" deep = 30 cm x 20 cm x 5 cm (2 litres)
9" x 13" x 2" deep = 33 cm x 22 cm x 5 cm (3 litres)
9" pie plate = 22 cm
10" pie plate = 25 cm

## Food Equivalents

### lemon

1 medium juice =2–3 Tbsp
1 medium rind = ½–1 Tbsp

### Orange

1 medium juice = 5–6 Tbsp
1 medium rind = 1–2 Tbsp

# Index